The
Geopolitical Orbits
of Ancient India

The
Geopolitical Orbits
of Ancient India

The Geographical Frames
of the Ancient Indian Dynasties

Dilip K. Chakrabarti

OXFORD
UNIVERSITY PRESS

OXFORD
UNIVERSITY PRESS

Oxford University Press is a department of the University of Oxford.
It furthers the University's objective of excellence in research, scholarship,
and education by publishing worldwide. Oxford is a registered trademark of
Oxford University Press in the UK and in certain other countries

Published in India by
Oxford University Press
2/11 Ground Floor, Ansari Road, Daryaganj, New Delhi 110 002, India

ISBN-13 (print edition): 978-0-19-806989-8
ISBN-10 (print edition): 0-19-806989-8

ISBN-13 (eBook): 978-0-19-908832-4
ISBN-10 (eBook): 0-19-908832-2

Typeset in Minion Pro 10.5/12.5
by Le Studio Graphique, Gurgaon 122 001

To

*the memory of Ramesh Chandra Majumdar, Hem Chandra
Raychaudhuri, Kallidaikurichi Aiya Nilakanta Sastri,
and Dinesh Chandra Sircar, whose works have taught me
the basics of the political history of ancient India.*

Contents

Preface

F.J. Richards' (1933) essay, 'Geographical Factors in Indian Archaeology' has long been a major influence in the study of Indian archaeology. In the first edition (1954) of his *India and Pakistan: A General and Regional Geography*, O.H.K. Spate depended for his chapter on 'historical outlines' on Richards' concepts, especially on Richards' idea of the 'centres of population and trade' as the focal points of the course of Indian history. With some modifications, B. Subbarao in the two editions (1956, 1958) of his *The Personality of India* introduced the geographical ideas of Richards and Spate to the study of Indian archaeology. In 1988, in the chapter on 'geographical approaches' in my *Theoretical Issues in Indian Archaeology*, I pointed out the inadequacies of such notions as 'areas of attraction, relative isolation and isolation', and so on. I argued that no part of the subcontinent can be such hierarchically labelled with any historical or archaeological justification.

In this volume, I have elaborated how the political history of ancient India has been enacted in various geographical orbits and how these orbits have kept on interacting throughout this history and how, contrary to general impressions, there has not been any fixed boundary line or 'divide'.

This volume was written in June–August, 2007, at the Asia Centre of the University of New England in Armidale, Australia, with the help of a fellowship from the Centre. I am deeply indebted to Professor Howard Brasted and Professor Ian Metcalfe for this privilege. The image of a quiet campus with vistas of wide and open undulating horizons, splendidly colourful birds, kangaroos, deer, and occasional possums persists in memory.

1

Introduction

The present work is rooted in the following idea. If one takes into consideration the focal geographical points of the ancient Indian dynasties and the geographical orbits within which they tried to expand their political power and interacted with the other contemporary dynasties, it should be possible to gain a long-term perspective of the historical–geographical configurations of ancient Indian political history. The perspective that we are seeking is not a static one. We are not primarily concerned with whether only a limited number of areas were the foci of major power centres throughout the course of ancient Indian history. We expect that all the major regions of India will have their quota of power centres in various historical phases. From our point of view, we find no especially valuable insight into the geographical dimensions of ancient India by emphasizing that there were only a finite number of geopolitical areas of the sub-continent, such as North-West, North-Centre, North-East, West and South.[1] To us, historically the more interesting question is to determine the degree of fluidity with which such areas and their power centres have interacted, imparting no absolute value to any given region. Our aim is to find out if there is a recurrent pattern in this interaction, defining certain historical orbits.

The definition of such orbits has long bothered scholars. Among them, the Oxus–Indus orbit is best known and well understood. The idea goes back to T.H. Holdich in the late nineteenth century when the question of delineating a permanent border between British India and Afghanistan was paramount.[2] In 1977, I pointed out how the data of both political and economic histories underlined the significance of this orbit as one political and economic interaction zone. I also thrashed out its implications in assessing those archaeological data which are cited frequently as evidence of migration to India from Central, and West Asia.[3]

The Oxus–Indus orbit is unlikely to be the only orbit of this kind in ancient Indian history. Scholars have occasionally juxtaposed this against a generally undefined 'Gangetic' or 'inner', or even, 'true' India.[4] In the same context, emphasis has also been placed on the significance of the 'Indo-Gangetic divide', that is, the area between the Sutlej and the Yamuna, which has been said to be the meeting ground of influences both from the East and the West.

Are such orbits fixed entities in our geographical understanding of Indian archaeology and history, or should they be considered nothing more than useful concepts to understand the geography of the flow of historical events in India? This question can be answered only when we can historically trace the persistence of all such orbits throughout the course of political events in ancient India. How many such orbits can be traced in the first place and how have they defined the geographical parameters of interaction between different geographical areas and kingdoms? It is their interaction rather than their areas on the ground which is important to understand how the different parts of the subcontinent formed one integrated geopolitical whole rather than being an agglomeration of many regional units.

On a different level, the internal geographical configuration of the individual political units can throw a lot of light behind the location of their places—capitals and smaller centres alike. A good source of the list and distribution of such places in a given kingdom is its inscriptions, but detailed research on the inscriptional placenames and their identifications on the ground is still a major desideratum of ancient Indian historical research. Similarly, archaeological field-investigations still have a long way to go in this direction. However, certain general observations may be made even now on the basis of what is known about the distribution of various raw materials, the location of major trade centres, and the broad alignments of routes. Even the location of battlegrounds will throw light on how the kings were moving about with their armies and if they were following specific routes. Even cursory references to such geographical features and issues are likely to make the geopolitical pulses of ancient Indian history a bit more alive. In the long run, this may be more revealing historically than the counting and gradation of power centres of various areas. First, political power centres cannot be said to have developed in any absolute sense; their character depended on the nature of the political force concerned. Two power centres of two widely separate times may be located in the same place but apart from sharing the same geography, they may share very little else. If a particular area has thrown up more political power centres than many other areas, will it mean that this particular area possessed any immutable quality and has to be graded accordingly in relation to the rest?

I have argued elsewhere that the concept of 'perennial nuclear regions' is a flawed concept in the study of Indian history and archaeology.[5] The historical and archaeological focus of importance has never been static; it has varied from time to time and area to area. Even the so-called 'backward' areas—a label which is frequently and readily attached to the forested and 'tribal' parts of the subcontinent— are the major repositories of natural resources, and historically these areas have always been closely linked with the developments in their neighbouring agricultural areas. An easy way to argue in favour of this idea is to point out that some of the major trade routes of the subcontinent passed through such 'backward' mineral and timber rich belts. They were most unlikely to have remained immune to the spread and impact of ideas from outside.

We also do not propose to bolster the claim of any arbitrarily drawn line on the map of India as a significant boundary-marker in her cultural or political history.[6] For instance, we shall not argue that the Vindhya-Satpura line marked one of the great divides of Indian history. For one thing, this cannot be backed by archaeological and historical data, and for another, claims like this cannot be said to provide any insight into the process of history along such divides.

Our main concern in this volume is to note how the different parts of the subcontinent have interacted throughout its ancient history, and one of the surest ways to assess such interactions is to trace how its political units—or dynasties or kingdoms, if one prefers—have tried to expand and configure themselves within the broad limits of the subcontinent's boundary. If they have done so in a number of orbits, it is also our concern to define them and underscore their historical ramifications.

Notes

1. Schwartzberg (1992: 254, Fig. 14.1). In different forms this idea has been expressed by earlier scholars including O.H.K. Spate (1957: 148):

We have thus three great divisions: the Indus valley, open to cultural and political influences from central and SW Asia; Hindustan, accessible only when the Delhi gateway has been forced, and more receptive than the S, to which it has acted as a shock-absorber; the Peninsula S of the Narbada, which, except in Maharashtra, has been far more resistant to influences from Asia; largely no doubt, owing to mere distance, but to some extent owing to the barriers of hill and jungle, especially in the NE. It is noteworthy that the Deccan Lavas extend far N of the Narbada in Malwa; this is the great passageway from Hindustan into the Deccan, and on its glacis in Maharashtra alike the Aryans, the earlier Muslims, and the Moghuls established their first serious lodgements in the Southland. The pattern of the subcontinent as a whole—diminishing ripples of alien influence radiating from an entry in the NW—is thus repeated in the Deccan.

There is, of course, no reason why the geographical zoning of the subcontinent's history should be dependent on the 'diminishing ripples of alien influence radiating from an entry in the NW'. Still earlier, Richards (1933) mentioned four such zones, 'in order of size': the Gangetic plain, the South, the Kistna-Godavari delta, and Gujarat.

2. Holdich (1910).

3. Chakrabarti (1977).

4. The concept of 'inner' India lying to the east of a line from Mathura to the Gulf of Cambay along the Aravallis finds mention in Spate (1957: 148): 'N and W of this the generally arid physical environment and the Islamic heritage combine to produce a cultural landscape strongly reminiscent of SW Asia; it has been said that the true India does not begin before the temples of Muttra, birthplace of Krishna.'

5. Chakrabarti (1988: Chapter 4, pp. 50–64).

6. cf. Day (1949).

2

The First Orbits—the Dominance of the Gangetic India

Legendary Beginnings to c. 200 BC

The Domain of Tradition: The Earliest Political Canvas

Dynasties and kingdoms occur quite early in the Indian historical record. Scholars like F.E. Pargiter and A.D. Pusalker have shown how the *Purana*s contain references to various kings and dynasties, some of which are also corroborated by the Vedic texts and epics. However, many of them suffer from the absence of such corroborative sources and have to be relegated to the domain of mythology or tradition.[1] This is a point which has also been made clear by H.C. Raychaudhuri who has tried to reconstruct our traditional history from the legendary king Parikshit to the well-known Magadhan king Bimbisara.[2]

The first phase of this traditional history in Pusalker's analysis takes one back to the legendary progenitor of all the subsequent Indian dynasties, Manu Vaivasvata. What is interesting is that even in this completely shadowy phase there are references to individual dynasties, their locations, and struggle for power. For instance, the king Yayati of the Lunar dynasty with its seat at Pratisthana (in this case, modern Jhusi) was a powerful king, bequeathing to his five sons five kingdoms, which between them covered the whole of the Doab and the territories which lay broadly to the west of the Doab. The youngest, Puru, got control of the ancestral seat of Pratisthana, which would roughly mean control of the southern Doab. The upper Doab went to Anu. The valley of the Chambal, Betwa, and Ken—roughly the area of modern Bundelkhand, the centre of which is modern Jhansi—went to Yadu. The Baghelkhand territory around Rewa fell to the share of Turvasu, with the territory west of the Yamuna and north of the Chambal going to the control of Druhyu. The account may be mythical, but the geographical configuration, although not detailed, stands out and makes sense: broadly the Doab and the territories flanking it on the west—five kingdoms of Yayati's sons, which, in fact, become seven if the kingdoms of Kanyakubja and Kasi in the same general region are taken into account.

The possessions of the Solar dynasty lay between Ayodhya and Vaisali, with Videha and its capital Mithila forming a third focal point. Between them, the Lunar and Solar dynasties seem to have controlled a very large section of northern India. In the legendary Puranic accounts this was the core area of political history at its earliest, with ties to the Narmada area where Mahishmati was a centre of political power, Gujarat, and Panjab. As the original dynasties proliferate into various branches around the successor kings, more geographical names get added to the list. Even in the succeeding phase 'from the accession of Parikshit to the end of Barhadratha dynasty' (of Magadha), which Pusalker depicts as tinged with more historical reality, the basic geographical focus of India's political history did not change much. According to him, the detailed history of this phase, as recorded in the Puranas, is 'confined more or less to the region now represented by the United Provinces and South Bihar'.[3]

He highlights the following major kingdoms throughout this region during this phase—Kuru which lay between the Sarasvati in modern Kurukshetra to the uppermost part of the Doab, Kosala which lay along the Ghaghra and included large territories both to its north and south, and Magadha or south Bihar. What is intriguing is that the Kurus had advanced as far west as Taxila, thus establishing a long-standing pattern of interaction between the North-West and the head of the Ganga-Yamuna territory. Many other kingdoms also emerge into significance during this phase—Panchala, Surasena, Vatsa, Avanti, Videha, Kasi, Kosala, Anga, Kalinga, Gandhara, and Kamboja, all of which figure in Pusalker's description of the period.

It has been assumed that the traditional history of India from the royal progenitor Manu Vaivasvata to the phase marking the dominance of Magadha is earlier than anything else which has come down politically to us. There is no specific reason why it should be so, especially when the Puranas are notoriously undependable chronologically, but it is interesting to reflect that this essentially Puranic story moves up and down the Ganga-Yamuna plain, incorporating in it the whole area north of the Narmada and up to the North-West. The Puranic sources did not apparently have a wider geographical applicability. Nor do the Puranas throw much light on the interrelationship between these kingdoms during this phase except to emphasize power struggle between such kingdoms as Kosala and Kasi.

Depending principally on the *Brahmana*s and the *Upanishad*s, Raychaudhuri[4] points out the existence of nine states of considerable importance in northern India in the post-Parikshit period—Gandhara, Kekaya, Madra, Usinara, Matsya, Kuru, Panchala, Kasi, and Kosala. If the location of Gandhara is in the Rawalpindi-Peshawar section, Kekaya and Madra lay between the Jhelam and the Chenab and between the Chenab and the Ravi respectively. Usinara has been placed in the modern Haridwar section and Matsya in the general area of Alwar. Raychaudhuri puts Parikshit in the fourteenth century BC, following a Puranic tradition, and thinks that Janaka, the famous legendary king of Videha, of which Mithila was the capital, should be put in the twelfth century BC. There may not be any special logic behind these dates but they convey the idea that we are still in the traditional phase of ancient Indian history. In Raychaudhuri's map of 'India in the age of Janaka' three more kingdoms are added to the above-mentioned list of important north Indian states during this period: Chedi (basically the Baghelkhand area of Rewa), Vatsa (northern bank of the Yamuna with Kausambi as the centre), and Kikata (south bank of the Ganga, East of Kasi, which should make it geographically overlapping with Magadha).

The upshot of this evidence from the present point of view is that even in the traditional and thus generally legendary phase of ancient Indian history, we find virtually the whole of northern India fairly open and divided into a number of states, especially along the sweep from the North-West (Gandhara) to Magadha and Anga. The other indications which emerge are the following—the North-West and the upper Ganga-Yamuna stretch (Kuru) were closely linked, and second, Mahishmati on the northern bank of the Narmada, the Bundelkhand, and Baghelkhand areas west of the Yamuna, the Mathura, and Alwar stretches of Rajasthan, and even Gujarat were all within this north Indian network.

There are also reasons to believe that various states had developed south of the Narmada and elsewhere during this traditional period. In the section 'the Deccan in the age of the later Vaidehas' Raychaudhuri combines various sources[5]—mostly the Brahmanas, Upanishads, *Jatakas*, and Puranas—to argue for the existence of the following kingdoms in 'ancient Dakshinapatha': Vidarbha (capital Kaundinyapura), Kalinga (capital Dantapura), Assaka (capital Potana or modern Bodhan), Bhojas (capital Bhojakataka between Ajanta and Aurangabad), Dandaka (Nasik area?), Andhras, Savaras (the Dandakaranya area north of Vizianagram) and Pulindas (south of the source area of the Narmada), and Mutibas (modern Hyderabad area?). In addition, Raychaudhuri's map of the region shows Mekala (the Maikal hills) and Mulaka (roughly the middle Godavari). Looked at closely, this is not the whole of the Deccan. This is Vidarbha and north Deccan including the Nasik area, possibly the whole of Andhra and Kalinga, and the source area of the Narmada. The regions further to the south are not mentioned in these sources which apparently have their geographical limitations.

The Historical Beginning

The period of the 'sixteen Mahajanapadas' around the period of the Buddha, the knowledge of which is primarily derived from the Buddhist and Jaina sources, is said to mark the first demonstrably historical phase of ancient Indian political history. I have elsewhere argued that the archaeological beginning of early history in the subcontinent covers the period from *c.* 800 BC to *c.* 500 BC.[6] Assuming that the Mahajanapada phase which bears a clear literary testimony, falls in the sixth century BC, the domain of tradition that we have alluded to earlier should be pre-sixth century BC. Without putting too fine a point on chronology, this may generally be accepted as a valid historical statement. The point which we would like emphasize is that by the time the political history of India assumes a concrete shape, as it obviously does from the phase of the 'sixteen Mahajanapadas' onwards, there is a motley of clearly defined political units in India covering not merely the Indo-Gangetic plain and the rest of northern India but also large parts of the Deccan. If the areas further south do not enter the picture by then, it is possibly because the sources dealing with northern India and the Deccan are silent about them. One would assume that visible geographical and political units had emerged by this time also in the Kaveri valley and elsewhere in the south. In any case, the evidence of these states and the geographical nature of interaction between them is certainly not elaborate during this phase, but whatever it was, it was on the basis of the emergence of these political units and their geographical interactions that the shape of the later political India emerged.

The fact that the Buddhist and Jaina sources list only sixteen 'great principalities', although with some variations between the two lists, it does not necessarily mean that India in the sixth century BC or somewhat earlier was divided only into sixteen great states. The lists possibly indicate nothing more than the Buddhist or Jaina religious interests in them. However, these lists consolidate and support the evidence of the existence of many principalities, large or small, in pre-Buddhist (or what has been said to denote the traditional) phase of Indian history.

The states in the Buddhist list are Kasi, Kosala, Anga, Magadha, Vajji or Vriji, Malla, Chedi, Vatsa, Kuru, Panchala, Matsya, Surasena, Asmaka, Avanti, Gandhara, and Kamboja. The Jaina list mentions Anga, Vanga, Magadha, Malaya, Malava, Achchha, Vachchha or Vatsa, Kochchha (Kachchha?), Ladha (Lata or Radha), Padha (Pandya or Paundra?), Vajji, Moli or Malla, Kasi, Kosala, Avaha (?), and Sambhuttara (Sumhottara?). There are obvious problems of identification in the Jaina list which has also been suggested to be later without any convincing argument. There is no reason to argue that this list is later simply because this shows a wider geographical knowledge than the Buddhist one.

The focal point of Kasi was Varanasi, and this kingdom interacted with Kosala on the one hand and Magadha on the other. The extent of the Kasi kingdom must have included modern Jaunpur which is at the doorstep of Ayodhya/Saketa, the earlier capital of Kosala, and it is natural that Kasi would have political struggle with Kosala, which it eventually lost. The same is true of Magadha of the modern Patna-Gaya area. The Magadhan border in the direction of Kasi possibly came up to the Karmanasa river which again is very near modern Chakia at the gate of Banaras. When Magadha was on a path of expansion, Kasi literally fell on the way. Although the interaction of Kasi with Kosala and Magadha is not a matter of surprise, some sources refer to the subjugation of Anga, which lies to the east of Magadha, by Kasi and the subjugation of the Haihayas of the Narmada valley, also by Kasi. Even the Asmaka capital on the Godavari has been described by one source as a city of the kingdom of Kasi.[7] To subjugate Anga, one had to pass

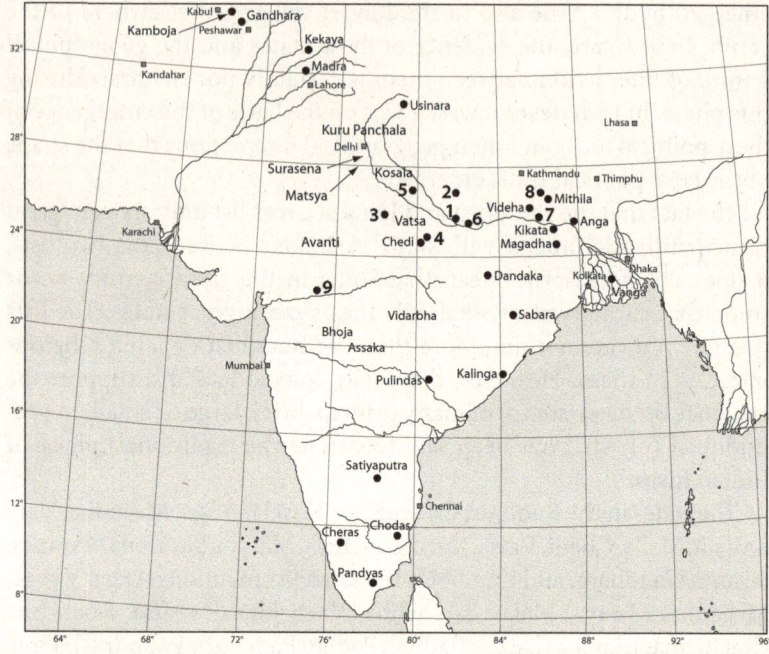

1. Jhusi (Pratisthana)   6. Kasi
2. Ayodhya   7. Vaisali
3. Jhansi (Bundelkhand)   8. Mithila
4. Rewa (Baghelkhand)   9. Mahishmati
5. Kanyakubja

Map 2.1   Location of Some Major Sites and Areas Mentioned in Chapter 2

through Magadha and thus a victory over Magadha was necessary. The alluded campaign against the Haihayas of the Narmada valley is decidedly intriguing. The upper reaches of the Narmada are accessible from Banaras across the forested Sarguja and Shadol areas of central India but to reach the Haihayas around their capital Mahishmati or modern Maheshwar from Banaras, one has to follow the route through Malwa. It is very unlikely that Kasi would try to invade the Haihayas of Mahishmati, which would involve sending army across other kingdoms and over a long distance. In any case, Banaras was a major terminal point of the routes which linked the Ganga plain with the Deccan, passing through various stretches of central India, Andhra, and Maharashtra. The fact that the capital of Asmaka on the Godavari has been described as a city of Kasi possibly indicates nothing more than the mutual links these places had by virtue of their positions on the Deccan routes. However, literary references like this need not be taken at their face value.

Lying on either side of the Ghaghra, Kosala must have covered a very large area and could not consequently escape having borders with the following states—Kasi and Vatsa to the west and south-west, the Mallas and the Sakyas and others to the East, and possibly Panchala to the north and north-west. The historical sources, however, seem to refer only to its struggles first with Kasi and later with Magadha. The Mallas and the other political units such as the Kalamas and the Sakyas on its eastern border were much smaller units and easily incorporated in the domain of Kosala. It is not easy to define the borders of Kosala in specific geographical terms, but there is no difficulty to accept Raychaudhuri's definition of its area—the Gomati in the west, the Sai in the south, the Sadanira or Burhi Gandak in the east and the Nepal Siwaliks in the north.[8] The dominance of north Bihar was apparently her immediate bone of contention with Magadha. In the struggle with Kasi, Kosala won, and as Raychaudhuri points out,[9] the annexation of the kingdom of Kasi by Kosala could not have happened long before the rise of Buddhism 'because the memory of Kasi as an independent kingdom was still fresh in the minds of the people of the Buddha's time and even later when the Anguttara Nikaya was composed'.

The Vatsa kingdom, of which Kausambi was the capital, extended possibly on both sides of the Yamuna, including a solid chunk of territory bordering the western limits of Kosala. As the literary sources suggest, it had interaction with Anga, Magadha, and Avanti, although in the case of Avanti, there was hostility. It is possible that the contact with Avanti was maintained through the Betwa valley which joined the Yamuna near Hamirpur. Another route through Baghelkhand, that is, the modern Rewa area, was possible, but in that case the literary sources were likely to have referred to the relationship of Vatsa with the Chedi kingdom, of which Rewa was the centre.

Not much has been stated about the interaction of the rest of the 16 principalities. Anga lay to the east of Magadha, and although its fluctuating relationship with Magadha is known, nothing is indicated of its relationship with its eastern neighbours such as Paundra and Vanga. Vajji, of which Vaisali was the centre, was targeted by Magadha. Malla is recognized as a separate territory, but lying at the eastern fringe of Kosala, it was likely to have been dominated by it even before it was annexed by Magadha. The fact that Panchala was divided into north and south Panchala is said to have been supported by the testimony of the Mahabharata, the Jatakas, and the *Divyavadana*, but the details of its political history during this phase are not available. King Avantiputra of the Surasena kingdom was one of the chief disciples of the Buddha, which would mean that the Mathura area lay in the vanguard of early Buddhist expansion. King Pukkusati of Gandhara sent an emissary to the king Bimbisara of Magadha, and this implies that there was no barrier in interaction between the north-western subcontinent and the southern section of the Ganga valley. Interestingly, Avanti, which had its capital at Ujjayini and Pradyota as its king, figures as a hostile power in relation to Magadha. The point is that Avanti could exert influence on Magadha only when the Vatsa kingdom, and at least a part of the kingdom of Kasi, were under its control.

On the whole, what is obvious is that the basic political focus of north India in the sixth century BC and later was at least in three directions. First, there was a straight sweep of communications from the North-West to Magadha, implying the openness of the whole of the Indo-Gangetic plain and the area of Panjab and beyond. Second, there was another sweep of movement from Anga to Avanti, that is, from the modern Bhagalpur-Rajmahal hills zone to western Malwa, implying that the whole of the intervening area in modern Madhya Pradesh was a part of this sweep too. Third, the tradition that Banaras or the kingdom of Kasi had links with the Narmada valley and even the capital city Bodhan of the Asmakas in Andhra suggests that the Gangetic valley network covered not merely western Malwa but some parts of the Deccan as well. There is little doubt that early historic India begins not merely with some major principalities and many smaller geopolitical units but also had a clear-cut historical–geographical configuration of power.

It is important to appreciate this configuration before turning to the geography of the Magadhan expansion. The history of the first Magadhan dynasties after the legendary Barhadratha dynasty is reconstructed principally on the basis of the Puranic and Buddhist sources including the testimony of the Sri Lankan chronicle *Mahavamsa*. The first major king was Bimbisara of the Haryanka dynasty. Anga was annexed to Magadha and at least a part of the kingdom of Kasi came under the Magadhan domination. Bimbisara contacted alliances with the Madras of Panjab, Kosala, and Vaisali.

Under his successor Ajatasatru, wars were waged against possibly the combined forces of Kosala, Vaisali, and the confederate clans of the region, leading eventually to the victory of Magadha. The city of Pataliputra was founded under Udayin, Ajatasatru's successor. With the transfer of capital to Pataliputra, Magadha was centrally placed to control things in various directions—the traffic along the Ganga, north Bihar plains, the plain of modern Balia and beyond in Kosala, and easy movement from Pataliputra in the direction of central India and the Deccan along the course of the Son which joined the Ganga then at Pataliputra. Besides, Magadha had always enjoyed easy access to the east, including the resource-rich Chhotanagpur plateau. A source suggests that by this time Avanti annexed Vatsa, and thus Magadha and Avanti came face to face, so to speak. Magadha turned victorious in the struggle with Avanti under Udayin's successor Sisunaga.

The general scholarly consensus is that the accession of Bimbisara to the throne of Magadha took place in 544/545 BC.[10] The dynasty which he represented, that is, the Haryanka dynasty, came to an end around 430 BC. The Magadhan line was then followed by Sisunaga who founded the Saisunaga dynasty. This dynasty came to an end around 345 BC or 364 BC[11] after which Magadha passed into the control of the Nanda dynasty, the first king of which was Mahapadmananda.

The chronology of this period is, because of the discrepancies among the sources, somewhat uncertain, but the chronology offered by scholars like Raychaudhuri is without doubt in the right direction. About 519 BC, Gandhara was annexed by the Achaemenids, but in the Buddhist sources we read that the Gandharan king Paushkarasarin or Pukkusati sent an emissary to Bimbisara, suggesting that when this happened, Gandhara was an independent kingdom and thus we are dealing with a context before 519 BC. Bimbisara who was a contemporary of the Buddha was no doubt a sixth century BC king.

The Puranic sources credit the first king of the Nanda dynasty, Mahapadmananda, with victory over a large number of kings— Ikshaku, Panchala, Kasi, Haihaya, Kalinga, Asmaka, Kuru, Mithila, Surasena, and Vitihotra. The Ikshakus were based in the lower Krishna valley of Andhra in the AD second–third century and this Puranic list may refer to this sector or even the area of Ayodhya which was the capital of the legendary Ikshaku dynasty. On the whole, however, the list clearly suggests that Mahapadmananda became the undisputed sovereign of the Ganga-Yamuna plain, the Narmada valley (cf. the Haihayas and Vitihotras), and parts of the Deccan (cf. Asmakas) and the East coast (cf. Kalinga). It was not a radical departure from the geographical pattern that we have noted earlier. However, one broadly accepts the general scholarly opinion that Mahapadmananda was 'the first great historical emperor of India'.[12] The claim gains an extra focus when we remember that the second/first century BC Hatigumpha inscription of Kharavela mentions the activities of the Nanda kings in Kalinga in the fourth century BC or about 200–300 years earlier.

From the Oxus to the Indus: The Achaemenids and Alexander

It is now time to reflect that along the geopolitical orbit which came up in the Ganga-Yamuna plain, central India up to western Malwa, and the Deccan and parts of the eastern coast, there was another orbit which was a major component of the overall Oxus to the Indus interaction zone. Historically, this emerges into view with the Achaemenid annexation of the Indus valley which, as the mention of Gandhara as a subject territory in the Behistun inscription of Darius indicates, should have taken place before 519 BC, the probable date of the Behistun inscription. Gandhara was one of the three Achaemenid satrapies in India, the two other satrapies being Satyagdia (capital Akra in Bannu) and the one in the lower Indus valley or Sindh. It is probable that the capital of Achaemenid Gandhara was the Bhir mound of Taxila. The capital of the Achaemenid Sindh cannot yet be determined because of the lack of details on the early historic sites of the region. The only reported early historic site of Sindh is Brahminabad in the Indus delta, but the site is not properly excavated.

There is no doubt that the Achaemenid control of the region was not accidental. They controlled the entire area of the Oxus-Indus orbit, and to do so they were likely to have controlled the routes to central Asia from Chitral and Gilgit-Hunza. As the whole of Afghanistan was their territory, they naturally controlled the Hindukush passes to north Afghanistan. If they could control the routes across the Karakoram and the Pamirs to north-east Afghanistan and Chinese Turkestan, they could protect the Central Asian trade circuit in its entirety. Further, the very location of the Achaemenid satrapies in the Indus valley from the Rawalpindi-Peshawar area to Sindh shows that their control of the valley was complete. This is something which is also suggested by the exploration of the navigability of the Indus by Scylax of Caryanda, a Greek who was sent by Darius for the purpose.

He explored the navigability of the river from Caspatyrus (somewhere in the upper reaches of the valley) downward.

The Achaemenids were likely to have maintained communications with their Indian territories mainly in two ways—by travelling from their base in the Fars plain through Kirman to Baluchistan, and by going to Kandahar (the capital of their satrapy of Arachosia) first, and then following a pass to the Indus plain.[13]

The Oxus-Indus orbit came into distinct prominence in the wake of Alexander's invasion of the Indus valley as the successor of the Achaemenid power in the east. The petty principalities which covered the entire area from Swat to the Indus delta and were described by the historians who accompanied Alexander suggest that the area was not a political wasteland during the time of Alexander's invasion and that it was unlikely to be so even in the Achaemenid time.

Alexander came to India as the inheritor of the Achaemenid power in the region. The fact that it was the Gandharan region which was possessed first by Cyrus implies that the Achaemenids entered the region via the Kabul valley. This entrance was also used by Alexander. He sent two of his commanders, Hephaestion and Perdiccas, through this, and he himself campaigned in the valleys of Kunar, Panjgora, and Swat which lie broadly to the north-east of Peshawar. This concern with occupying the hilly region to the north-east of Peshawar seems to have a geographical implication. Alexander and the Achaemenids before him established control over the southern section of Central Asia including the Oxus valley. The hill valleys north-east of Peshawar lead to Central Asia both via the Pamir plateau and the north-east Afghanistan area of Badakhsan. Thus, the hill valleys which lead in the direction of the Pamirs and Badakhsan had considerable geopolitical significance for Alexander for maintaining the security of his Central Asian possessions. One can be certain that the area had similar significance for the Achaemenids too. The pattern of Achaemenid and Macedonian invasions of the subcontinent categorically demonstrate the historical emergence of the Oxus to the Indus interaction zone. That Alexander did not move further east from the Indus valley shows that like the Achaemenids before him he also was interested in retaining supremacy only over this zone.

The detailed accounts that one gets in the contemporary Classical sources of the movements of Alexander and his generals impress one, first and foremost, by the sheer number of the various principalities which stretched from one end of the Indus valley to another. It is apparent that about two centuries of Achaemenid rule over the region could not curb the emergence and consolidation of various small principalities all over this sector. Such states as Gandhara, Kamboja, Madra, and Kekaya which basically covered parts of the north-west and Panjab were, as we have seen before, known in the Vedic and generally Brahmanical and Buddhist sources. What the Classical sources show is the sheer scale and extent of the formation of such states. The number of principalities must have been much more in the sixth century BC India than the generally accepted number of 16, despite our traditional sources being silent about them. While looking into the details of the Achaemenid and Macedonian control of the north-western area of the subcontinent up to the Indus, it also becomes clear that India even then was not an area which was isolated from the cross-currents of historical affairs in Central and West Asia extending right up to the Mediterranean zone.[14]

Mauryan India

These two geopolitical orbits—the one consolidated by the Magadhan expansion and the one highlighted by the Achaemenid and Macedonian invasions—are the earliest discernible major geographical foci of state power in ancient India. These two orbits coalesced under the Maurya dynasty to form an overarching orbit from the Hindukush to Karnataka.

The area south of Karnataka seems to have had an orbit of its own, although it is difficult to make out when that emerged. The fixed historical reference point is the Asokan inscription (RE II) which mentions the Satiyaputras, Keralaputras, Cholas, and Pandyas. Thus, by the third century BC the south Indian orbit was in place, and the problem is to determine how far back can one trace it. It has been argued elsewhere that there is good reason to date the beginning of early history in the Kaveri delta and elsewhere in the south at least about 500 BC. The Satiyaputras, of which the notable chief was Atiyaman/Adigaman, had their focal point around Takadur in the modern Dharmapuri area. Keralaputras or Cheras occupied at least the Periyar valley in which their first capital Vanji is supposed to have been located. It appears that a part of Kongunadu or modern Coimbatore-Salem region was within the Chera domain because their second capital Karur was located in this sector. Basically, the Chera or Kerala kingdom denoted 'the western coastal strip above the northern limit of the Pandyan kingdom' and 'a notable inward extension by way of the Palghat gap'. The lower Kaveri valley, the coastal plain between north Vellar and south Vellar, the former joining the sea near Porto Novo and the latter flowing through the Pudukottai area, formed the Chola territory, which would mean roughly the Thanjavur-Tiruchirapalli segment. The Pandya area 'included the modern districts of Tirunelveli, Madurai, and Ramnad, besides south Travancore, often called Nanjilnad, plough-land'. The early history of these kingdoms has been reconstructed on the basis of the Tamil Sangam literature, 'the most significant part of which', according to K.A.N. Sastri's detailed comparative study, reflects 'the history of the period ranging from AD 130 to about 230'. However, there is no reason why this literature cannot contain the echoes of an earlier tradition. The sheer fact that the states mentioned in the Sangam literature find mention in RE II proves that the history of these states certainly goes back to the third century BC. The Cheras, Cholas, and Pandyas, each with their list of kings, indulged in substantial fighting among themselves and with various chieftains who possibly represented

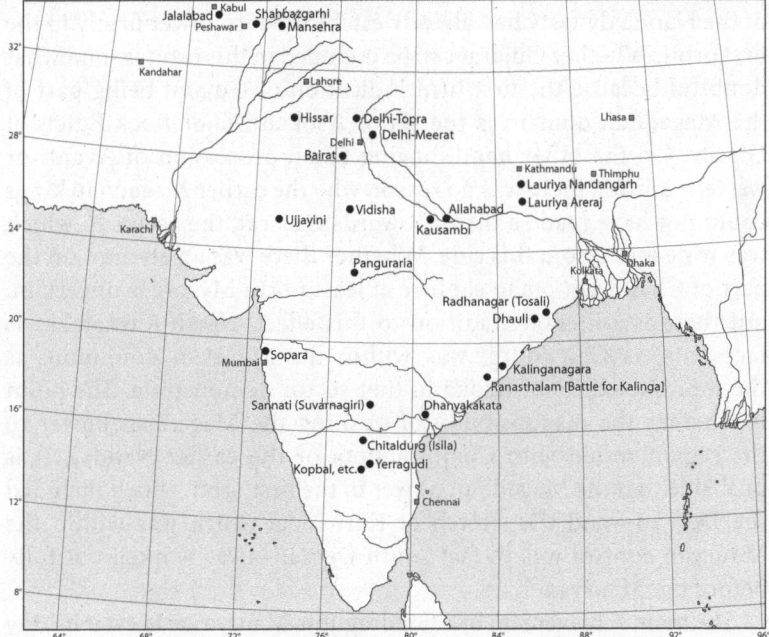

Map 2.2   Location of Some Major Sites in the Context of Asokan Edicts

small regional pockets of territory. There are references to some lesser principalities along with references to the three major ones in the Sangam literature. The identity of these three major political units of the south is firmly established not merely on the basis of the Sangam literature but also on the basis of their inscriptions and coins.

It appears that the southern orbit of power was in its first phase somewhat self-contained, concerned mainly with the establishment of suzerainty within the region itself. The only major region outside it, with which it interacted, seems to be Sri Lanka. However, this may be a wrong impression. In the Sangam literature, in any case, we find the Chola king Karikala credited with the conquest of the whole of India up to the Himalayas. The concept of *Digvijaya* (conquering the world) was undoubtedly there. Besides, geographically it does not make any sense that the three major south Indian kingdoms of the day were fighting only among themselves. On the model of the later historical developments in the south, it can safely be asserted that all of them took a lot of interest in extending their belt of influence northward to south Karnataka and north-eastward to the Andhra coast.[15]

We have noted that the Magadhan power under Mahapadmananda of the Nanda dynasty had already established its power firmly in the first orbit. Whether Gujarat can be included in this orbit is somewhat doubtful because the first firm indication of Gujarat being part of the Magadhan domain is the set of Asokan Major Rock Edicts at Girnar. On the other hand, having taken possession of Avanti or western Malwa, there was no reason why the earlier Magadhan kings could not have made a thrust towards Gujarat, the access to which was wide open from this side. Whether there was an attempt on the part of Chandragupta to capture at least north Mysore is uncertain, but there is a literary tradition to this effect. North Karnataka, as far south as Chitaldurg, was within the Mauryan dominion, as the multiple edicts of Asoka in that sector demonstrate. The point is whether the responsibility of pushing the Magadhan power to the region rested with Chandragupta or the earlier Nandas. It is probable that the Magadhan power in the first orbit, which included the Deccan—and the stretch of Karnataka which was within the Mauryan control was in fact south Deccan—was worked out fully before the Mauryas.[16]

The main achievement of Chandragupta Maurya lay in establishing a firm hold over the second orbit, that is, the Oxus to the Indus orbit. It is not that the whole of this orbit came under the Mauryan control, but the Hindukush is the natural boundary of South Asia in this direction, and Chandragupta established Magadhan suzerainty up to the Hindukush, which would mean that the Kabul-Kandahar stretch of south Afghanistan came under the Mauryas. This he did by thwarting the ambition of Selecucas Nicator, the inheritor of Alexander's empire in the east, in the direction of the Indian territories. One is not sure if the area up to Herat went to Chandragupta; that would not make much sense because in that case, the Mauryas would have controlled Bactria or North Afghanistan as well, but the latter idea is unacceptable because Bactria was the heartland of the Greek power in the east. Regarding Makran coming to the Mauryan control, it is not inherently improbable. Right up to the southern slopes of the Hindukush, the Oxus to the Indus orbit was under the Mauryan power, and Baluchistan and its coast, the latter known as Makran, was a part of this orbit.

At this point, one has to raise the issue of the eastern territories of Bengal and Assam—were they parts of the Magadhan dominion? If so, when did this come about? The most important evidence of the Magadhan presence in these eastern territories is the Mahasthangarh Mauryan inscription which shows that the Pundra territory was in any case under the Mauryan control. The location of Mahasthangarh is in the Karatoya valley which is historically linked with the Brahmaputra valley, and the very fact that the Mauryas were established in the Karatoya valley denotes that some parts at least of the Brahmaputra valley were under Mauryan domination. Similarly, after the discovery, and the dating of the early historic urban site of Wari-Bateshwar located near an old channel of the Brahmaputra near Dhaka in the mid-fifth century BC, it is possible to argue that 'Samatata' as a geographical unit may date from the Mahajanapada period, and considering that there was no major geographical barrier between Mahasthangarh and the area of Wari-Bateshwar, one would argue that the Mauryan domination extended up to Samatata. At present, the Brahmaputra separates the former Pundravardhana territory from the Samatata territory, but this Brahmaputra is the result of a comparatively recent shift in this river's course. The old channel of the river can still be seen further east, and Wari-Bateshwar is located near the mouth of this old channel before it joins the Meghna near Bhairavbazar in Bangladesh and the combined stream moves towards the Bay of Bengal. Again, if Samatata was under the Mauryan control, there was no geographical hindrance to their possible movement right up to the Chittagong coast, just as there was no hindrance to their movement through the broad sweep of the northern bank of the Brahmaputra right up to the Sadiya frontier from their base in Mahasthangarh in the Karatoya valley. As far as modern West Bengal is concerned, there is no Mauryan epigraph from the area, but it is against common geographical sense to believe that Magadha, having annexed Anga, which would take it to the mouth of entry to West Bengal near the Rajmahal hills anyway, would stop here and not come down to the mouth of the Bhagirathi or the original course of the Ganga, especially when the West Bengal area lies on the path to Orissa or Odra which had been under Magadhan control since the days of the Nandas.

We are assuming that the basic historical-geographical configuration of the Magadhan power was achieved before the beginning of the Maurya dynasty, whose founder Chandragupta Maurya simply added to it the stretch from the Indus valley to the southern foot of the Hindukush, giving the Mauryan India a strong foothold in the Oxus to the Indus interaction zone of Indian history. The evidence is in some cases, as in the cases of Gujarat, Bengal, and Assam, shadowy, but if Chandragupta had undertaken expeditions in these directions, there would have been echoes of these expeditions in the literary traditions.

There is no evidence that the second Maurya king Bindusara added anything to the Mauryan territory, but the fact that the Mauryans kept on maintaining interests in the direction of Central and Western Asia is clear from the literary tradition that he wrote to Antiochus of Syria asking him to buy and send him sweet wine, dried figs, and a sophist. Besides, the classical sources mention other links between the Magadhan court and the Hellenic world during this period.

Bindusara's successor Asoka maintained these Hellenic links, and this is evident from the list of kings mentioned in his Rock Edict XIII. These kings have been listed by Raychaudhuri[17] as 'Ptolemy II, Philadelphos, king of Egypt (BC 285–247); Magas, king of Cyrene in North Africa (who probably died not later than BC 258; Antigonos Gonatas, king of Macedonia (BC 277 or 276–239); and Alexander who ruled over Epirus (BC 272–c. 255) or Corinth (BC 252–c. 244)'. What this list makes clear is that the Mauryan India was perfectly at ease in its knowledge of, and links with, various states lying to the west of its border and extending as far west as the lands around the Mediterranean. Similarly, links with the states beyond the southern frontier were maintained, including those with Tamraparni or Sri Lanka where Devanampiya Tissa (date of accession *c.* 250/247 BC) was his contemporary king. The Sri Lankan chronicles speak of his sending Buddhist missionaries not merely to Sri Lanka where they were headed by his son Mahendra but also to Suvarnabhumi or lower Myanmar and Sumatra. Buddhist missionary activities under Asoka are specifically mentioned by the Sri Lankan chronicles in certain southern areas of his own kingdom (Mahishamandala or Mysore, Vanavasa or Banavasi near the Karnataka coast, Aparantaka or North Konkan, and Maharashtra) and in the Yona or Yavana lands (most likely the territories at the foot of the Hindukush), Kashmira, and Gandhara. One would suggest that Kashmir came under Mauryan control in the time of Chandragupta himself when he took control of the area up to the Hindukush.[18]

The true indicator of the extent and nature of the Magadhan control under Asoka is the distribution of the different categories of his inscriptions—Major Rock Edicts, Minor Rock Edicts, Major Pillar Edicts, Minor Pillar Edicts, and individual rock inscriptions. The north-western extent is clearly marked by the cluster of inscriptions in south Afghanistan—RE XII–XIII in Greek at Kandahar, Pillar Edict VI at Kandahar, Shahr-i-Kuna bilingual Greek and Aramaic inscription resembling MRE from Kandahar, Pul-i-Darunta inscription with quotations from Asokan edicts in Afghanistan, and two separate inscriptions, both mentioning 'Priyadarsin', at Lamghan and Kandahar. Considering the general distribution of Asokan edicts in the whole of the subcontinent, this is a very impressive cluster in south Afghanistan, especially around Kandahar which, if the hypothesis of the existence of PE VI there is true, must have had an inscribed Asokan pillar too. An Aramaic inscription is also reported from Taxila, and attention has been drawn to the occurrence of a fragmentary Asokan PE VI in Buner, again suggesting the existence of an inscribed pillar there. Besides these, there are Major Rock Edicts written in Kharosthi for the benefit of his subjects in the North-West at Shahbazgarhi in Peshawar and Mansehra in Hazara. In a comparatively limited sector of the north-western Frontier and south Afghanistan, these form a solid cluster of edicts and suggest Asoka's special concern in preaching his *Dhamma* or moral code of conduct in an area which was demonstrably diverse, ethnically and linguistically. However, the Kandahar and south Afghanistan distribution may also suggest, however faintly, that this was an area where the royal message of

Dharma needed repeated highlighting. It is possible that this was a frontier of unrest. Looking at the precise locations of Shahbazgarhi and Mansehra edicts, it has been said that they lie on the route which led in the direction of the Pamirs and thus Central Asia.[19] The report of PE VI from Buner also supports the premise that the Mauryan India was familiar with the route which went from the north-west through Hunza and Gilgit to Kashgar and Yarkand. This, in turn, implies that it was familiar with China, and thus the argument that China could not have been known to the *Arthasastra* is wrong.[20] Besides, if a route passed through Gilgit and Hunza to Central Asia, that was most unlikely to be unrelated to Kashmir, and thus the tradition that Kashmir was within Mauryan India is historically valid.

Lest we over-signify the occurrence of Asokan edicts in the sense that we attach significance only to those areas which have edicts and underplay the significance of those which have none, we must remember that these edicts came up only after Asoka converted to Buddhism, developed his moral code and decided to propagate that in various ways, only one of which was the putting up of edicts on rocks. It is unlikely that Asoka had the time to give the whole of the territory under him a systematic coverage of inscriptions. We also do not know why Major Rock Edicts were set up in some places and Minor Rock Edicts in others. Similarly, we do not know how the sites of pillar edicts were selected. We do not even know if edicts were engraved on pillars which were already existing or Asoka himself had ordered them to be set up and inscribed. There are certainly many uncertainties regarding the locations and other related issues of Asokan edicts, but still, a careful perusal of these locations is likely to provide an insight into how the vast Mauryan territory made a geographical sense.

In the eastern region, it is the inscribed pillars of Lauriya Areraj, Lauriya Nandangarh, and Rampurva which dominate attention. This particular cluster of pillar edicts and pillars is occasionally supposed to mark a route to the Nepalese *tarai* area beyond Rampurva, and considering that there are two pillar remains at Rampurva at the present border with Nepal, there may be some truth in this idea. When one comes to the details, one notes that the Kolhua pillar, which is uninscribed, is located in a Buddhist structural complex including a stupa and monastery. The associated archaeological relics, if any, of Lauriya Areraj seem to be unclear, but in the case of Lauriya Nandangarh, we are aware that the site as a whole contained a row of presumably early mud stupas and a later terraced temple/stupa and was apparently an important sacred centre either after the beginning of Buddhism or before it. Regarding the Rampurva remains such details are missing. In the east again, a few miscellaneous remains call for attention—fragments of pillar capitals from Masarh between Patna and Arah and Salem near Hajipur; unconfirmed report of the discovery of a pillar at a ghat in Patna where the Buddha crossed the Ganga when Pataliputra was being built; and the stump of a presumably Mauryan but uninscribed pillar at Sikligarh near Banmankhi in Purnea. The Sikligarh pillar stands outside a large mud fortification which is undated but may belong to the early historic period. There are some structural remains in the place where this pillar stands. Sikligarh lies on the direct route going from Pataliputra in the direction of Mahasthangarh.

One may also put the inscribed pillars at Lumbini and Nigliva in the Nepalese tarai in the context of the general eastern region. The major settlement centre of this sector lay at Tilaurakot on the bank of the Banganga river, which may be given the status of a Maurya administrative centre, although not of the capital of the Buddha's father Suddhodana. The impressive pillar capital from Bansi which falls in the modern Basti district (or a modern sub-division thereof) and lies on the direct route from Pataliputra to Lumbini also highlights the significance of the Nepalese tarai complex in this area. Further along this route in the direction of Pataliputra, there is a monolithic pillar with its capital missing on the opposite bank of the Ghaghra from Khairadih which is an ancient centre and a noted town of the early centuries AD. The pillar is narrower than the average Asokan pillar and less polished, but it is monolithic and the trace of abacus on the top of the pillar is still there. We do not know of any other early phase of Indian history when monolithic stone columns were made except the Mauryan period.

Thus, looking at the present corpus of Mauryan lithic remains in the eastern region including the tarai region of modern Nepal, what can be positively said in historical terms is not much. Nepal was significant, in ways of which we are still unaware, in the Mauryan scheme of things. The route from Pataliputra to the Lumbini sector is clear; the Ganga was crossed at Buxar and the Ghaghra at Khairadih to go in the direction of Basti from where there is a clear route towards Lumbini via Kopia, an early historic fortified town, and Bansi. The Rampurva, Lauriya Areraj, and Lauriya Nandangarh monuments and pillars also indicate the contemporary significance of Nepal, although suggesting that the modern route from north Bihar to Nepal via Raxaul was not the ancient route in this direction. Its place was taken up by the Vaisali>Kesariya>Areraj>Nandangarh>Rampurva alignment. In this context, one also notes the literary tradition that Asoka built a stupa at Pasupatinath near Kathmandu. The pillar at Sikligarh suggests some significance for the eastern route from Pataliputra to Mahasthangarh. The Masarh find lies between Pataliputra and Buxar, itself an ancient town, and Salem near Hajipur lay on the route from Pataliputra to Vaisali. The inscription that Asoka left behind as the memory of the donation of a cave in the Barabar hills near Gaya is the only dedicatory inscription of the kind left by him.

In Bihar, Minor Rock Edict I has been found at two places, first, at Sasaram in a small hilltop cave overlooking the road towards Banaras via Bhabua and Chakia, and then at Ghurhupur near Basaha in the Kaimur area. From Bhabua, the road goes to the hills in which the site of the eighth century temple Mundesvari is located, and having crossed it, goes in the direction of the Karamnasa which is crossed at Manglaur, giving access to the Chakia area. Nindaur, a major early historic site, lies in this sector between Bhabua and Chakia and underscores the significance of this route. Ahraura, another hilltop site of Minor Rock Edict I, is a communication node to the west of Banaras. From Ahraura there is a straight road to Banaras, with the Ganga being crossed probably at Ramnagar, and from Ahraura the road coming from the direction of Pataliputra keeps on going towards Mirzapur and beyond. Ahraura is a kind of crossroad, whose importance called for the setting up of a small mud fort of the Mauryan period, the ruins of which can still be traced in the old locality of modern Ahraura. The significance of Banaras in the Mauryan period is obvious from the Sarnath pillar, but the significance of the old city is also highlighted by the surviving stump of the Lat Bhairon pillar which is supposed to be surviving relic of an Asokan pillar after it was destroyed in comparatively recent times due to a public disturbance or fire. Banaras lay at a major junction point of routes—towards Ayodhya via Jaunpur; towards the trans-Sarayu plain via Ajamgarh; towards the Deccan via both Ahraura and Mirzapur; towards the Doab via Allahabad; and towards the east both by the river and via Ahraura and Chakia.

There is no special reason to argue that the Allahabad pillar inscription, on which the famous Samudragupta inscription was engraved later, was shifted to its present position near the confluence of the Ganga and Yamuna from Kausambi which has an in situ Asokan pillar fragment of its own. From Allahabad one moved up both the Yamuna and the Ganga to reach Bhita and Kausambi along the Yamuna and Sringaverapura along the Ganga. The Allahabad-Bhita-Kausambi alignment also led to the Rewa plateau climbing the Vindhyan scarp at Sohagi ghat and Baldaha ghat and was overlooked at the former by the third–second century BC stupa of Deur Kothar.

It is important to note that fragments of at least one pillar which is identical in shape and size with the classic Asokan columns have been found at this site, and what is more important is that an inscription of a Buddhist monk in the script of the third century BC has been found engraved on it. The implications of this discovery do not seem to have sunk in; the existence of a third century BC 'private' (not royal) inscription on a monolithic stone column identical with the typical and well-known Mauryan columns brings us back to the idea that such stone columns pre-existed Asokan rule and that only on some of them he decided to have his inscriptions engraved. The Deur Kothar stone column bears no trace of a capital and no trace of a capital could be detected at the site either. Till further discoveries are made, the issue of the inscribed Deur Kothar 'Mauryan' monolithic stone column should be left unsettled.

From Ahraura, a road ascends the Vindhyan scarp to move in the direction of the Robertsganj or Sonabhadra plateau on the way to Sarguja and Chhattisgarh, which in turn would give access to the Deccan (both Andhra and Maharashtra). In the Garra dam area outside Ahraura there is a monolithic stone column of thinner proportions than the classic Mauryan specimens. The inscription it currently bears is early mediaeval but was possibly engraved long after the column itself was created.

There is an Asokan capital used as the base of the *linga* (the phallic stone of Siva) of the Nageswarnath Siva temple at Ayodhya, and some excavations at the mound which abuts this temple should result in the discovery of the associated pillar too. Beyond the Ghaghra, the existence of a Mahamatra, a principal royal official, at Sravasti, is known from the Asokan edicts, although no Asokan inscription has been directly discovered at Sravasti. Kausambi has a pillar, now surviving as a stump. Further up the Ganga-Yamuna plain, there is an Asokan pillar capital at Sankisa, but there is no pillar and the quality of the capital is far removed from the quality of the classic Asokan pillar capitals elsewhere. A similar type of Asokan pillar capital has been noted in the collection of *Gujari Mahal* in Gwalior and it is known to have come from Udayagiri in Vidisa area. We have Asokan edicts in situ at Kalsi in Uttaranchal. The place lies at the spot where the Yamuna comes out from the hills to the plain and marks a route which follows the river to the interior of the hills and eventually can give access even to Tibet. The fact that a set of major rock edicts was located here suggests that this route was indeed important during Asoka's time. An Asokan inscribed pillar also existed at Meerat, although it was removed by Feroz Shah Tughlak in the fourteenth century to Feroz Shah Kotla of Delhi. The exact location of the pillar is uncertain, but Meerat lies on a route which leads to Nazibabad in Bijnor, and slightly beyond Nazibabad, to Kotdwar in Uttaranchal. Kotdwar takes one to Pauri and joins the broad alignment towards Badrinath and Kedarnath. Topra in Haryana, more or less in alignment with the Paonta Saheb and Kalsi, is another site from which Feroz Shah Tughlak removed an inscribed Asokan pillar to Delhi (his hunting lodge on the Delhi ridge). Its exact spot in the modern Topra village is uncertain but the villagers themselves seem to be very aware of the tradition that an Asokan column had once existed in their village. This awareness may be due also to the fact that schoolbooks mention that an Asokan column was removed from Topra to Delhi. There is some confusion about the identification of this Topra. There has been a suggestion that the column once stood in the area of Paonta Sahib. There is another claimant for an Asokan pillar in Haryana; a pillar in a mosque at Fatehabad is supposedly monolithic and of Asokan origin. In recent times, B.C. Chhabra was certain on this point, and it is interesting to note that the place lies on a route which came out of Delhi and went via Rohtak, Jind, Hansi, Hissar, and Sirsa in the direction of Bahawalpur and eventually Sindh, Multan, and Afghanistan via the Gomal valley. This was an important route, and one need not be surprised if there was a Mauryan period pillar on this route. Delhi itself has an Asokan edict (Minor Rock Edict I) engraved on a rocky outcrop in Srinivaspuri, testifying to the age-old significance of the Delhi area as a communication node. Equally interestingly, the Delhi edict lies below the ridge which contains the Kalkaji temple, the most important and presumably the oldest mother goddess shrine of the area. Whether the edict was set up at a place where the devotees of this timeless goddess would congregate in strength is, of course, uncertain, but there can be an argument in this direction.

Rajasthan has reported two Asokan edicts, both from Bairat, a major early historic city of the time. The so-called Bhabru edict was found loose and thus its exact find-spot remains uncertain. The second edict lies on a rocky outcrop in the outskirts of modern Bairat by the side of the road coming from Delhi via Alwar. In Gujarat, Asoka decided to carve a set of major rock edicts in the Girnar hill, possibly because of the sacred association of this hill.

In Madhya Pradesh too the occurrences of Asokan edicts are sporadic and limited only to Minor Rock Edicts with the exception of the pillar edict found in the Buddhist complex of Sanchi. Minor Rock Edicts occur at Gujarra near Datia, Rupnath near Kakrehta between Bharhut/Satna and Jabbalpur, and Panguraria near Nindore on the north bank of the Narmada near Hosangabad. Gujarra lies on the route which comes out of Gwalior and goes towards Jhansi and is possibly also linked with a route which comes out of the early historic site of Chakranagar, south of Etawah, and goes in the direction of the Betwa valley (cf. Ehrich and further down). Sanchi too was a communication node, marking a move in the direction of Ujjayini in western Malwa on the one hand and towards the upper reaches of the Betwa which has some major early historic sites including Eran, on the other. Sanchi has a Minor Pillar Edict. Panguraria, in the hilly belt north of Hosangabad and south of Bhopal, marks a major Buddhist complex in the general neighbourhood of the fortified early historic site of Nadner and the immediate neighbourhood of the unfortified early historic mound of Ninnore, the latter presumably the major early historic crossing point of the Narmada in this sector. In Madhya Pradesh, excavations in the outskirts of Ujjain have revealed an Asokan pillar capital (now kept in the Ujjayini University museum) but the sculptural quality is bad and cannot be compared with the classic specimens.

In Maharashtra, Major Rock Edicts have been found at Sopara, North of Mumbai. The area is full of creeks, and although archaeological research here has been scrappy, leading hardly to an integrated picture of such a textually famous port as Sopara, the occurrence of Major Rock Edicts at this place adequately suggests its importance as possibly the most important port of the time on the West coast. In Maharashtra, there is only one other reported occurrence of an Asokan edict, a Minor Rock Edict in the Chandrapur or Chanda area of Vidarbha. The report seems to be unconfirmed but A.K. Mitra-Sastri published it, and cannot be readily ignored.[21]

The fact that this comes from the Chanda area makes sense because the Chanda district lies on the route which comes from the north through Balaghat, crosses the Wainganga river at Pauni, and moves further south to Andhra through Chanda. In Andhra, the route passes through Karimnagar and Warangal to reach the Amaravati sector of the lower Krishna valley. In Andhra, Amaravati is one of the three places to have yielded parts of an Asokan edict (Minor Pillar Edict). As in Sanchi, the inscription was apparently a part of the famous Buddhist complex at Amaravati which is in the vicinity of the major fortified early historic complex of Dhenukakata. The two other places in Andhra which have yielded Asokan edicts are Yerragudi (both Major and Minor Rock Edicts) and Rajula Mandagiri (Minor Rock Edicts I and II), both in the Kurnool district, near its borders with Tamil Nadu and Karnataka. At Yerragudi there is a low hill, part of a long ridge set in the midst of a wide plain. The edicts occur on the face of a rock cliff. Rajula Mandagiri is a more or less flat-topped hill and the Asokan edicts are carved on the rocky floor by the side of a small pool which is currently overhung by a tree. In the case of Rajula Mandagiri, it is possible to claim that the place was chosen as the site of Minor Rock Edicts because this pool on a flat-topped, open hill was a cult centre where on certain days of the year people used to congregate. In the case of Yerragudi it is not easy to make such a statement. First, there is no archaeological site in the neighbourhood; at least we did not find any. Second, the cult association, if any, of the spot is not quite obvious. Some scholars have tried to locate Suvarnagiri of the edicts at this place. The point is that Suvarnagiri was an important enough place to have a Mahamatra. Considering that places like Sravasti, Ujjayini, Taxila, and so on, had Mahamatras of their own, the general significance of Suvarnagiri as an urban centre in Mauryan India becomes obvious. There is no such urban site in the neighbourhood or even in the general area of Yerragudi. We find no reason why Yerragudi should denote the location of Suvarnagiri. The most important urban site of the Maurya period, south of the sites in Maharashtra, is Sannati (Karnataka) and from this point of view alone, Sannati can be identified with the Asokan Suvarnagiri. Regarding Isila, the other southern site mentioned in the Asokan inscriptions, our assumption is that the site of Chandravalli near Chitaldurg (and not Brahmagiri, as frequently argued) has a better chance of being identified with it.

In Orissa, Asokan edicts occur at Dhauli and at Jaugada, the former in the outskirts of modern Bhubaneswar and the latter in Ganjam. The historical geography of these two places is important. The Bhubaneswar area was within the territory of Odra which had its capital at the site of Radhanagar near Jajpur which lies somewhat to the east of Bhubaneswar. The size and character of Radhanagar as an urban site suggests to us that the territorial unit of Odra, although not mentioned as one of the 'sixteen principalities' in the Buddhist or Jaina sources, dates from the period of the Mahajanapadas. We further believe that the site of Sisupalgarh came up as a Mauryan administrative centre, with possibly not a good deal of antiquity behind it. The set of Major Rock Edicts that one finds at Dhauli and which has a background of a rock-cut elephant suggesting the aura of an elephant emerging from the rock mass does not necessarily imply that the battle for Kalinga was fought by Asoka in this section. Of the two places, Sisupalgarh and Radhanagar, it was Radhanagar which represented Tosali which was important enough in Mauryan India to have a Mahamatra ruling from it.

It is Jaugada, ancient Samapa, which is ancient Kalinga straddling the modern Ganjam and Srikakulam areas of Orissa (Ganjam) and Andhra (Srikakulam). The Kalinga battle could have been fought not near Bhubaneswar but in this sector. Some centuries later, another king of Magadha tried his power in the area of ancient Kalinga, and from the *Allahabad Prasasti* of this king Samudragupta we know the route taken by the Magadhan army to reach the Kalinga area. The first king who is mentioned to have been defeated by him in this context is Mahendra of Kosala, which would mean basically the modern Chhattisgarh area of Bilaspur and Raipur (if not the adjacent areas of Sambalpur as well). This is South Kosala or Mahakosala with a rich early historic growth behind it. The chief archaeological site of the early historic period is Malhar near Bilaspur, and the massiveness of the site indicates to us that this region too formed a principality of the Mahajanapada period, although remaining unmentioned in the relevant Buddhist or Jaina sources. The ancient route crosses the Mahanadi near Malhar and proceeds up to Raipur beyond the archaeological complex of Sirpur. Beyond Raipur, a route proceeds west on the way to Vidarbha, but another route turns south, with a branch going to Sambalpur and other areas of Orissa. Another branch moves in the direction of modern Vizianagram across the forests of Dandakaranya. Vizianagram lies in Kalinga, with Srikakulam, its western boundary lying further to the west. It is interesting that the second king mentioned by Samudragupta's inscription in this connection is Vyaghraraja of Mahakantara. This Mahakantara or 'great forest' plainly stands for the forested tract of modern Dandakaranya. To reach Chhattisgarh from where the Magadhan army proceeded to the Kalinga coast through Dandakaranya, the Magadhan army could have travelled from the area of Banaras to the Sarguja plain and entered Chhattisgarh from there. This was a major route to the Deccan from the Banaras area. Or, they could have followed the Banaras-Mirzapur-Rewa-Katni alignment and proceeded from the area of Satna-Katni to the Amarkantak section and Shadol before they could reach the area of Bilaspur in Chhattisgarh.

The capital of ancient Kalinga was at modern Dantavaktrunikota which even now shows a large fortification encircling the place. This is the largest early historical site of the area. To reach it, the Magadhan army must have turned to the east from the area of Vizianagram, and the Kalinga army must have come out to meet them. There is still a place called Ranasthalam (or 'the place of the battle') between the site of Dantavaktrunikota and Vizianagram. We suggest that the name carries the folk-memory of the battle between the Mauryan army and the Kalingas. This may be nothing more than a speculation but in the light of the probable route taken by the Mauryan army to reach Kalinga, this makes sense. In any case, there is no reason to argue that the Kalinga battle took place near modern Bhubaneswar.

In Karnataka, there is a veritable cluster of Asokan rock edicts— Major Rock Edicts at Sannati and Brahmagiri, and Minor Rock Edicts at Maski Gavimath and Palkigundi (the last two on two sides of the town of Kopbal, one on the top of a reasonably high hill and the other at the opposite end of the town in a rocky complex), and Minor Rock Edicts at Nittur, Udegolam, Brahmagiri, Siddapur, and Jatinga Rameshwar (the last three in the neighbourhood of modern Brahmagiri). The Maski edict lies at the mouth of a small rock-shelter at the foot of a low hill, the mouth of the rock-shelter currently being overhung by a tree. At both Nittur and Udegolam there are bouldery outcrops in open fields. The edict is engraved on one of these boulders at both places. The Brahmagiri edict figures on a large boulder set in the open, whereas the Siddapur specimen lies about a mile to the west. Jatinga Rameshwar is about 3 miles to the south of Brahmagiri, with the edict lying in a temple compound. The Sannati find of Major Rock Edicts (XII, XIV, and a separate edict replacing RE XIII) is not in situ; they occurred in rock slabs found below the pedestal of the deity in a local temple. They were collected from somewhere else and put there in a later period. In this sense, these inscribed slabs are portable antiquities, which no Asokan inscription is, except the Bhabru edict.

This broad discussion on the distribution of all categories of Asokan edicts in different parts of the subcontinent may lead to a few intriguing issues. Why is it that in two sectors—south Afghanistan and south Karnataka—the density of their find-spots is distinctly more than we notice elsewhere. In the case of south Afghanistan, we have suggested that at the frontier of the Mauryan state, it was a sensitive and possibly not a very peaceful area—an area where the royal message of piety could have had a special significance of its own. This is pure speculation, but it may not be useful to contend that the Mauryan state during Asoka's time faced no challenge whatsoever. The conquest he made was limited by his own admission to Kalinga, but this need not mean that he had no challenge at all within the frontier he inherited from his Mauryan predecessors. The focus on Kalinga itself was likely to be due to a geopolitical purpose. First, this region is known to have had a maritime tradition, and assuming that this maritime history goes back to the Mauryan period and earlier, the Mauryan state would naturally like to have it incorporated within it. Second—and we believe it to be more significant—Kalinga straddles a very important position in ancient India's geography route. It controls the route to the south along the coast, and equally importantly, it controls the route which comes down from south Kosala to the modern Vizianagram area. With Andhra and the upper segment of Orissa's coast in its possession, the Mauryan state could not afford to keep Kalinga unannexed.

In Karnataka, the inscriptions are confined only to Gulbarga and Chitaldurg which have traditionally played a very important geopolitical role in the Deccan's history. As we shall see later, both the south Indian and Deccan powers have had their eyes on the control of this sector. Among other dynasties, the Pallavas with their base at Kanchipuram had their northern border extended up to Bellary, and if one follows the history of the western Chalukyas of Badami and the Rashtrakutas of Manyakhet, we shall see that they made repeated sweeps of the Chitaldurg area to control the areas further South. It was not a peaceful frontier. Scholars have tried to say that the edicts occur here because this was a gold mining area in the Maurya period, as shown by the dates of the pre-Christian era from the Hatti mines which, in fact, are not far from Kopbal. But why people of a gold mining area should be exposed more to Asoka's concept of Dhamma than his subjects in the non-gold mining areas? On the other hand, if it was a tension-prone frontier, there would be some reason of proclaiming the Mauryan royal presence rather loudly here.

Whatever it is, the Asokan edicts were not territory-markers. All the places where they occur seem to have an importance of their own, but these places do not form a specific pattern. For instance, the location of the Minor Rock Edicts at Sasaram, Ahraura, Rupnath, and Panguraria, and the pillar edict at Sanchi may be said to lie along the route which came from Magadha and went in the direction of the Deccan. However, these inscriptions cannot be given the status of Kos Minars of the Delhi-Agra sector of Mughal India. The edicts were not intended to mark trade routes; if they came up as markers of trade routes, there would have been other routes and other places along the same route which would have the Asokan edicts. The inscriptions at Shahbazgarhi and Mansehra may be located at two places on a major route which would eventually cross the Pamirs but we do not know why only these two places were selected as suitable locations in this sector. The same is true of Kalsi which lies at one of the entry points of the Uttaranchal Himalayas, but why the other entry points (cf. Hardiwar, Kotdwar, and so on) were not selected as the locations of such edicts? Sikligarh certainly lay on the Pataliputra-Pundravardhana route but why was only Sikligarh selected as the site of a pillar?

We are unlikely to have answers to these questions, but we should know that too much should not be read into the distribution of the Asokan edicts which in a sense seem to be fairly widespread in all the major sectors of his pan-Indian dominion. We can ask separately what was the importance of an individual site with an Asokan edict, and in many cases, although though not in all cases, this question can be answered. Among the cases where this cannot be answered, Brahmagiri is one and Yerragudi is another. Just because the site has a neolithic antecedence and possesses many megaliths in a subsequent stage, Brahmagiri cannot be said to be a site of much local or regional significance. We have noted the same thing about Yerragudi.

Occasionally, questions have been asked about the nature of centralization in the Mauryan kingdom. The elaborate bureaucracy, as attested in the sources of the period including Megasthenes and *Arthasastra*, testifies that the kingdom was as centralized as it could be in a pre-modern technological context. Among other things, different versions of the edicts could not have been engraved in different parts of the subcontinent unless there was a centralized machinery for the purpose in place. There is no reason to claim that the vast spaces of hilly and forested central India lay outside the Mauryan rule. If this were the case, we would not have found the chain of edict sites along the Kaimur and central Indian section of the Deccan routes—Sasaram, Ahraura, Rupnath, and Panguraria. Nor would have been possible the march of the Mauryan army through Sarguja and the hilly jungle which separates it from Chhattisgarh, and finally through the forests of Dandakaranya to the Kalinga coast. Of course, this reconstruction of the march of the Mauryan army from Pataliputra to the Kalinga coast is hypothetical but logical and probable in view of the fact that a few centuries later, Samudragupta of Magadha followed the same route to march to the Kalinga coast and further south.

The more one thinks of the Mauryan India geographically, the more one realizes that this brought under historical light not merely the entire length and breadth of the subcontinent but also its links with Sri Lanka and Suvarnabhumi on the one hand and the territories arranged around the Mediterranean. The four southern states—the Cholas, Cheras, Pandyas, and Satiyaputas—receive their first clear historical attestation in the Mauryan record. We have seen that the geography of the Mahajanapada period was also pan-Indian arranged from Gandhara and Kamboja in the North-West to the Malaya hills region of south India, but it was under the Mauryas that this took a well-lit historical shape. We know during this period virtually each and every part of ancient India and the basic orbits of her interaction with other parts of Asia.

This is, of course, not to argue that the innumerable political units of various scales—large, medium, and small—that one could trace in the Mahajanapada period and even during the time of Alexander's invasion of the North-West and the Indus valley got wholly subsumed under the Mauryan rule. In the south, which lay outside the Mauryan rule, such units were clearly there, but even within the Mauryan territory such units are unlikely to have lost all their force. One does not know when all the different groupings of people and the political units that one finds in the Puranic sources took shape, but their fairly persistent presence in the sources suggests that they were long-lived and unlikely to have vanished with the establishment of the pan-Indian rule of Magadha under the Mauryas.

At the same time, we do not have to assume that the Mauryan rule did not bring about some basic changes in the structure of ancient Indian regionalism. For instance, the geographical foci of the old Mahajanapada states lost their force by this time. We no longer hear of such states as Vatsa, Kosala, and Kasi as forces in ancient Indian history. The territorial units of the Mallas, Sakyas, Koliyas, and so on, in the eastern fringe of Kosala lost their significance in the Mahajanapada period itself.

The kingdom such as that of the Mauryas could not have come about without a clear geopolitical sense of the significance of each of its component areas from south Afghanistan and Nepal to the bouldery outcrops of south Deccan. By the sheer fact of putting such a vast area in the framework of a single state, this must have acted as a catalyst of unleashing regional and local political and economic forces which naturally led to the formation of multiple states after its overarching framework disappeared. As far as 'orbits' go, the Gangetic orbit under the Mauryas covered the whole of north India and the Deccan, and in the case of the Oxus-Indus orbit, it pushed up to the natural frontier of the subcontinent, that is, the Hindukush. The south Indian orbit retained its identity. In the south Indian case, not all problems have been sorted out. For instance, what should be the most logical boundary of Mauryan territory in Karnataka? One can safely assume that it must have extended up to the Chitradurg/ Chitaldrug>Shimoga line, including the coast. From Chitaldurg we have direct evidence, and we suggest the coast as well because, on the analogy of later historic parallels, the political powers based in Gulbarga-Bijapur invariably tried to annex the north Kanara sector. Banavasi or ancient Vaijayanti with its links with the trade of the south Konkan coast was an important place to control. The more southern districts of Karnataka, that is, South Kanara (Mangalore), Tumkur, Hasan, Mandya, Kolar, and Mysore, are a problem. The south Indian kingdoms which have been specified in RE II do not mention this area. However, there is no assurance that this sector did not come under their influence. The Mauryans, on the other hand, would not have liked to leave the gold-field of Kolar alone. There cannot be a clear solution of this issue. We would put this belt down as the Mauryan frontier zone on the south.[22]

Except the Tamil Nadu and Kerala coasts, and possibly the coast of South Kanara, the Mauryan state controlled the entire coastline of the subcontinent and the bulk of its mineral resources.

Notes

1. Pargiter (1913, 1922); Pusalker (1951a).

2. Raychaudhuri (1953: 1–84). In the first section (pp. 1–11) he discusses the sources. In the second section (pp. 12–47) he discusses the period from the king Parikshit onwards. The third section (pp. 48–84) is titled 'the age of the great Janaka'.

3. For the details, Pusalker (1951: 268–318).

4. For the nine states of the Post-Parikshit period, Raychaudhuri (1953: 58–84).

5. For 'the Deccan in the age of the later Vaidehas', Raychaudhuri (1953: 85–94).

6. For the development of early history, see Chakrabarti (2006).

7. 'Kasi' as Asmaka capital, Raychaudhuri (1953: 144).

8. Raychaudhuri (1953: 77–8, 99).

9. For the conquest of Kasi by Kosala, Raychaudhuri (1953: 153–5).

10. For Bimbisara on the throne of Magadha, Raychaudhuri (1953: 205–9).

11. For the Saisunaga dynasty, Raychaudhuri (1953: 225–8).

12. Majumdar (1953: 33).

13. On the Achaemenids in India, Chattopadhyay (1974); Dandamaev (1989); Vogelsang (1992); Magee et al. (2005).

14. On Alexander's invasion of India, for a comprehensive discussion, Smith (1924: 52–120), also, McCrindle (2004).

15. Majumdar (1953: 228–33); Sastri (1958); and Mahadevan (2003).

16. For the question of Mauryan expansion in the south, Raychaudhuri (1953: 310–13).

17. For the Greek kings in the Asokan inscriptions, Raychaudhuri (1953: 331–2).

18. For the Mauryan control of different areas, see (Thapar 2002: chapter 4) on internal administration.

19. For the locations of Shahbazgarhi and Manserah, see Falk (2006). Regarding Shahbazgarhi, his map clearly shows its position on the Peshawar> Nowshera>Mardan>Shabazgarhi>Ambala pass>Buner pass alignment. On the position of Manserah, he writes:

The place obviously was chosen because it marks the diversion from the main valley to the upper regions leading to Kashmir and to Gilgit via Balakot over the Babusar pass along the Kundar. The southern road led to Taxila. Coming from China, however, there was also the possibility to turn west at modern Haripur and to proceed via Shabazgarhi towards Pushkalavati.

Manserah lies a little to the north of Abbotabad, which offers possibly the easiest route to Kashmir from the plains. It is probable that Manserah came up because of the significance of this route to Kashmir.

20. It is well-known that the *Arthasastra* mentions Chinese silk— 'Chinapatta'.

21. An incomplete copy of MRE was acquired from the Chanda/ Chandrapur area, and A Mitra-Sastri published it, but this has since then been missing.

22. Apart from Hultzsch (1925), Sircar (2000) and Falk (2006) contain detailed lists of Asokan inscriptions. For reading, Hultzsch and Sircar are more secure and dependable. For the 2009 discovery of MRE I at Ghurhupur (near Basaha) in the Kaimur district of Bihar, see *Sanatan* (electronic journal of Indian Archaeology). For a damaged edict from Deotek in the Chandrapur district of the Vidarbha area of Maharashtra see Sastri (1997–8), with earlier references to it; also see Sastri (1997–8) for the probable find of an edict from Ghuggus in the Chandrapura district:

The record commences with the mention of the emperor Asoka as Priyadarsi, the king of Magadha. He salutes the Buddhist order and enquires about its well-being. He next expresses his high esteem for the Buddha, Dhamma and Sangha, the well-known Buddhist trinity in the prescribed order. After this it is impossible to make out anything from the Xerox though there is absolutely no doubt that many more lines must have followed.

3

The Shift of the Focus to Orissa, the Deccan, and Malwa

c. 200 BC to c. AD 300

The Post-Mauryan Political Scenario in North India: The Decline and Fragmentation of the Gangetic Orbit

There is a lack of consensus among the various Puranic and other texts about Asoka's successors. The sources disagree even about the number of sons he had. The Kashmir chronicle *Rajatarangini* mentions that one of his sons, Jalauka, became king of Kashmir and tried to establish control in the Ganga-Yamuna plain up to Kanauj. He also reputedly defeated an attack by the Mlechchhas, which could mean an invasion of the north-west and Panjab by the Bactrian Greeks. According to the Tibetan writer Taranatha, Virasena, another of his successors, became the king of Gandhara. According to Kalidasa's *Malavikagnimitram*, the Vidarbha area also seceded from the Mauryan state. In the Classical sources, there is a mention of an independent king, Subhagasena, in the north-west about this time. Whatever may be the element of truth in these traditions, there is no doubt that the regional pressures were on, but it appears that these pressures were not principally along any geographical fault line. For instance, Kashmir reputedly became an independent political unit in the post-Asoka period but the fact that the post-Asokan Kashmir had in its sight the control of the Ganga-Yamuna plain up to Kanauj suggests that even the regional units developed wider geographical frames of their own. More than that, the idea that the Gangetic valley can be penetrated by a thrust from the north-western direction is interesting, and was widely accepted in later times.

The principal inheritors of the Mauryan power seem to be the Sungas who ruled from Pataliputra but do not appear to have retained the former Magadhan control of even the core of northern India. In Central India, their power did not extend beyond eastern Malwa which had Vidisa as its capital; southward their control ended on the Narmada. North-East from Pataliputra, Kosala with its principal centre of Ayodhya, was under the Sunga control, and so presumably was Ahichchhatra of north Panchala. The Sunga control also extended up to Panjab and the Indus. Pushyamitra Sunga, the first king of the dynasty, usurped the Mauryan power in c. 187 BC. He was a contemporary of the Sanskrit grammarian Patanjali who belonged to Gonarda which lies between Ujjayini and Vidisa. There are allusions to the Yavana or Greek invasions during his time. The Greeks apparently laid siege to both Madhyamika (modern Nagari between Chitorgarh and Kota) and Saketa or Ayodhya. These invasions were possibly nothing more than lightning thrusts but it may be noted that these thrusts came from the north-west (possibly the Gandhara area) and followed two alignments, one directed at the heart of the Ganga valley and the other directed against Malwa through Rajasthan. The Greeks of the north-west had also ambitions beyond their own centre, just as Asoka's successor in Kashmir eyed the Gangetic area up to Kanauj.

There are also indications that even within the territory the Sungas are supposed to control, their hold was becoming tenuous. For instance, the inscription of Asadhasena, maternal uncle of the king Brihatsvatimitra or Brihaspatimitra of Ahichchhatra, at Pabhosa near Kausambi suggests that there were local kings in the Gangetic territory. Similarly, the Heliodorus pillar inscription mentions an apparently local king, Bhagabhadra Kasiputra, at Vidisa in about the same time.

It is interesting that the vast regions of eastern India—Bengal and Assam, for instance—drop out of the radar of the contemporary sources. The Kanvas who came in about 75 BC possibly held on to the territory ruled by the Sungas, but this is not the time when the Gangetic India was the primary focus of ancient Indian history. The focus shifts elsewhere—the north-west including the Oxus to the Indus zone, the Deccan, and Malwa. It is a long period, from about the first century BC to about AD 300 when Magadha and thus Gangetic India became powerful again.

The Oxus to the Indus zone played during this time a major role in the Indian history. Although it is common to refer to this phase as a phase of foreign invasions when the Greeks, Parthians, Scythians, and the Kushanas marched across the Hindukush and carved out their areas of influence not merely in the Indus valley but also in various other parts of northern India. However, an examination of the geographical stages by which they advanced will show that they attempted to secure the Indus valley only when they secured a foothold south of the Hindukush. It was this southern Hindukush area which was the spring-board of their thrusts against India. From this point of view, these 'invasions' do not emanate from an orbit which is geographically separated from the subcontinent.

The Greek chapter in ancient Indian history is clearly divided into two phases. In the first phase, the centre of power was the Greek kingdom of Bactria which fell to the lot of the successor of Alexander's kingdom in the east, coming under the control of this Greek power based in Syria. Controlling north Afghanistan from a base in Syria could not be easy, and the relationship between the Syrian overlord and the Bactrian power was always a fluctuating one. The cut-off point of this relationship and the declaration of Bactria as an independent Greek kingdom took place possibly around the middle of the third century BC under Diodotus I of Bactria. Diodotus II was replaced on the Bactrian throne by Euthydemus, during whose time the Syrian overlord Antiochus III tried to re-exert his authority. Eventually the independence of Bactria was recognized, with the focus falling on Euthydemus' son Demetrius. It is under Demetrius that the Bactrian Greeks enter Indian history.

However, Antiochus III is known to have undertaken an expedition to the Kabul valley where the name of a king called Subhagasena (Sophagasenus) figures. Euthydemus himself, as the distribution of his coins suggests, is likely to have extended his power to south Afghanistan and the contiguous territory in eastern Iran, and possibly parts of the north-western subcontinent.

Under Demetrius, a considerable part of the Greek power centred in north Afghanistan seems to move to the south of the Hindukush and especially India. The most important part of the references to Demetrius in Indian sources relates to the allusions in Patanjali's *Mahabhashya* which says that the Yavanas or the Greeks (in this case) attacked Nagari or Madhyamika in Rajasthan and Ayodhya or Saketa in the heart of the Ganga plain. More detailed is the reference in the *Yuga-Purana* section of the *Gargi Samhita* which says that in addition to Ayodhya, the Greeks also attacked Panchala (possibly the Rohilkhand portion), Mathura, and even Pushpapura or Pataliputra. This is said to have happened after the reign of the king Salisuka who belonged to the Maurya line and was fourth in descent from Asoka according to a puranic evidence. It is possible that Demetrius' invasions happened twice, once when the Mauryan fabric still retained a shape, and once it had completely disintegrated and Magadha was under the rule of Pushyamitra Sunga. The *Mahabhashya* mentions only Nagari and Ayodhya. Nagari could have been invaded during Pushyamitra's reign, that is, during the lifetime of Patanjali. Whatever might have been the exact period of Demetrius' expeditions against India that took place towards the very end of the third century BC or the early years of the second century BC. What deserves notice is that from his base in south Afghanistan he could carry out raids as far deep in the Ganga valley as Ayodhya and Pataliputra. Raids such as these seem to establish a pattern which, as we shall see later, continued long in the Indian history.

One would think that by this time Demetrius had his control firmly established in the Indus valley. This would also mean that his position was getting weak in north Afghanistan where Bactria fell to Eukratides who survived Demetrius' attempt to re-assert his sovereignty. The major challenge to Eukratides' power came from Parthia or north-eastern Iran or Khorasan under Mithradates I (*c*. 171–36 BC) and possibly also from the nomads of Central Asia who in the Chinese sources were known as the Yueh-chi. Eukratides' successor Heliocles was the last Greek king of Bactria who, after being ousted from north Afganistan, had to depend on his territories in south Afghanistan and the Indus valley. What is important is that this marks the beginning of the rule of the Indo-Greeks in the north-west.

Unstratified coin-finds have played a dominant role in the reconstruction of the Greek dynastic history in the Oxus to the Indus zone. Among the many Indo-Greek kings identified in the numismatic record, possibly most were ruling contemporaneously as minor chiefs in different parts of the Indus valley and the adjoining hilly region from the north-west to Panjab and Sindh. Of them, possibly the most important was Menander (*c*. 115–90 BC?) who figured prominently in the Buddhist text of *Milinda-Panho*. On the basis of the distribution of his coins it has been argued that he extended control over central Afghanistan (somewhat indeterminate but must mean the central area south of the Hindukush), North-West Frontier Province, Panjab, Sindh, Rajasthan, Kathiawar, and even parts of western Uttar Pradesh.[1] What this argument does not envisage is that it is crediting Menander with his capital at Sakala or Sialkot ruling a large compact territory from the south of the Hindukush to the gates of Delhi, covering the whole of the Indus valley and the Indo-Gangetic divide with the addition of Rajasthan and Gujarat. No king with his capital in Panjab has ruled over such a large territory in the Indian history. Whatever may be deduced from the coin distributions, the fact that a coin issued by a king is found somewhere does not necessarily mean that the find-spot in question belongs to the territory administered by that particular king. Menander was no doubt an important Indo-Greek king, and because of his conversion to Buddhism and his being the central character of *Milinda Panho*, he has figured prominently in the Indian tradition, but that does not mean that he was the only Indo-Greek king of his time from the north-west to Delhi on the one hand and to Sindh, Rajasthan, and Gujarat on the other.

Geographically, the rest of the Indo-Greek kings are not interesting. They have been assumed to belong either to the house of Euthydemus or to the house of Eucratides. They must have dotted the entire stretch of the Indus valley and the adjoining hills up to the Hindukush with their small principalities just like the situation which the historians accompanying Alexander found earlier. A few names like Menander and Antialcidas stand out; Antialcidas because he is known to have ruled from Taxila and was the king of the emissary Heliodorus who came to the court of the king Kasibhadra of Vidisa. Towards the end of the pre-Christian era, their power in the region was usurped by the Parthians and Scythians, although there was a period in which all three of them—the Indo-Greeks, Scythians, and Parthians—seem to have interacted and vied for supremacy.

Going through the historical literature one would think that the whole of the north-western slice of the subcontinent from the Panjab hills to Sindh was then being colonized on a large scale by the Greeks, Scythians, and Parthians appearing from north Afghanistan and north-eastern/eastern Iran. Succeeding generations of historians and archaeologists who have tried to visualize this process as the great eastward civilizing thrust of Hellenism in the direction of India have forgotten that the Indian side of the story is hardly known. The Indian sources virtually throw no light on the history of this period in this sector. One would safely assume that the north-western subcontinent of the period was far more densely dotted with kingdoms ruled by Indian kings than it was by the kingdoms ruled by the Indo-Greeks, Scythians, and Parthians.

Eastern Iran was the spring-board of both Parthian and Scythian powers in India. As early as the second century BC, Mithradates I of Parthia is known to have extended Parthian control to eastern Iran which itself is only a narrow strip of territory except in the south-east where the territory expands to form the valley of the Helmand and Seistan in general. With their base in Seistan, the Parthians of that time could have extended their influence to the lower Indus valley and perhaps also to the Kutch area, if not to Kathiawar. Raychaudhuri believes that Mithradates I 'penetrated even into India', meaning thereby a stretch of Panjab.[2] The names of two Parthian kings figure later in the Indian context—Vonones who is placed by Sircar entirely in the first century BC and Gondophernes whose reign is dated *c.* AD 21–46, according to him.[3] There is, however, a debate about the Parthian/Scythian lineage of Vonones who, with his base in eastern Iran, ruled over south Afghanistan and had his viceroys ruling in the (unidentified) eastern part of his dominions. Gondophernes is a more visible figure because he figures in an inscription from Takht-i-Bahi in the Mardan area of the north-west and also because he is known in the Christian tradition to have received Saint Thomas, an Apostle, in his court around the middle of the AD first century. Broadly, his control was limited to the Kabul valley and parts of the north-west.

The Scythian rulers seem to have a sharper profile. The classic Saka country from the Indian point of view was Seistan. The first prominent ruler of this group, Maues (*c.* 20 BC–AD 22, according to Sircar[4]), assumed the title 'great king of kings' on his coins, possibly after extending his control over large parts of north-western India and also as far east as Mathura where there is an inscription of the time of Saka Mahakshatrapa Sondasa which has been placed by Sircar around AD 15.[5] Azes I, Azilises, and Azes II figure among Maues' successors, and although their territories and even mutual relationships are somewhat uncertain, there are reasons to believe that the Saka viceroys/rulers or Kshatrapas/Mahakshatrapas became features of the political scene of the Taxila and Mathura regions during this time. The Satraps of the Taxila region include such names as Satrap Aspavarman, Liaka Kusulaka, and so on. The principal Satrapa names from Mathura are

Ranjuvala, Sondasa, Hagana, Hagamasha, Sivaghosha, Sivadatta, and others. It appears that the Mathura area was ruled by a Satrapal family who declared themselves free from the Saka suzerainty and were later supplanted by the Kushanas.

The Greek, Indo-Greek, Parthian, and Scythian chapters of ancient Indian history are geographically interesting in their own right. They are clear demonstrations of the fact that one of the most significant geopolitical orbits of India in the post-Maurya period was the Oxus to the Indus orbit. However, and this is an important point to remember, the political history of this period demonstrates that it was not a monolithic orbit but divided into a number of distinct segments—Khorasan or north-eastern Iran or ancient Parthia with a part of Turkmenistan thrown in; north Afghanistan or Bactria; north-east Afghanistan or Badakhsan/Kafiristan; south Afghanistan; Seistan or the Helmand basin and the adjoining desert area; the Peshawar plain and the mountain valleys to the north and north-east of Peshawar; Baluchistan including the Makran coast; the lower Indus valley or Sindh; the upper Indus valley or Panjab; and finally possibly Kashmir, although under the Parthians and Indo-Greeks this does not figure much in political history. No political power was systematically successful over this orbit; they fought among themselves and had to be satisfied with the control of only a few sections of it. More importantly, the Saka thrust towards Mathura categorically demonstrates that during this period the area between the Sutlej and the Yamuna, that is, the area of what is called the Indo-Gangetic divide in Indian geography became subject to the influence of political factors emanating from the Oxus to the Indus orbit. This scenario becomes far more clear under the Kushan dynasty. Under them, the Oxus to the Indus orbit, including Kashmir and the sub-orbit of the Indo-Gangetic divide, became one political unit and came to dominate the political history of northern India in a big way.

The rise of the Kushana power was not dissimilar to what happened before in the case of the Greeks, Indo-Greeks, Parthians, and Scythians. Known as the Yueh-chi in the Chinese records which mention that after they got dispersed from their original land of Chinese Turkestan or the modern Chinese province of Sinkiang, they initially settled in Bactria and established their capital in the Bokhara area which lies in the southern section of Central Asia. Their territory was divided into five principalities, the chief of each of these principalities being known as *Yabgou* or *Yabagu* of the coin legends. The Kuei-shuang or the Kushanas formed one such principality. Their chief, later known as Kujula or Kujula Kadphises I, established his power over the rest of the principalities, attacked Parthia, and wrested control of the Kabul valley and its adjoining regions including Kafiristan. His son, later known as Wima Kadphises, possibly conquered the Panjab region.

The nature of Kujula's interaction with India is clear from the fact that he converted to Buddhism and describes himself on one of his coin legends not merely as 'the great king, king of kings' but also as one 'steadfast in true faith' (*Satya Dharma Sthita*, *Satya Dharma*—in this case, meaning Buddhism). Wima Kadphises, who possibly annexed the Indus valley or at least its Panjab part, was a worshipper of Siva, one of his coin legends mentioning Mahesvara or Siva clearly. Even in this, the nature of Kushana interaction is exactly similar to the interaction which took place between the Indian culture and the Indo-Greeks, the classic case in this regard being the Heliodorus pillar inscription of Vidisa where a Greek declares himself as *Bhagavata* or a worshipper of Vishnu. The problems of Kushana history, of which there are many, including the relationship of its greatest king Kanishka with his predecessor Wima Kadphises, are not relevant here, but it appears that the story of Kushana expansion in India cannot be clearly understood because of the lack of suitable sources. Under Wima Kadphises only Panjab is mentioned as his area of control in India whereas Kanishka's kingdom was undoubtedly of much greater extent in the subcontinent:

Epigraphic records of the reign of Kanishka himself prove his control over the U.P., Punjab, N.W.F.P. and the Bahawalpur region North of Sindh. Officers like the Dandanayaka Lala and the Kshatrapas Vespasi and Liaka were serving in north-western India while parts of eastern Uttar Pradesh were under the joint rule of the Mahakshatrapa Kharapallana and the Kshatrapa Vanasphara. The discovery of a large number of Kanishka's records at Mathura, with one from Sui Vihar 16 miles from Bahawalpur and of an epigraph of one of his immediate successors at Sanchi ... near Vidisa, the ancient capital of East Malwa, as well as the establishment of a satrapal house of the Sakas in Western India about his time seems to suggest that Sindh, Rajputana, Malwa and Saurashtra also came under the sphere of Kanishka's influence. The find of an inscription of another of Kanishka's immediate successors near Kabul and a tradition recorded by Alberuni point to Kanishka's rule over Afghanistan and the adjoining parts of Central Asia.[6]

His records have also been obtained from Sravasti and Sarnath.

Some inferences regarding the extent of Kushana rule at its heyday may be made in more clear geographical terms. The whole of the Oxus to the Indus zone, including Kashmir and Ladakh, must have been under its control. This should also suggest some area north of the Oxus in Central Asia and perhaps some area of Sinkiang as well. Towards the east, there is a clear thrust up to Mathura where the strength and consolidation of the Kushana power is manifest in the number of its inscriptions and the images of the Kushana kings. With their base in Mathura the Kushanas could easily exert influence both over east Rajasthan and Malwa. The Sui Vihar inscription near Bahawalpur shows that the idea of the Kushana control over Sindh and Panjab is justified. Bahawalpur lay on the direct route to the area of Delhi from the Multan area on the one hand and Sindh on the other. This route came up the dried bed of the Ghaggar-Hakra from Sindh to Rajasthan, and having entered Haryana it followed the Sirsa-Hissar-Hansi-Jind-Rohtak alignment. At each of these places there are still large mounds, testifying to the importance of this alignment in the Indian history. From Mathura another route must have followed the Delhi-Karnal-Kurukshetra alignment to Panjab, as among other things, the location of the Kushana period stupa of Sanghol testifies. From Sindh, influence could be exerted both on Kutch and Kathiawar.

The Rabatak inscription suggests Kushana penetration up to the core of Uttar Pradesh and Bihar. Whether this was something like the thrust of Demetrius towards Ayodhya or turned out to be more durable is impossible to say. Considering the length of the line required for the penetration of Kushana arms to such a distance from Mathura, one would think that the Kushana thrust up to Pataliputra and beyond had possibly nothing more than an expeditionary character. However, one can assume that the area up to Banaras could be under the direct Kushana control and similarly, this area of direct rule may also be extended up to Sravasti, which would mean that the Kushana occupation of Mathura was not in the form of a wedge but covered a large chunk of the Indo-Gangetic plain up to the trans-Sarayu area on the one hand and Banaras on the other.

The basic historical significance of the Kushana rule in India was that under them virtually the whole stretch from Central Asia to Mathura, Sravasti, and Banaras formed one political unit. The significance of this happening in terms of trade and cultural exchange must have been remarkable. This was the heyday of the Silk Route trade which was joined by many routes from India including that across the Pamirs. The motley of deities of various areas that one finds in the Kushana coinage makes sense in the light of the cultural interaction this compact political unit had with various areas in all directions. The sheer list of these deities makes for interesting reading. The reverse of Kanishka's coin-types show deities of Greek, Sumerian, Elamite, Persian, and Indian origins and the same trend is continued in the coins of his successors.

The Kushana power is said to have declined after the reign of Vasudeva who, according to Sircar, ruled from *c.* AD 145 to 176.[7] So, from the last quarter of the AD second century the Kushana power was on the decline, especially in northern India where the Saka Satraps became powerful in western and central India, the local rulers began to show strength in Uttar Pradesh and Rajasthan, and the Nagas came to power in Mathura. It appears that the Kushanas retained their strength in Panjab, NWFP, and Afghanistan at least up to the middle of the AD third century. This was the time when the Sassanid kings of Iran began to exert pressure in this direction. North-East Iran, north Afghanistan, and south Afghanistan including Seistan slowly passed into the Sassanid control. Sircar[8] points out that the Paikuli inscription of the late AD third century 'appears to refer to several Indian rulers including the kings of the Surashtras, Avantis, Kushanas, Sakas and Abhiras, as subordinate allies, if not as feudatories, of the Sassanians'. It is possible that the Sassanids extended their direct rule beyond Seistan to at least the western part of Sindh.

The geographical process here is interesting. In a sense, the Sassanid influence on Indian political affairs towards the end of the Kushana rule is reminiscent of the control the Achaemenids who, like the Sassanids, had their base in the Fars plain of Iran. The Achaemenid control was direct over the Indus valley. Similarly, the Sassanids controlled a part of the lower Indus valley and had their eyes on the areas they could exert influence on with their base in the Indus, principally Kutch-Kathiwar peninsulas and Malwa.

The Kushana rule demonstrated the extent of the influence that the unified Oxus to the Indus orbit could exert on the political configuration of a very large part of northern India. The area up to Mathura could be brought under the direct control of this orbit, thus making the Gangetic heartland of Uttar Pradesh and Bihar virtually wide open to its thrusts. At the other end, the power was felt in Kutch, Kathiawar, Gujarat, Rajasthan, and Malwa. The Saka Kshatrapas who ruled initially on behalf of the Kushanas in this vast area of central and western India might have got Indianized to a great extent, their inscriptions and coins being a good indication of this process, but the geographical point which stands out is that this was a period when the Oxus to the Indus orbit completely overshadowed the Gangetic and generally inner Indian orbit.

The Coming Back of the Inner Indian Orbit into its Own

When the Oxus to the Indus orbit was triumphant over northern India, certain regional groupings which basically date from the closing centuries of the pre-Christian era made their appearance in the northern Indian historical record mainly in the form of their coins. As the related knowledge stands now, it has to be admitted that this is essentially a post-Mauryan development in which certain regional entities of northern India expressed themselves territorially. In a way, they hark back to the regional groupings of the Mahajanapada period, but they do not repeat in toto the earlier groupings and names. Considering that some of their coin legends mention them as particular groups of people, it has been assumed that these particular types of coins were issued by different tribal republics. The coins of the monarchical states have the names of the kings on their coins.

The change in the historical scenario is striking. It is apparent that even within the all-encompassing framework of the Mauryan rule, some regional identities lay dormant, and when that framework disintegrated, it did not take them a long time to consolidate themselves politically. They must have submitted themselves to the Kushana and associated Scythian and other dominance in the early AD centuries, but came back into their own as soon as this dominance was gone.

Rajasthan, Panjab, and the Himalayan belts of Kangra and Almorah seem to have most of the 'tribal states' whereas the monarchical groupings came up around certain major cities of the Gangetic plain. A large number of tribal states like those of the Arjunayanas (west of Agra-Mathura), Uddehikas (Bayana area of Rajasthan?), Malavas (between the Chenab and the Ravi in Panjab), Sibi (Shorkot area of the Jhang district of Panjab), Rajanyas (north or north-western Rajasthan), Yaudheyas (original core around Ludhiana?), Uttamabhadras (the Pushkar area of Rajasthan), and others are known, although the scholarly literature puts emphasis more on the Arjunayanas, Malavas, and Yaudheyas. The monarchical states include those of the Nagas around Mathura and in central India, Ahichchhatra, Ayodhya, and Kausambi. The list is not comprehensive but indicates the general geographic locale of this development.

The Arjunayanas, for instance, had their focal centre in the Alwar-Bharatpur section of Rajasthan, which abuts the Ganga-Yamuna plain in this section. This is more or less the ancient Matsya territory. They were a tribal republic, as their coin legend 'victory to the Arjunayanas' suggests. These coins belong to the end of the first century BC, but these chronologies depend almost exclusively on the palaeography of the script on coin legends. The Arjunayanas come back into their own after the Kushanas and find a mention in Barahamihira's *Brihatsamhita* of *c.* AD sixth century. The Malavas, originally confined to Panjab between the Ravi and the Chenab, may be one of the groups of people mentioned by historians accompanying Alexander and some Indian texts, but they are supposed to have migrated to Rajasthan from there and set up a capital city of their own at Nagar or Karkotanagara near Tonk and Bundi in Rajasthan. In the AD second century they reputedly fought with a similar group in the Ajmer area, the Uttamabhadras and their allies, the Saka Kshatrapas of western India. The coin legends specifically refer to the Malava territorial unit—*Malava-janapadasa*. They extended their control possibly to the Udaipur sector of south-east Rajasthan, and it is quite natural that from their location in Rajasthan they would exert influence on the Malwa plain of modern Madhya Pradesh. It is possible that the term 'Malwa' for the modern Malwa plain is derived from the Malavas as a group of people. It appears that the Malavas or one of their sub-groups, the Aulikaras, remained visible in the history of central India up to at least AD sixth century. That it was a group of people is denoted by one of their coin legends *Malavanam jayah*.

Panini's *Ashtadhyayi* included the Yaudheyas among the Kshatriyas who earned their living by the profession of arms. Coins and seals bearing their legends have been found in a large area from Ludhiana in Panjab, Rohtak-Bhiwani in Haryana to Bayana in Rajasthan, Saharanpur and Dehradun in Uttar Pradesh and Uttaranchal. Traditionally their centre is the modern Rohtak-Bhiwani area, where at Navrangpur near Bhiwani they were supposed to have their capital. It is possible that their capital was named *Bahudhanaka* or *Bahudhanyaka*, and *Karttikeya* figures as at least one of their important deities. One of their coin legends, *Yaudheya-ganasya-jayah* or 'victory to the Yaudheya republic' leaves no doubt about their non-monarchical character.

Among the monarchies which figure prominently in this period along with the republican states mentioned earlier, an important place goes to the Naga kings of parts of the Doab and central India. They were prominent in their areas in the AD third–fourth centuries, especially at Vidisa and Padmavati (modern Pawayya near Gwalior). The most important Naga centre was Padmavati which had a large number of Naga kings (that is, kings with their names ending with 'Naga'). The Pawayya area lies at the approach route to eastern Malwa from the Agra-Gwalior side, and it seems that the Naga area of influence lay between the Gwalior sector and the Vidisa area. The *Puranas* mention their rule at Mathura during this period, although Mathura does not seem to have yielded coins bearing the term 'Naga'. The coins of a king called Virasena have been found in the post-Kushana context in the Mathura, Bulandshahr, Farrukhabad, and Etah districts of western Uttar Pradesh.

The coins found at Ahichchhatra and the neighbouring areas indicate the presence of kings whose names end in 'Mitra', although other types of names are also known. Two coin types of Ahichchhatra bear the name Achyuta who has been identified with a king mentioned in the Allahabad pillar inscription of Samudragupta in the AD fourth century. According to Sircar,[9] the Ahichchhatra coins may be put in the three centuries after the middle of the first century BC. The coins from Ayodhya are similarly dated. Sircar[10] assigns them to the two centuries after the closing decades of the first century BC. Another series of coins appears at Ayodhya after the demise of the Kushana rule, with somebody called Kumudasena being mentioned in his coins as 'Raja'. It is possible that his kingdom was later incorporated in the Gupta dynastic territory.

The local series of coins found at Kausambi have been put between the first century BC and the AD fourth century.

Some of the royal names found on these coins have been corroborated by epigraphic records. A relevant dynasty is known as the Magha dynasty. Its coins and inscriptions have been found in the Allahabad and Fatehpur districts of Uttar Pradesh and at Bandhogarh in Madhya Pradesh, forming a well-connected stretch along one of the routes which travelled from the area of Allahabad-Kausambi to the Deccan through Chhattisgarh. A seal from Bhita in the Allahabad sector mentions a king called Vasishthiputra Bhimasena, and he is also mentioned in an inscription from Ginja (near Allahabad) and in an inscription from Bandhogarh, both the inscriptions falling in AD 129–30. There are six inscriptions of this king's son, Kautsiputra Prausthasri at Bandhogarh, with three of them dated AD 164, 165, and 166. In about this period there are also numismatic and epigraphic references to the king Kausikiputra Bhadramagha at Kausambi. Speculations have been made about the relationship between the kings of Kausambi and those from Bandhogarh. From the present point of view, more important is the fact that in the Kushana period itself there were kings ruling in the region from Allahabad-Kausambi to Bandhogarh. Such names keep on appearing in the numismatic and/or epigraphic sources till about the AD fourth century.

If one thinks of the regional foci of power in northern India even during the supremacy of the Saka Kshatrapas and Kushana kings, several areas thus stand out. Mathura, Kausambi, Ahichchhatra, and Ayodhya areas of the Ganga-Yamuna plain, and basically eastern Malwa and the area between this and Gwalior are the areas where the evidence of individual royal lineages can be corroborated mostly by numismatics but partly by epigraphy as well. Certain areas, such as Panjab-Haryana, Rajasthan, and even Malwa, had various tribal republics. It is thus obvious that the pressure of the Scythian and Kushana dominance notwithstanding, regional strands of power continued to survive in parts of northern India and apparently outlasted this long dominance. Nothing is really known about the situation elsewhere in northern India, especially in the regions to the east. As the mention of various eastern states like Samatata and Davaka in the Allahabad pillar inscription of Samudragupta indicate, there were regional foci of political power in that region as well.

In retrospect, the wide persistence of regional territorial forma-tions not merely in the Ganga valley but also in Malwa through prolonged spells of supra-regional powers indicates in a sense that the large orbits of interaction, as shown by the emergence of supra-regional powers, are not the only foci of ancient Indian geo-politics. These foci seem to have been held up always by regional territorial formations.[11]

Orissa, the Deccan, and Malwa

If the history of post-Mauryan India in the north was dominated by the Oxus to the Indus orbit and the emergence of small groupings of kings and tribal republics, vast stretches of the Deccan, western Malwa, and Orissa in the post-Mauryan context formed an orbit of their own within which a lot of interaction took place with some thrusts towards the north.

The dynasty which emerged in Orissa after its Mauryan rule was over was the Chedi or Maha-Meghavahana dynasty, of which the most important personage was its third king Kharavela known principally from his (now damaged) inscription in the Hatigumpha cave in the Udayagiri-Khandagiri cave complex near Bhubaneswar. The general scholarly consensus puts him in the first century BC. North of the coastal plain of Orissa, there is a large stretch of high ground which is even now largely forested and extends into Chhattisgarh in the north, Dandakaranya in the west and north-west, and the Chhotanagpur plateau in the north and north-east. There is no reason to believe that Orissa which stretches from Baleshwar to Ganjam was at any point a backwater and not linked in different ways with its neighbouring areas.

On accession, possibly sometime in the first century BC, Kharavela who called himself, among others, *Kalinga-chakravartin* or the 'universal emperor of Kalinga', undertook an expedition in the western direction, towards Andhra, reaching the valley of the Krishna. Soon afterwards, he is also known to have defeated a king called Vidyadhara (provenance unidentified) and the people known as the Rashtrikas and Bhojakas. Sircar[12] puts the latter in Vidarbha. If Kharavela had marched with his army as far as Vidarbha, that is, the area around modern Nagpur, he would first have emerged in the Raipur sector of Chhattisgarh passing through Sambalpur or Bhawani Patna, and then travelled west towards Vidarbha. It would have been a very long line of invasion. Kharavela also proceeded up to the Barabar hills near Gaya and attacked Rajagriha, the former capital of Magadha, in that connection. To proceed to the Gaya area from Kharavela's centre in the Bhubaneswar area, a march across the modern sector of Singhbhum and Hazaribagh would be necessary, and it appears from this that the Chhotanagpur plateau during this period was under Orissan control. He eventually proceeded up to the bank of the Ganga in Magadha, defeating the king Bahasatimita. Whoever this king was, he is likely to have belonged to the Mitra dynasty of Magadha, whose records have been known from the Gaya district. The success against Magadha at least in the Gaya sector must have given him easy access to Anga further east. It has been said that Kharavela included a few *Jaina* images in his booty from Magadha and Anga, thus avenging the defeat of Kalinga by the Nanda kings of Magadha 300 years earlier. These Jaina images were reputedly carried away by the Nandas from Kalinga. Kharavela's ambition in the western direction also became manifest in his conquest of the modern Masulipatnam area of Andhra where he destroyed the city of Prithuda (unidentified). The Hatigumpha inscription mentions that Kharavela went deep south, defeating the Pandya kings of the Madurai region. Looking at Kharavela's feat of arms in all directions, it appears that he ruled in the first century BC basically the kingdom of Kalinga which by this time comprised both the former Odra and Kalinga territories. With his border as far west as the modern Srikakulam-Vizianagram area, it is only natural that he fought in the area further down the coast. However, his expedition against the Pandyas could not be anything more than an opportunistic thrust aimed at gathering booty. The same must be said about his march against the Gaya-Rajgir sector of Magadha and Anga to its east. Maintaining a permanent control over this area across the difficult terrain of the Chhotanagpur plateau was difficult. With his territory stretched to the west as far as the Vizianagram area, he could easily have moved up to the Raipur area, from where the road to Vidarbha or the Nagpur area is open, without any major barrier. Again, the line of invasion would have been rather long, and a long-term control of the Vidarbha region was not possible for him.

One wonders why Kharavela did not turn his attention to the east. He could easily have marched across the Suvarnarekha up to the Bhagirathi. West Bengal's political history of the period is uncertain. This sector possibly continued to remain under Magadha, and if so, the tradition that Kharavela encountered the forces of a Magadhan king on the Ganga could well mean that this stretch of the Ganga was in the West Bengal section. Or, it was also possible that the area up to the Rupnarayan delta in West Bengal was already under the control of the political power of the Bhubaneswar sector. Whatever it was, the Orissan scenario becomes blurred after Kharavela.

The power which came up in the Deccan in the wake of the Mauryas was the Satavahanas who, as the evidence suggests, had within their orbit the whole of the Deccan including the present day Maharashtra, northern Karnataka, and Andhra beyond the coast. This is a vast area, and one would expect here as in the Ganga plain and elsewhere in northern India some smaller centres of power as well. Numismatically, it appears there were developments of local political units in some parts of this region. The Satavahana chronology has been seriously disputed, with some placing its beginning as late as the AD first century. However, this is unlikely to be the case in view of the political vacuum in the Deccan created by the demise of the Mauryas. The Satavahanas rose to power mainly because of this political vacuum, and if so, they were likely to have crystallized their position in the second century BC itself, that is, immediately after the disappearance of the Maurya rule in the Deccan. One is not sure how effective the Sungas and Kanvas were in maintaining the earlier hold of Magadha over the Deccan. There is no firm evidence that they held on to the Deccan territory previously held by the Mauryas.

In any case, there cannot be any objection to the coming of power of the first recorded Satavana king Simuka in about 30 BC (Sircar's chronology).[13] Sircar points out that there is reference to Simuka being a servant of the Kanva kings in the Puranas, which suggests that some kind of Magadhan hold was maintained in the former possessions of the Mauryas in the Deccan.[14] It is difficult to be certain of Simuka's power base; he is mentioned as a king in a Nanaghat inscription, Nanaghat being a pass which can be approached from Junnar to cross the Western Ghats and reach the Mumbai coast. It is also possible that he also came to control parts of Malwa and western India from this possible base in the upper Deccan. Both Malwa and Gujarat are within striking distance of this base. Little is known of Krishna, Simuka's successor, except that he is mentioned in epigraphic records. Krishna's son Satakarni I seems to be the first major Satavahana king with power over upper Deccan, and at least parts of Malwa and western India. That eastern Malwa was within the Satavahana orbit is clear from the dedicatory inscription on the southern gateway of Sanchi which mentions that it was the gift of Vasishthiputra Ananda, the foreman of artisans of the king Satakarni. A Nanaghat inscription celebrates the performance of Vedic sacrifices including one *Rajasuya* and two *Asvamedha* sacrifices by him, the inscription being known as the inscription of his queen Nayanika.

In the post-Satakarni I period, that is, in the AD first century, the Satavahana possessions in western India, Malwa, and upper Deccan passed into the hands of the Saka Kshatrapas who seem to have advanced to this region from their base in Sindh. The sources mention only two groups of the Satavahana lineage in this period—the Apilakas of possibly some area of modern Madhya Pradesh, and the Kuntalas who ruled over the Kuntala country which comprised north Kanara, Belgaum, and Dharwar, all in modern Karnataka. Scholars write of an eclipse of Satavahana power right up to the advent of Gautami Satakarni whose reign has been put by Sircar[15] between AD 106 and 130.

The power which caused this eclipse was the Sakas and testifies to their spread in Gujarat from Sindh and from Gujarat to western Malwa and the northern part of the Konkan coast. According to the Periplus, the Sakas or Scythians ruled Sindh from their capital at Minnagara (unidentified), and it has been inferred on the basis of the testimony of the Periplus that northern Konkan came under the Scythian control in the middle of the AD first century. Soon afterwards, the whole region including Malwa must have passed to the control of the Kushanas and the Saka Kshatrapas must have ruled this area mainly on behalf of their Kushana overlords.

Of the two groups of Saka Kshatrapas in western and central India, one was known as the Kshaharatas and the other as the Kardamakas. The Kshaharatas came first. The coins of the earliest known Kshaharata Kshatrapa was Bhumaka whose coins have been found in the coastal areas of the Gujarat mainland, Saurashtra, and Malwa-Rajasthan stretching as far as Ajmer. Whether he issued his coins as an independent power or as a provincial ruler of the Kushanas is difficult to say but it appears that he carved out a niche for himself in western India and Malwa. The coins of his successor Nahapana have been found more widely, from Ajmer to Nasik, thus suggesting his grip over a large but nonetheless compact region. The central point of his power is c. AD 119–26, and although the inscriptions mention him as Kshatrapa or Mahakshatrapa, his coin legends call him 'Rajan', thus implying that he was unlikely to have an overlord. The inscriptions of his son-in-law Ushavadata or Rishabhadatta in the Nasik and Karle caves give interesting details about his territorial possessions. They mention the districts of Govardhana or Nasik and Mamala or Pune, both of which were possibly under his control. But there are references in his inscriptions to Kapura (Baroda state), Prabhasa (south Kathiawar/Saurashtra), Broach, Dasapura (Mandasore in western Malwa; north of Ujjain), Sopara, and Pushkar. In the same context there are also references to some rivers of the region—Tapti, Barnasa or Banas (south-east Rajasthan), Parada (Par in Surat), and Damana (Damanganga near Daman). Dahanu, north of Mumbai, has been referred to as Dahanuka. Sircar[16] states that it is 'very probable' that Nahapana's terrtories included Malwa, Saurashtra, mainland Gujarat, north Konkan coast, northern Maharashtra away from the coast, parts of Rajasthan, and a portion of the lower Indus valley. When the Uttamabhadras of Rajasthan were besieged by the Malavas, Ushavadata went to seek help from the Kshatrapas and defeated the Malavas. The Kshaharata branch of the Kshatrapas was defeated by Gautamiputra Satakarni, possibly not long after AD 124–5.

Under the Kardamaka branch of the Saka Kshatrapas, the first of whom is Chastana, the Kshatrapa power witnessed a revival. Chastana's successor was his grandson Rudradaman I whom we find jointly ruling with Chastana in the Andhau inscriptions from Kutch. In about AD 140 Chastana has been mentioned as the ruler of Ujjayini by Ptolemy. Rudradaman I was a more important ruler. His Junagarh inscription refers to him as the ruler of various areas of western India and Malwa which he wrested from Gautamiputra Satakarni. Vasishthiputra Satakarni, a son of Gautamiputra, was his son-in-law. This is known from an inscription at Kanheri. At its height, Rudradaman's territories included Malwa, Gujarat mainland including the Sabarmati valley, north Konkan, the Mahishmati area on the Narmada, Kutch, Marwar, western part of the lower Indus valley, Sauvira or the eastern part of the lower Indus valley, and Nishada (the western Vindhyas and the Aravalli range). He also defeated the Yaudheyas based in southern Panjab. It appears that in north Maharashtra (Nasik and Pune areas) the Satavahanas continued in power.

Rudradaman I's rule came to an end about AD mid-second century. The Kardamaka branch of the Kshatrapas continued to rule different parts of their original kingdom till about the middle of the AD fourth century, but it was a far cry from their heyday under Rudradaman. Two ruling groups make their appearance in parts of the region in the early AD third century. The Abhiras carved out a kingdom in north Maharashtra by the middle of the AD third century and the Malava power became important in south-east Rajasthan in about this period.

What emerges is that basically in the AD first three centuries there developed a vast geopolitical orbit covering Sindh, the whole of Gujarat, Malwa, east Rajasthan and some parts of west Rajasthan as well, and north Maharashtra including the north Konkan coast. This geopolitical orbit remained independent of the Gangetic orbit. Originally its growth was due to an impact of the Oxus to the Indus orbit because the Sakas and Scythians emanate from the latter. However, it appears that but for the settlements of the Sakas in Sindh this orbit would not have come into existence. As time went by, the

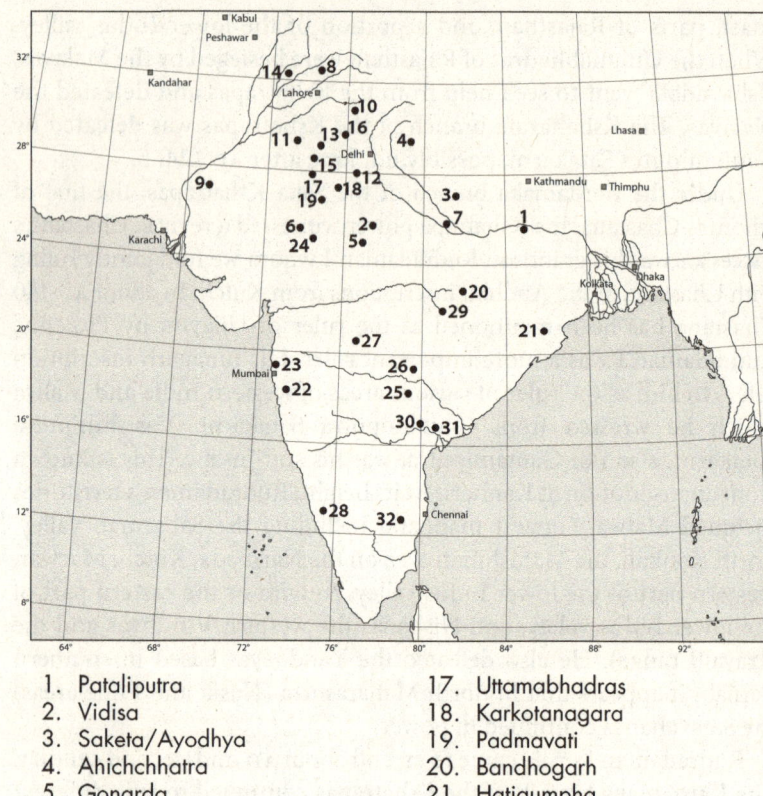

1. Pataliputra
2. Vidisa
3. Saketa/Ayodhya
4. Ahichchhatra
5. Gonarda
6. Madhyamika
7. Pabhosa
8. Sakala
9. Sui Vihar
10. Sanghol
11. Arjunayanas
12. Uddehikas
13. Malavas
14. Sibi
15. Rajanyas
16. Yaudheyas
17. Uttamabhadras
18. Karkotanagara
19. Padmavati
20. Bandhogarh
21. Hatigumpha
22. Nanaghat
23. Kanheri
24. Ujjayini
25. Bodhan
26. Adam
27. Devagiri
28. Banavasi
29. Shadol
30. Nagarjunakonda
31. Amaravati
32. Kanchipuram

Map 3.1   Location of Some Major Sites and Areas Mentioned in Chapter 3

area developed some sub-orbits. One such sub-orbit seems to have spread over north Maharashtra and Gujarat mainland and another orbit of this type came about covering south-east Rajasthan and parts of the desertic west Rajasthan.

That the Satavahanas and the Kshatrapas would fight over north Maharashtra, north Konkan, Malwa, and a fringe of Rajasthan is not unnatural. North Maharashtra controls the routes going further to the south, and north Konkan and the mainland Gujarat coast were among the pivotal points of India's Indian ocean trade. Apart from being a rich agricultural plain, Malwa controlled traffic both to west India and the Deccan, and stood guard at a major entrance to the Ganga valley, especially the upper Ganga valley, from the Deccan and west India.

The development of a sub-orbit in north Maharashtra under the Abhiras is interesting in its own right. The original territory of the Abhiras is uncertain but without looking for them in eastern Iran, Rajasthan desert, or between the lower Indus valley and Saurashtra, as Sircar[17] does, it may be more sensible to accept the Mahabharata evidence and associate them with Aparanta or north Konkan and possibly parts of northern Maharashtra or mainly the Nasik area. They are known to have served as generals of the Saka Kshatrapas of western India, and one Isvaradatta whose coins have been found in the Saka area could or could not have been an Abhira. It appears that the king Mathariputra Isvarasena who appears in a Nasik inscription of *c*. AD mid-third century was an Abhira king.

An unstated dimension of the rule of the Saka Kshatrapas and other related groups such as the Abhiras is that they appear in their epigraphic records completely Indianized. The Nasik inscriptions of Ushavadata with their list of gifts to the Brahmins and visits to different pilgrim places are an excellent indicator of this phenomenon. Similarly, Rudradaman I's Junagarh inscription written in excellent and poetic Sanskrit shows that there was nothing 'east Iranian' about these Sakas, at least by the time they came to flourish in Sindh, Gujarat, Malwa, parts of Rajasthan, and northern Konkan coast and northern mainland Maharashtra.[18]

A New Orbit: Maharashtra (both Vidarbha and Deccan inclusive of the Konkan coast), Andhra (both Deccan and the coast), and Karnataka (Deccan and the Konkan coast)

As the Satavahana ambition in the north was thwarted by the Saka Kshatrapa power, the Satavahana kings had to focus on the regions to the east and the south. This is what one discovers in Gautamiputra Satakarni's possessions outside Malwa and the rest—the Krishna valley, Asmaka territory (in the modern Karimnagar area of Andhra, around the site of Bodhan, although some scholars put it at Adam in Vidarbha), Mulaka with its centre at Paithan, and Vidarbha. It is a fairly compact unit south of the Vindhya-Satpuras stretching from Vidarbha to Konkan and from northern Maharashtra to the Krishna valley. The inscriptions of Gautamiputra's successor Vasishthiputra Pulumavi has been found at Nasik, Karle, and Amaravati, clearly suggesting that Gautamiputra's territory in this sector remained intact. Karnataka up to the Bellary district also came under his control. The Satavahanas forfeited their ambitions in India north of the Narmada, but the Deccan as a whole including Vidarbha and the Konkan coast came to constitute their pasture. It strikes one by its geographical compactness, with all its parts mutually well-linked. From Vidarbha there were at least two major openings to the Krishna valley, one through Chandrapuri to Karimnagar, and the other from the Amraoti-Buldhana sector of Vidarbha to Nizamabad and beyond. Bellary or the southernmost Deccan was accessible either from south-western Andhra or from the southern Maharashtra-Bijapur-Gulbarga alignment. The coins of Sivasri Satakarni, Pulumavi's successor, have been found in the Krishna-Godavari section of Andhra. Under Yajnasri Satakarni (c. AD 174–203) the Satavahana power gained some advantage at the expense of the Kshatrapas because his coins have been recovered from Baroda in the mainland Gujarat and even Saurashtra. His coins have also been found in the Krishna and Godavari districts of Andhra, the Chanda district and other parts of Vidarbha, and north Konkan. His inscriptions have been found at Nasik, Kanheri, and Chinna Ganjam in the Krishna district. The compactness of the area south of Vidarbha-north Konkan alignment up to north Karnataka remains undisputed. The Satavahanas were in fact the lords of Dakshinapatha which figures in this period as another major geopolitical orbit of ancient India.

It is equally important to remember that the Satavahana zone also developed various identifiable regional foci during the period of the Satavahana decline after Yajna Satakarni. Coins and an inscription of Chandra Satakarni have been found in the Godavari district of Andhra. An inscription of Puloma or Pulumavi, a later Satavahana king, has been found at Myakadoni of Bellary. The coins of one Rudra Satakarni have been found in Andhra. Andhra possibly passed from the Satavahanas to the Ikshakus by the middle of the third century and the Pallavas of Kanchi advanced up to northern Karnataka by the end of this century.

However, there were Satavahana successors elsewhere in the Deccan. A Satavahana group ruled in north Kanara, Belgaum, and Dharwar. This was the area of Kuntala whose capital was at Banavasi. From this area one also gets the coins and inscriptions of a branch of the Satavahanas who bear the term 'Chutu' in their names. The Konkan coast around Karwar and further south, and the adjoining areas of Karnataka seem to have been the centre of the Chutu clan. The Kuntala territory was possessed by the Kadambas in the middle of the AD fourth century. Some of the Kuntala kings could go back to the AD second century, which would mean that the Kuntala territory had a sub-group of the major Satavahana clan ruling in that area. A relevant inscription is the Banavasi inscription of Haritiputra Vishnukada Chutukulananda Satakarni. Sircar's analysis[19] of the Tarhala hoard of coins in the Akola district of the Vidarbha area of Maharashtra suggests that a branch of the Satavahana family continued to rule in Vidarbha and the adjoining areas of Madhya Pradesh up to the appearance of the Vakatakas in that area in the second half of the AD third century. Another Satavahana group seems to have ruled in the Chhattisgarh or the south Kosala area. Satavahana coins have been discovered in this sector. Further, the dynastic name of the Kuras appears on some coins of the Kolhapur area. According to Sircar, they were the local rulers of the Kolhapur region.[20]

One would suggest that the manifestation of several distinct areas within the territories of Vidarbha, south Kosala, Kuntala, and Kolhapur in the Satavahana-post-Satavahana context is an interesting process in itself and cast its shadow deep on the post-Satavahana history of the region. In a sense, the geopolitical identity of the Deccan became highlighted only under the Satavahanas. It is also important that the adjoining areas such as Vidarbha, Chhattisgarh (south Kosala), and the Krishna-Godavari delta emerge strongly as political entities during this period. The interrelatedness of each of these geographical components is obvious. From south Kosala one easily enters the Godavari delta, one of the lushest green deltas of the subcontinent. From Vidarbha, as we have noted, there are at least two main routes to the Andhra coast, one through Karimnagar and the other through Nizamabad. Within Andhra itself the districts of Anantapur and Kurnul lead to Bellary in Karnataka. On the other hand, from north Maharashtra there are different approaches to the Karnataka and Andhra sectors. The Konkan coast itself brings one in a straight line to the Kuntala territory of north Canara, Belgaum, and Dharwar. On the eastern side of the Western Ghats there is a straight route coming via Kolhapur. This route can take one straight to the Bijapur-Gulbarga section of Karnataka and the areas further south. Andhra is also easily approachable from the Bijapur-Gulbarga section. There is little doubt that the area of the Satavahana influence south of the Vidarbha-north Konkan alignment constituted a major geopolitical unit.

The two powers which developed in the earlier Satavahana domain were the Vakatakas and the Ikshakus. The name of the first Vakataka king was Vindhyasakti, which may evoke an association with the Vindhyan area. This may not be surprising because the records of one of the Vakataka feudatories have been found in the Bundelkhand area which lies in the eastern segment of the Vindhyas and imply that the area was within the area of the Vakataka influence. The core of the Vakataka power lay in the Nagpur and Akola areas. With this base they extended their power in parts of the Deccan and Madhya Pradesh. Vindhyasakti has been mentioned in an inscription from Ajanta which lies at the entrance to the interior of the Deccan. Vindhyasakti's successor Pravarasena I established Vakataka suzerainty from Bundelkhand to the Hyderabad sector of the Deccan. Vindhyasakti possibly ruled in the last quarter of the AD third century and the reign of Pravarasena I takes the chronology down to AD mid-fourth century. Pravarasena's successor Prithvisena I married a daughter of Chandragupta II (AD 376–414), a famous Gupta king of Magadha. It is probable that the Vakatakas and the Guptas were contenders for power in the Malwa region of Madhya Pradesh, which is natural in view of their control of the Bundelkhand area. It also appears that the control over Bundelkhand also gave the Vakatakas control of a large, hilly, and forested section of the Satpura-Maikal belt. It is said[21] that the last reference to the Vakataka power was in an AD sixth century inscription of the Vishnukundin kings of the Krishna valley in Andhra. Thus, on the whole, the Vakatakas ruled from the middle of the third to the middle of the AD sixth century or thereabouts.

An interesting aspect of the Vakataka rule is that after Pravarasena I the kingdom was divided into two parts, one centred around Nagpur, and the other based at Basim in Akola. These two units must have had different geographical possibilities. The Nagpur branch is considered the main branch where after Pravarasena I, the king was Rudrasena I who was followed by Prithvisena I, two records of whose feudatory

Vyaghradeva have been found in Bundelkhand. One is from Nachna, the site of a famous Gupta period temple and the other at Ganj near Ajaigarh in the Panna area. Rudrasena II married Chandragupta's daughter Prabhavatigupta who ruled for a long time on behalf of her minor sons, one of whom was Pravarasena II (AD mid-fifth century). The Poona grant of Prabhavatigupta was issued from Nandivardhana, possibly the capital (modern Nagardhan or Nandardhan) of the main branch of the Vakatakas near Ramtek. Ramagirisvamin (Vishnu) of Ramtek itself is mentioned in another inscription of Prabhavatigupta. Pravarsena II's inscriptions have been found in the areas of Wardha, Chhindwara, Seoni, Nagpur, Balaghat, Amraoti, and Betul, showing clearly that the Vakataka dynasty of the Vidarbha area was also controlling the intervening areas between Bundelkhand and Vidarbha. Balaghat and Seoni control the route which came towards Vidarbha through the central Indian jungles. It appears that Pravarasena II established a new capital called Pravarapura which possibly lay in the Wardha area and has been tentatively identified with modern Paoner. His inscriptions suggest that the territories ruled by his representatives or feudatories were given the status of *rajya*s or kingdoms. For instance, the Amraoti area was called Bhojakata rajya and the Chhindwara area Arammi rajya. Narendrasena, Pravarasena II's successor married a princess of the Kuntala territory. He was succeeded by Prithvisena II whose inscriptions have been found in the Chanda and Bhandara districts, one to the south and another to the east of Nagpur. The main branch of the Vakatakas passed into oblivion after him.

Harisena of the AD mid-fifth century seems to be the most powerful among the Vakataka kings of Basim or Vatsagulma. The Ajanta record caused to be incised by one of his ministers, a devout Buddhist called Varahadeva, mentions Harisena as having influence in the Kuntala territory, Avanti or west Malwa, Kalinga, (south) Kosala, the Traikutaka territory of north Konkan, Lata or the Navsari-Broach area of Gujarat, and Andhra. It is possible that this Vakataka king interacted with the kings of all these areas, but nothing can be claimed beyond this.

In the Nasik area, the Satavahana power was finally supplanted by the Abhiras, who from this base, could exert influence along the alignment of the Western Ghats and the Konkan coast. An advance along the Gujarat coast was probable, and similarly, they could come in the way of the expansion of the Kadamba power in the

Kuntala territory of the southern segment of the Konkan coast and the adjoining area. The Abhiras were powerful at least between the AD mid-third century and the AD fourth century when they came in conflict with the Kadamba king Mayurasarman. Some parts of north-western Deccan also witnessed the growth of a separate but short-lived dynasty during this period—the Bodhi dynasty which is known from their coins and had kings called Sribodhi, Sivabodhi, Chandrabodhi, and Virabodhi.

In Andhra, the Ikhsvakus were the most powerful of the Satavahana successors. Their capital was at Nagarjunakonda or the ancient Vijayapuri. The founder of this dynasty, Chantamula I, is dated in the second quarter of the AD third century. As the distribution of their inscriptions suggests, the Ikhsvakus remained principally a power of the Krishna valley in Andhra, most of their inscriptions being found in the Amaravati, Jaggayyapeta, and Nagarjunakonda areas. Although they were pushed into the background by the advent of the Pallavas of Kanchipuram in Tamil Nadu towards the end of the third or the beginning of the AD fourth centuries, they maintained their separate identity possibly at least till the AD fifth century. The Pallava occupation of the area is proved by the Mayidavolu copper-plate inscription which records an order of the Pallava crown-prince of Kanchi Sivaskandavarman to his provincial governor of Andhrapatha in Dhanyakataka or the present-day Amaravati.

Towards the end of the AD third century or thereabouts, the Machlipatnam area was under the rule of the Brihatphalayana dynasty, of which only one king, Jayavarmana, is known. His Kondamudi copper-plate grant calls him 'Rajan' and 'Maharaja' and mentions his 'camp of victory' at Kudur which may be located in the Machlipatnam or Ghantasala area. The power of this dynasty also seems to have fallen to the advent of the Pallavas of Kanchipuram who advanced up to the Krishna valley (*Andhrapatha*), the Bellary district of Karnataka (Satavahaniya province), and the Kuntala territory, also in Karnataka.[22]

Notes

1. See Sircar (1953a: 115) for Menander's territory; for the earlier phase, Professor Jagannath (1957); for the Indo-Greeks as a whole, Banerjea (1957a) provides steady and clear guidance.

2. On Mithridates, see Raychaudhuri (1953: 425–8); for the Scythians and Parthians in India, see Sircar (1953b) and Banerjea (1957b).

3. On Vonones, see Sircar (1953b: 123–5) and Banerjea (1957b: 201–4). On Gondophares, see Sircar (1953b: 128–32) and Banerjea (1957b: 209–15).

4. On Maues, see Sircar (1953b: 125–6) and Banerjea (1957b: 194–201).

5. On Sodasa, see Sircar (1953b: 132–5) and Banerjea (1957c: 269).

6. For the quotation, Sircar (1953c: 141). For some comparatively important developments in the Kushana studies, see Mukherjee (1988); Sims-Williams and Cribb (1995–6); Falk (2001, 2004); and Mukherjee (1995) (for a complete translation of the Rabatak inscription). Also, for the general details, Banerjea and Professor Jagannath (1957).

7. For the date of Vasudeva, Sircar (1953c: 151); for Falk's dating of Vasudeva at AD 225, see Falk (2001, 2004).

8. For Paikuli inscription, see Sircar (1953c: 152).

9. For the date of Ahichchhatra coins, see Sircar (1953d: 172) and Professor Jagannath (1957: 105–6).

10. For the date of Ayodhya coins, see Sircar (1953d: 173).

11. For these regional territorial formations, see Sircar (1953d).

12. For Bhojaka, see Sircar (1953e: 214); for Kharavela, see also Professor Jagannath (1957). According to Professor Jagannath, 'everything points to the beginning of the second century BC as the date of Kharavela's accession to the throne'. There is no scholarly consensus on this issue.

13. For Simuka, see Sircar (1953e: 195). For the Satavahana phase as a whole, see Gopalachari (1957: 293–327). Gopalachari puts the date of Simuka at 235 BC. For a recent volume dealing with the Satavahanas, Sastri (1999) (opting for a late Satavahana chronology).

14. Sircar (1953e: 196–7).

15. Ibid., pp. 200–4; Gopalachari (1957: 312–15).

16. Sircar (1953f: 180–2); Banerjea (1957c: 274–8).

17. Sircar (1953g: 221–3); Sircar (1957: 331–3).

18. Sircar (1953f: 184–5); Banerjea (1957c: 281–3).

19. Sircar (1953e: 209) (for the Tarhala hoard).

20. Sircar (1957: 338).

21. Sircar (1953g: 207).

22. Ibid., pp. 226–7.

4

The Re-emergence of the Gangetic Orbit and the Regional Power Centres

c. AD 300 to c. AD 800

The Re-emergence of the Gangetic Orbit under the Guptas

Magadha and its capital Pataliputra come back into focus under the Gupta dynasty. Initially, the dynasty establishes its base by coming into a matrimonial alliance with the Lichchhavis of Vaisali or north Bihar. At this stage, it is likely that the Gupta power was stretched along the northern and southern banks of the Ganga in modern Bihar. Whether it incorporated Magadha as whole or extended east into parts of Bengal is impossible to say. R.C. Majumdar[1] thinks that, although no confirmatory evidence exists, the kingdom of Chandragupta I, who married a Lichchhavi princess, comprised 'nearly the whole of Bihar and portions of Bengal and Awadh'. If true, this was a compact unit and made possible for his successor Samudragupta to undertake conquests in different directions, of which his Allahabad pillar inscription (also known as *Harisena prasasti* because this was composed by Harisena in the form of an eulogy) is the most authentic evidence. Nine north Indian kings, who are specifically mentioned, were defeated and their kingdoms annexed. Two of these kings—Nagasena and Ganapati Naga—were members of the Naga family of Padmavati (Pawayya), Vidisa, and

Mathura. Two more, Achyuta and Chandravarman, ruled respectively in the Ahichchhatra region and West Bengal. The territories of the remaining five kings (Rudradeva, Matila, Nagadatta, Nandin, and Balavarman) cannot be satisfactorily located but are clearly suggestive of the fact that in different parts of northern India there were various ruling families in the post-Kushana context. Much regarding these families remains unknown. The five political units at the boundary of Samudragupta's kingdom came to acknowledge his sovereignty but were basically left alone. Three of these units—Samatata, Kamarupa, and Nepal—denote the Meghna-trans-Meghna territory of modern Dhaka and Comilla, parts of the Brahmaputra valley, and parts of Nepal up to the Kathmandu valley. The fourth such unit, Davaka, has been assumed to denote the Nowgong district of Assam, and the fifth, Kartripura, has been identified with the Kartarpur area of Jalandhar. The inscription also mentions ten feudatory tribal states along with the five units located along the kingdom's boundary. Among them, the Malavas, Arjunayanas, Yaudheyas, and Madrakas are known to have been located in various parts of Rajasthan and Panjab. Of the rest, the Sanakanikas were located near Vidisa and the Abhiras possibly in a neighbouring area. The remaining three—Prarjunas, Kakas, and Kharaparikas—cannot be located with certainty but have been put by Majumdar to the north and east of Vidisa in the eastern Malwa area itself. Majumdar's description of the territory directly under Samudragupta's administration is as follows:

In the east it included the whole of Bengal, excepting its southeastern extremity. Its northern boundary ran along the foothills of the Himalayas. In the west it extended up to the territory of the Madras in the Punjab and probably included its eastern districts between Lahore and Karnal. From Karnal the boundary followed the Yamuna up to its junction with the Chambal, and thence along an imaginary line drawn almost due south to Bhilsa. The southern boundary ran from Bhilsa to Jubbulpore and thence along the Vindhya range of hills.[2]

This would mean the whole of the Indo-Gangetic plain up to nearly the Indus and a large part of Rajasthan and eastern Malwa.

Samudragupta also defeated kings all along the route to the south from south Kosala, that is, the Bilaspur, Sambalpur, Raipur, and Durg sector. The defeated king of this area was Mahendra. The next king along the route was Vyaghraraja of Mahakantara which should denote the extensive Dandakaranya area stretching up to the

Vizianagram area of the Andhra coast. The places along the Andhra coast were Pithapuram in the Godavari district (the defeated king Mahendragiri), Vengi or Peddavegi near Ellore (the defeated king Hastivarman), a succession of other kings and areas along the Andhra coast up to Nellore (Damana of Erandapalla, Kuvera of Devarashtra, Mantaraja of Kaurala, Svamidatta of Kottura, Nilaraja of Avamukha, and Dhananjaya of Kusthalapura), Nellore (the defeated king Palakka), and finally, Kanchipuram (the defeated king Vishnugopa). This could mean nothing more than a raid, but to those who know the entire route from Magadha to Kanchi will appreciate the clarity with which the route of the attack was planned and its logistics organized. This certainly was the most ambitious of the military expeditions undertaken in ancient India, both before and after Samudragupta who ruled approximately between AD 320 and 380. Little is known of his immediate successor Ramagupta, although he is now known to have existed as a Gupta king. The next ruler Chandragupta II who ruled up to about AD 415 is more famous. Western India in general—western Malwa and Gujarat—was wrested from the Saka Kshatrapas by him. Equally intriguing is the evidence furnished by the famous Meherauli iron pillar inscription which mentions the king Chandra and his exploits against the kings of Bengal and his advance beyond the Indus up to Bahlika or Balkh/Bactria in north Afghanistan. If the palaeography of this inscription is Gupta period palaeography, no other 'Chandra' of this period except Chandragupta II could be credited with such victories both in the east and the west. The western expedition remains somewhat problematic in the sense that there is no special reason why Chandragupta would decide to carry his western expedition up to north Afghanistan. Did 'Bahlika' mean some other territory in the north-west during this period?

At its height under Chandragupta II, the Gupta kingdom comprised virtually the whole of northern India from Bengal to Gujarat and from the Vindhyas to the Indus and beyond. Chandragupta II's successor Kumaragupta who ascended the throne in c. AD 415 and ruled up to c. AD 455 maintained this possession intact. It was only towards the end of his rule that under the leadership of the crown prince Skandagupta, an attack by the White Huns from the north-west was defeated and a major danger averted. Skandagupta died in c. AD 467; the Hunas possibly weakened the Gupta military fabric but was not successful till the end of the fifth or the beginning of the AD sixth century. A major light of Skandagupta's reign is the inscription of his Gujarat governor

Parnadatta and Parnadatta's son Chakrapalita, which narrates how the dam of the Sudarsana lake in the Girnar hills, dating from the time of Chandragupta Maurya, came close to bursting because of the excessive rains and was repaired by these officials of Skandagupta. When this dam was repaired by Parnadatta and Chakrapalita, it was about 800 years old, and the fact that this dam was looked after by the various kings over such a long period throws some interesting light on the maintenance of important public works in ancient India.

Among Skandagupta's successors the important one was Budhagupta (c. AD 477–500), and although the Gupta king still remained the acknowledged monarch of Aryavarta, different regional powers had already begun to make themselves felt. In the Kathiawar peninsula, the Maitrakas of Valabhi assumed the title 'Maharaja' and their records claim that Dronasimha who first assumed the title was installed in royalty by the paramount ruler (that is, the Gupta king) himself. Two powers of Bundelkhand—the Parivrajaka Maharajas (roughly north of Satna) and the power which had Uchchakalpa (modern Uchahar, west of Satna?) as the capital—do not mention in their records the Gupta king as their suzerain. The Panduvamsa kings of Kalinjar or Kalanjar area and Baghelkhand zone assume royal titles towards the end of the AD fifth century. The two records of Maharaja Lakshmana found near Allahabad and Rewa of about this period do not mention the Gupta suzerain and the same is true of Maharaja Subandhu who issued a land-grant from Mahishmati on the Narmada in the late AD fifth century. It is apparent that some areas of the Gupta kingdom were slowly passing out of the Gupta control by the end of the AD fifth century.

The Gupta power disintegrated roughly by the middle of the AD sixth century, and to a great extent this was due to the invasions of the Hunas from the north, first under Toramana and the second under Mihirakula. By the beginning of the AD sixth century, Toramana was well installed in Panjab and apparently took control of central India up to Eran near Bina in East Malwa. His son Mihirakula had his capital at Sialkot or Sakala and thus controlled the Indus region, possibly including Kashmir. An inscription dated c. AD 530 states that Mihirakula's power came up to Gwalior.

In a sense, it is interesting to observe how the forces emanating from the Oxus to the Indus orbit were exerting influence on the course of history in the Gangetic inner Indian orbit in the form of the Hunas. However, by coming up to Gwalior, Mihirakula confronted the ambition of the king Yasodharman of Malwa who was based at Mandasore between Ujjayini and Rajasthan. Mihirakula was defeated, and thus ended the impact of the Hunas on the history of inner India.

Yasodharman's Mandasore eulogy depicts him virtually as the successor of the Gupta power between the Himalayas and the Kalinga coast and between the Brahmaputra river and the Arabian sea. Much of this claim has to be treated as an exaggeration, although for a brief period, possibly between AD 530 and 540, he was the most powerful king of northern India.

The Gupta kings certainly receded into background by this period, a process which was helped by the rise of the Maukharis and Later Guptas in the Gupta heartland by the middle of the AD sixth century. Similarly, one hears of a king called Vainyagupta in the eastern part of Bengal, possibly outside the main Gupta lineage.

Narasimhagupta was the last major Gupta king, although his direct control need not have extended beyond Magadha and its immediate neighbourhood. His suzerainty was possibly still invoked on a large part of the former Gupta dominions. Possibly, he also played a role in stalling the progress of Mihirakula towards the Ganga valley. Narasimhagupta was followed by Kumaragupta III and Vishnugupta, the last two of the recorded Gupta kings. Dated between *c.* AD 535 and *c.* 570 they still issued gold coins, suggesting that the fabric of the Gupta power had not completely collapsed even by then. Majumdar[3] points out that Kalinga and northern Bengal had acknowledged Gupta suzerainty till about the AD mid-sixth century and possibly somewhat later.

Geographically speaking, the rise of the Gupta power in the middle Ganga plain and its expansion throughout the whole of northern India up to the Indus valley and possibly beyond was somewhat sudden, if not a little surprising. After the fall of the Mauryas, the Ganga plain had been subject to almost continuous pressure from the Indus to the Oxus orbit in various forms, with the Kushanas establishing themselves up to Banaras and conducting forays further east. The regional political entities that one encounters in this plain in the post-Kushana context give no indication of the role that the valley will play in Indian affairs under the Guptas soon afterwards. One does not find Chandragupta II's annexation of western Malwa and Gujarat surprising; that came logically in the sequence of events, but what is somewhat unique is Samudragupta's thrust as far south as Kanchipuram across south Kosala and the entire stretch of the Andhra coast, and the move across south-west Andhra (Nellore, Anantapur) to Kanchipuram. Possibly, he did this because he found the routes to the Deccan blocked by the Vakatakas and others.

North India after the Guptas: Various Sub-orbits of Power till the Eighth Century

A number of regional power centres emerged in northern India from Gujarat to Assam and from Nepal to Orissa after the end of the paramountcy of the Guptas. In the early to mid-seventh century, Harshavardhana tried to impart some political unity to north India, but in the history of post-Gupta northern India, it is the regional powers which deserve main attention along with the establishment of Arab power in Sindh.

The centre of the Maitraka dynasty power was at Vala/Valabhi in the Bhavnagar sector of the Kathiawar peninsula. Till the Gupta period the centre of political power in Gujarat was the area of the Girnar hills in Junagarh. Why the focus shifted to Bhavnagar under the Maitrakas is not clear. The Bhavnagar area which lies on the Gulf of Cambay possibly offered certain maritime advantage to the Maitraka rulers. As we have noted, the Maitraka kings initially owned suzerainty to their Gupta overlord, although they came to style themselves as 'Maharaja'. From the time of Guhasena in the mid-sixth century onwards, the Maitraka kings shed their Gupta links. The extent of the Maitraka power is not easy to ascertain. It has been pointed out that the early Maitraka land-grants all refer to villages in Bhavnagar, but in a record of one of the Maitraka feudatories in *c.* AD 574, it is stated that a king of the area of Dwaraka in the north-western part of the Kathiawar peninsula was defeated by that feudatory. It is probable that by the last quarter of the AD sixth century, the Maitrakas had extended their power over the whole of the Kathiawar peninsula. It is likely that their hold over Kathiawar enabled them to control the situation in the Gujarat mainland and possibly in parts of western Malwa as well. Kutch also was likely to have been under the Maitraka control. The Maitraka power reached its apogee under Siladitya who ruled around AD 580.

The rise of the Gurjara power in Rajasthan had its focus around Jodhpur (the first capital at Mandor 5 miles north of Jodhpur) in the Marwar sector of west Rajasthan. This also happened around AD mid-sixth century. The origin of the Gurjaras has excited a lot of historical speculation but to no purpose. What is important is that under them the desert tract of Rajasthan comes for the first time in sharp focus in Indian history, just as the Kathiawar peninsula became a power centre in its own right under the Maitrakas. A Brahmin named Harichandra established the first Gurjara kingdom in the AD mid-sixth century, but his four sons seem to have ruled separately with different capitals, the existence of at least one of which has been historically attested. This was at Medantaka or possibly modern Merta, 70 miles north-east of Jodhpur. These kings continued to rule for the next 200 years.

The shifting of the political focus of Rajasthan to the Marwar section possibly calls for an explanation. It is possible that certain trade routes through the desert, especially the ones which led to Sindh and also to the area near Delhi became prominent during this period and the Gurjara rulers decided to take advantage of that. However, this is nothing more than a speculation.

Another Gurjara branch established power at Nandipuri near Broach. The place has been identified satisfactorily with Nanded/Nandod on the bank of the Karjan river in the former Rajpipla state. Their earliest records date from the first half of the AD seventh century and during this period, this Gurjara principality extended between the Mahi and the Kim rivers on the coast and between the coastline of this sector and the borders of Malwa and Khandesh. The stretch between Mahi and Kim includes the mouth of the Tapti as well, that is, the modern Surat area from where there was an easy route to the Burhanpur area of Malwa. From Burhanpur, one could easily enter both Khandesh and Malwa. Again, there may be a connection between the possible mercantile importance of this area and the associated routes and the growth of a separate nucleus of power here under a branch of the Gurjara dynasty.

The power which emerged prominently in the Uttar Pradesh-Bihar section of the Ganga-Yamuna plain during this period, that is, the AD mid-sixth century and later, was that of the Maukharis. *Maharajadhiraja* Isanavarman, the first Maukhari king to bear this sovereign and independent title, has his first secure date at AD 554 and claims to have defeated the Vishnukundin kings of Andhra, the Sulki kings of Orissa, and certain unspecified kings of Bengal. If there is any truth in this claim, one would think that Isanavarman's kingdom included south Bihar from where both Orissa and Bengal were accessible. The road to Andhra in his case must have lain through Orissa. Whether Kanauj was the capital of the Maukharis is a disputed point. On the whole, the base of the Maukhari power seems to be more of south Bihar or Magadha than Uttar Pradesh. If they had their capital at Kanauj they would have had a kingdom covering the better part of the Doab and the Ganga valley. On the other hand, it is not impossible to postulate the existence of such a large Maukhari kingdom for a very brief period.

The Later Guptas who may or may not have been linked in some way to the Guptas were the main contenders of the Maukhari power in Magadha. The Aphsad inscription which is found in the Nawada area of south Bihar gives the Later Gupta genealogy and was issued by Adityasena, the eighth ruler of the dynasty. Kumaragupta, the fourth king of the lineage, defeated the Maukhari Isanavarman and advanced up to Prayag or Allahabad. The Maukharis were also defeated by Kumaragupta's son Damodaragupta. The Later Gupta power seems to have reached its height under Mahasenagupta, Damodargupta's son. In Bana's *Harshacharita* he is called the king of Malwa, which is not an impossibility provided he could retain his control over the Allahabad region and proceed from there to Malwa. According to the Aphsad inscription he advanced up to the Brahmaputra and defeated the king Susthitavarman of Kamarupa.

This seems to be a fairly fluid period politically in the Gangetic India. Towards the end of the AD sixth century, presumably between AD 567 and 597, the Ganga plain was attacked by the Chalukyan king Kirtivarman who claims to have defeated the kings of Anga, Vanga, and Magadha. Considering that he had to come a very long way from his base at Badami in south Deccan, this implies that the political lines of the period were very fluid indeed. Further, between AD 581 and 600 there was an incursion to possibly parts of Bihar and Uttar Pradesh from the Tibetan king Sron-btsan-sgam-po.

There is apparently some confusion about the territories the Later Guptas ruled. The Aphsad inscription found in the Nawada sector east of Rajgir in Bihar testifies to their rule in the eastern part of Magadha. There is no difficulty in postulating the presence of the Maukhari power in the Gaya sector which lies to the west of this belt. The Later Gupta presence east of Rajgir suggests that the ancient Anga area which lies further to the east and the modern Santal Pargana area would have been included in their kingdom. In fact, there is an inscription of a Later Gupta queen from the Mandar hills near Deoghar in Santal Pargana.

If south Bihar was the focus of tussle between the Maukharis and the Later Guptas, Bengal was no less a witness of various political tussles during this period. Two political centres make their brief appearance in Bengal in the immediate post-Gupta context—Vainyagupta who left behind his inscription from the Brahmanbaria section of the Tripura district of eastern Bengal, and the three kings—Gopaditya, Dharmadeva, and Samacharadeva—of the Kotalipara sector of the Faridpur district of eastern Bengal, who are known principally from their coins. Unless one thinks that Vainyagupta's power base was the Samatata tract, there cannot be any explanation of the Brahmanbaria section to form a focus of power in any period of the Indian history. The Faridpur district as a post-Gupta power base is more problematic; how and why it happened, as it undoubtedly did because the gold coins (based on the imitation of Gupta gold coins) of the Kotalipara group of kings and presumably their successors have been found extensively in eastern Bengal (modern Bangladesh). On the whole, one may assume that in the sixth–seventh centuries there were distinct political developments in eastern Bengal, one in the Dhaka-Tripura or ancient Samatata sector and the other in Faridpur, the latter apparently based in the Vanga region.

In the seventh century Bengal there was also a kingdom in the old Gauda section, with its base on the northern bank of the Ganga/Bhagirathi in the Murshidabad district. Sasanka, the lone known major king of this kingdom with its capital at Karnasuvarna (Chhiruti in Murshidabad), figures in the political struggle between Pravakaravardhan, Rajyavardhan, and Harshavardhana of Thaneswar, Devagupta (presumably of the Later Gupta connection) of Malwa, and the Maukhari Grahavarman of Kanauj. The combined forces of Devagupta and Sasanka uprooted Maukhari Grahavarman of Kanauj who was married to the Thaneswar princess Rajyasri. This brought the Thaneswar forces in, and it appears that the result of the conflict between them and Sasanka of Gauda was inconclusive. This power struggle forms a major theme of Bana's *Harshacharita*. Sasanka has had his seal matrix on the rocks of Rhotasgarh, and his inscription has been located in the Midnapur district of south-west Bengal. His presence in Orissa is known from the records of his officers and feudatories in northern and southern Orissa.

In the political context of the time when the lines of domination were changing fast, Sasanka must be credited with the carving out of a kingdom which was reasonably coherent geographically. The alignment along the western bank of the Ganga/Bhagirathi from Karnasuvarna to Medinipur and from Medinipur to Orissa is clear and has been a major line of movement in the Indian history. The extension up to Rhotasgarh suggests that his kingdom also included the entire highland area from the western part of modern West Bengal to the Gaya-Sasaram sector of modern Bihar. Rhotasgarh is approachable from Sasaram, with the Son flowing around Rhotasgarh. This area gives direct access to the Palamau section of the Chhotanagpur plateau, and a major route from south Bihar to the Banaras area via Bhabua and Chakia passes through this general area. The configuration of Sasanka's kingdom involves segments of two distinct routes of ancient India. It is not clear, however, of the other areas likely to have been under his control. The lower stretch of West Bengal, that is, the eastern bank of the Bhagirathi offers a distinct possibility, and similarly, the Maldaha section of northern Bengal could have lain within this kingdom because traditionally Maldaha has been considered part of Gauda in Bengal. Besides, according to Bana's *Harshacharita*, Sasanka met his nemesis in the hands of the king Bhaskaravarman of the Brahmaputra valley, and it is probable that his kingdom included considerable parts of north Bengal, through which the Brahmaputra valley was easily approachable. The length of Sasanka's kingdom which stretched in a sense from the borders of Assam to the Ganjam area of Orissa was wholly undefendable for any length of time. Similarly, the extension of his power up to the hills of Sasaram and Rhotasgarh, that is, the Kaimur section of the Vindhyas, comes as a surprise. The highlands which dot the western part of modern West Bengal and continue right through the Santal Pargana, Hazaribagh, and Palamau sectors of modern Jharkhand up to the Gaya-Sasaram sector of south Bihar must have been incorporated in this short-lived political complex. It appears that in the post-Gupta scenario of north India, the geographical alignments of power had begun to take fast-changing and unusual shapes.

Kamarupa as a kingdom gains an authenticated status in the Allahabad pillar inscription along with another Assam kingdom Davaka. The existence of two independent kingdoms in the Brahmaputra valley, one around Nowgong and the other around modern Guwahati, is interesting in its own right. The antecedence of these kingdoms is not known, but one would not be surprised if they went back to the post-Mauryan period. We have already argued that the Brahmaputra valley was within the Mauryan political orbit. The available royal genealogy of Kamarupa begins with Pushyavarman, but of the first six rulers of this dynasty nothing is known except their names. The seventh king Narayanavarman reputedly performed two *Asvamedha* sacrifices. By the time of the eighth king Bhutivarman, which may be around the middle of the AD sixth century, that is, after the decline of the Gupta power, Davaka and the Surma valley of lower Assam were incorporated in the Kamarupa kingdom. The traditional boundary of Assam was the Karatoya valley of east Bengal, and it is possible that the Kamarupa territory was expanded up to this valley in about this period. By the beginning of the AD seventh century, Bhaskaravarman, well-known because of the importance of his role in north Indian dynastic politics of this time, was on the throne of Kamarupa.

Orissa of this period had also witnessed independent political developments, although the inscription of a king called Prithvi-Vigraha, found near Khallikote and dated *c.* AD 569–70, acknowledges Gupta suzerainty. This allegiance to the Guptas, however nominal, was shaken off by the Mana dynasty of north Orissa and the Sailodbhava dynasty of south Orissa in the last quarter of the AD sixth century. A king called Sambhuyasas of the Mana dynasty ruled both north and south Tosali, that is, the area from Balasore to Puri sometime between *c.* AD 580 and *c.* 603. The Sailodbhavas ruled in the Kangoda territory, that is, the territory between the Chilka lake south of Puri and the western part of the Ganjam district. Its founder was the king Ranabhita (or Aranabhita) who possibly flourished sometime in the second half of the AD sixth century. Orissa succumbed to the king Sasanka of Gauda by the early part of the AD seventh century. In an inscription of the Sailodbhavas of *c.* AD 619, one finds them acknowledging the suzerainty of Sasanka. However, the rule of Sasanka in Orissa lasted for only his lifetime, and the most powerful dynasty in Orissa in the post-Sasanka stage was the Sailodbhavas who soon succumbed to the influence of Harshavardhana of Thaneswar and Kanauj.

The rise of a powerful principality at Thaneswar in the outskirts of Kurukshetra harks back in a sense to the early Kuru kingdom of a much earlier era. In fact, the first Kuru capital Asandvivat (modern Asandh) is not far from Kurukshetra. From here, one could follow the Ghaggar-Hakra alignment to Sindh and also pass easily into Rajasthan, and from Rajasthan, into Malwa. Also, there was a straight line of movement to Panjab through Ambala. In the east, Delhi was almost at the doorstep, and from there the Ganga-Yamuna plain was open. Apart from the inscriptions of the period and Bana's *Harshacharita* which is only a panegyric in favour of Harsha, an important source is Hsuang Tsang's testimony of the political condition of northern India in the first half of the AD seventh century. His travels lasted from AD 630 to 644. There was a kingdom south of the Hindukush ruling basically in the former Gandhara territory. There was another kingdom in Swat. Kashmir kingdom of this period also included a considerable part of Panjab. The Sialkot area was the major political nucleus of Panjab during this period. There were states, although none powerful, in the hilly region of Panjab (modern Himachal). East of the Yamuna there was a state in Rohilkhand and another in the neighbouring Himalayan belt. Nepal and Kamarupa figure prominently in Hsuang Tsang's scheme and there are references to various states in the Ganga-Yamuna plain and the states in Bundelkhand, Gwalior, and Ujjain. The Valabhis controlled virtually the whole of western India, but there were kingdoms near Broach, in the Gurjara country of west Rajasthan, and in Sindh or the lower Indus valley. Thaneswara's political ambitions were framed in this political context.

R.C. Majumdar makes the following assessment of the boundaries of Harsha's kingdom:

... at first Harsha's kingdom comprised merely the territories of the old states of Thaneswar and Kanauj, though he probably added some small principalities to the north and west. It may be said to have comprised Eastern Punjab and Uttar Pradesh. Towards the close of his reign, he had annexed Magadha and even pushed his conquests as far as Orissa and Kongada. It is not definitely known, however, whether the last two with the intervening territory were ever incorporated in his kingdom.[4]

Harsha was thus basically successful in eastern Panjab and the Ganga-Yamuna valley, with a short-lived spell of dominance in Bihar and Orissa, and probably Bengal, because he must have marched to his Orissan conquests through Bengal, that is, along the Gauda-Orissa alignment of his adversary Sasanka's kingdom. He tried but had no success in the direction of Rajasthan, Malwa, and the Indus valley. The Chalukyan Pulakesin II thwarted his Malwa and west Indian ambition by defeating him in that sector.

The most striking thing about Harshavardhana's political interaction was that with his base in modern Haryana he made himself the most important monarch of his time in northern India from eastern Panjab to south Bihar. He also advanced up to the Orissan coast presumably through the territory of Sasanka. He made alliance with the king Bhaskaravarman of Kamrup, and it is this alliance which makes me feel that his route to Orissa possibly lay through the Kajangala area and thus through the former Gauda territory. The fact that he tried to draw political lines over such a vast region is far more important than the degree of his success or failure in a given area.

North India after Harshavardhana was dominated, till about the middle of the AD eighth century, by various dynasties which had already appeared in the scene before his reign. Thus, in a sense, Harshavardhana's attempt to carve out a kingdom over most of the Gangetic valley, Orissa, Malwa, western India, and Rajasthan was a kind of short-lived interlude. There is a tradition of a Chinese attack under a Chinese official Wang-Hiuen-Tse who is supposed to have been aided by the Tibetan king Sron-btsan-sgam-po and the king of Nepal Amsuvarman. The attack was apparently against north Bihar and Magadha. Victorious, according to the Chinese tradition, the invader returned to China in AD 648. Whether there is an element of truth or not in this tradition, the fact that the middle Ganga valley could be attacked from beyond the Himalayas through Nepal surely marks an expansion of the geopolitical probabilities in this phase of Indian history.

In Magadha, or at least in the eastern part of it, the Later Guptas continued to rule well into the AD eighth century. Adityasena, the king who is known mainly from his inscription at Aphsad, ruled in the third quarter of the AD seventh century. One supposes that the Later Guptas were busy trying to keep their power intact against the Maukhari kings on the one hand and the kings of Gauda on the other. The boundaries of the kingdom were possibly changing rapidly, and eventually the Later Gupta power was put to an end by the invasion of Yasovarman of Kanauj. A Sanskrit poem composed by Vakpati describes the path of Yasovarman's conquest. He first reached the Vindhyas, that is, the Kaimur range which lies on the route to Magadha and is a part of the Vindhyas. He worshipped the goddess Vindhyavasini whose temple is at the foot of the Vindhyas near Mirzapur. Having defeated the king of Magadha, he received the submission of the kings of the Deccan and advanced as far south as the Malaya hills and the southern seas. He then marched against the Parasikas (possibly the Arab invaders who were trying to reach inner India after their conquest of Sindh in AD 712) and defeated them. The regions protected by the Western Ghats (that is, the Konkan coast) gave him tributes. He then came to the Narmada valley and proceeded by the sea coast to enter the desertic west Rajasthan. From there he came to Thaneswar, proceeding to Ayodhya, from where he went to the Mandara hill region of Santal Pargana and eventually went to the Himalayan region. According to the poet Vakpati he thus conquered the world.

This must be an amazing military manoeuvre starting from Kanauj and may be discounted forthwith. The only element of truth is possibly that he defeated the kings of Magadha and Gauda, although Gauda is not specifically mentioned in this list of conquest. It is also possible that he defeated the attempts of the Arabs to reach Kanauj. Yasovarman's reign may be placed between c. AD 700 and c. 740 and his power was uprooted by the king Laltaditya of Kashmir.

Kashmir came into prominence during this period under the Karkota dynasty, which ruled, in addition to Kashmir, the Rawalpindi, Salt Range, Abbotabad or Hazara, Punch, and Rajouri sectors of western and north-western Panjab. The king Chandrapida of this dynasty sent an emissary to the Chinese emperor in AD 713, seeking help against the Arabs who possibly had reached the borders of his kingdom by that time. The Chinese help did not come but Chandrapida could keep the Arabs at bay. Laltaditya Muktapida was the next important king. He ascended the throne in AD 724. He sought Chinese help against Tibetans whom he defeated later on his own. The people living on his borders—Dards, Kambojas, and Turks—were also defeated by him. Kalhana's *Rajatarangini* describes his chain of conquests—Kanauj, where Yasovarman was overthrown, eastern coast and Kalinga, Gauda, Karnataka including the Konkan coast, Dwaraka in the north-west Kathiawar peninsula, Avanti or western Malwa, and the north-western hills where the Kambojas, Turks, and Tibetans were defeated. Again, this is an amazing claim— the fact that a king could go around, with his base in Kashmir and the adjoining areas of Panjab, virtually the whole of the subcontinent is inherently improbable. He could have undertaken a victorious thrust in any one direction far from his base. He could have been victorious against Kanauj and Gauda and also against people nearer home such as the Kambojas and others. What is interesting in such panegyrics is their composers' notion of geography and the expanded geopolitical consciousness of the time when a king, wherever he was based, had to undertake expeditions in all parts of the subcontinent. Lalitaditya died in AD 760, and the power of the Karkota dynasty lingered on till the AD ninth century.

Politically, Assam and Bengal were not doing well during this period. For about a century after the reign of Bhaskaravarman, not much can be known about the individual geopolitical exploits of the kings of Assam. Similarly, the period following the rule of Sasanka has to be considered in Bengal a period of various local chieftains of whom one knows very little. The Khadga dynasty ruled in the second half of the seventh century in south-eastern Bengal and there was a post-Sasanka king called Jayanaga in the region of Karnasuvarna. The region also became subject to the invasions of Yasovarman and Lalitaditya. There are also references to the Rata dynasty and Chandra dynasty in the AD eighth century in south-east Bengal.

The Sailodbhavas of Orissa came back to power in the post-Harshavardhana era of Orissa and possibly extended their kingdom beyond Kangoda to the Mahanadi delta. Kakatabhukti or the modern Cuttack area came under the Sailodbhava control. The Maitrakas of Valabhi came to an end about AD 766, but before that they defeated an attempt by the Arabs to advance as far as Ujjayini. The Gurjara kings continued to dominate in western Rajasthan, possibly shifting their capital to Bhillamalla or modern Bhinmal. In fact, scholars have postulated that there were Gurjara kings ruling over parts of Rajasthan, Malwa, and Gujarat. One of their main achievements was that the Gurjara-Pratihara king Nagabhata rolled back the Arab invasion which came in the direction of Ujjayini, overrunning the Jodhpur area and other parts of Rajasthan. About the middle of the AD eighth century the Gurjaras of Rajasthan lost their ascendancy. Around this time, the Gurjaras who were based near Broach lost their power, mainly because of the expansion of the Chalukya power from the Deccan to the Navsari area of the Gujarat coast.

In eastern Rajasthan there emerged three new powers in the eighth century, although all possibly had earlier antecedents—the Guhilots of Mewar, whose most famous king is Bappa Rawal (the first half of the AD eighth century); the Mori Rajputs who are recorded from Jhalrapatan and Kota, and the Chahamanas who had their base at Sakambhari. In addition, there were various minor states in Rajasthan, such as the one in Sirohi in the seventh century. In Gujarat, the Chapas or Chapotkatas began to rule from Anahilapataka or Patan North of Ahmedabad.

Sindh witnessed Arab invasion as early as AD 643, only eleven years after the death of Mohammad the Prophet in AD 632. This was undertaken by the Caliphate of Umar against Thana, Broach, and Debal, all on the West coast. In the next stage, the Arabs tried to establish their control in Kabul and Zabul, the latter in Seistan. None of these early attempts was successful in the long run. The attacks against the west coast ports were not successful at all whereas Kabul and Zabul slipped out of the Arab control. In AD 643 there was another unsuccessful naval raid against Debal. In AD 660 the Arabs advanced by land up to the Bolan Pass where they were defeated. In the next twenty years there were six more invasions against the Bolan Pass area which was no doubt a frontier post of Sindh. During this period the Arabs came to control the Makran coast. Debal was raided again twice around AD 708 but without success. It was under Muhammad-ibn-Qasim that Debal fell to the Arabs, and from there he advanced inland to Hyderabad in lower Sindh and Sehwan. He then crossed over to the eastern side of the Indus and defeated the army of Dahir, the king of Sindh. The fort of Ror/Raor was captured and the Arab army proceeded to Brahminabad from where Alor, the capital, was captured. It also seized Multan in lower Panjab. Muhammad-ibn-Qasim seems to have been recalled from India in 714–15. Alor was reoccupied by the Sindh forces after his departure, but by the mid-eighth century the Arab power in Sindh got stabilized.

There seems to be a qualitative difference between the post-Gupta north India and what happened in the same region in the post-Harshavardhana period. The force of the regional powers came to the forefront in both contexts but the political lines were more volatile in the post-Harsha context when there developed almost an ideal of what an all-conquering king should do. The panegyrics of Vakpati in praise of Yasovarman of Kanauj and those of Kalhana in praise of Lalitaditya Muktapida of Kashmir seem to be good indicators of this trend. Besides, less than 100 years after the end of Harsha's rule the Arabs carved out a kingdom in Sindh.[5]

Post-Sixth Century Deccan and the Related Areas

In the Deccan, the Vakatakas went on the decline in the beginning of the AD sixth century. In their heyday under Harisena they carved out an integrated kingdom—the Kuntala territory in the southern section of the Konkan coast in Karnataka, Avanti or western Malwa, Kalinga or the Srikakulam-Ganjam territory, south Kosala or the Raipur-Bilaspur-Sambalpur area, the Traikutaka territory in north Konkan, Lata or the Navsari-Broach area, and Andhra or the mouth of the Krishna. By any standard, this is a huge territory. From their base in Vidarbha, they could go south and control the Krishna mouth. From the western borders of Vidarbha also they could enter Andhra through Nizamabad. From Vidarbha they could move west and control the Traikutaka area of Nasik-Junnar and north Konkan. This gave them a base to control the whole of the Konkan coast up to Karnataka in the south and move north along the coastal alignment up to the Navsari-Broach area of Gujarat. From the eastern part of Vidarbha, through the modern Bhandara and Durg areas, they could proceed up to the south Kosala segment of Raipur and Bilaspur, and move down south-west from this section to Kalinga. Geographically, they could control such a widespread kingdom from their Vidarbha base, but when one thinks of the administrative and other logistical network to keep such far-flung territories together, one cannot but be impressed.

In the first half of the sixth century when the Vakataka power was on the decline, a dynastic unit came to be formed in the Jeypore-Bastar territory which lay on the path from south Kosala to the Kalinga coast and the Krishna mouth. However, they established their control at least over a part of the former Vakataka territories such as Vidarbha itself. The Kadambagiri grant of the king Bhavatta (or Bhavadattavarman) records the grant of the Kadambagiri village which has been identified with Kalamba in the Yeotmal district. The grant itself was issued from Nandivardhana, the former Vakataka capital near Nagpur. The capital of the Nalas was presumably Pushkari or modern Podagarh in Bastar. The Nala kings issued gold coins and this suggests that, although located in the comparatively narrow area of Jeypore-Bastar, they wielded considerable economic and political power. From their home base they could easily come to south Kosala; an inscription from Rajim shows their presence near Raipur. The Nalas continued to remain powerful in this segment for a long time.

Another dynastic unit, although possibly with a much earlier antecedence, lay rooted in the western segment of Vidarbha, around the present Amraoti district. A branch of the dynasty apparently established itself in Goa in the Konkan coast. It is probable that they were in that area earlier, but the Bhoja kings have been specifically identified in the Goa territory in the AD seventh century. Chandrapura or modern Chandor has been identified to be the capital of the Bhojas in Goa.

The Traikutakas seem to have got their hold in north Konkan and the adjacent areas of inland Maharashtra and the Gujarat coast as early as the AD fifth century, the importance of the dynasty being traceable from Maharaja Dharasena (second quarter of the fifth century). There is a Traikutaka grant from Kanheri in AD 493. The Traikutaka capital was possibly Amraka or Amraka-nagara which remains unidentified.

The Kalachuris were initially in occupation of northern Maharashtra, Gujarat, and parts of Malwa as early as AD fifth century. The first major king of the dynasty was *Parama-mahesvara* Krishnaraja who issued silver coins which were known in that sector as *Krishnaraja-rupaka* as late as the early AD eighth century. Towards the end of the sixth century, the Kalachuri territory seems to have been limited to the Nasik-Aurangabad sector of Maharashtra and parts of Malwa. From their base in Nasik-Aurangabad, they were more likely to have been limited to the southern part of Malwa. If there is any truth in the assumption that the Aulikara dynasty of Mandasore was subdued by them, it is likely that they extended their control over the whole of western Malwa. From here it is probable that they extended their power to Gujarat by the mid/late AD sixth century. It also appears likely that under the king Buddharaja, the Kalachuri power included eastern Malwa as well, and this would be around the beginning of the AD seventh century.

In about this period, the Chalukyas of Badami became the main contenders for power against the Kalachuris.

This was also the period when one can trace the early Rashtrakuta lineage in various parts of the Deccan before the collapse of the Chalukyas of Badami in the mid-eighth century. They appear in the Satara-Ratnagiri region of Maharashtra and also in the Betul-Elichpur sector of eastern Vidarbha or Khandesh. The more powerful part of the family possibly flourished in the upper Deccan as feudatories/viceroys of the Chalukyas. Similarly, there was a branch of the family in the more southerly area of the Deccan, around Manapura, which has been identified with Man in the Satara district. The Rashtrakuta grants in the Betul-Elichpur sector seem to belong to the early AD eighth century. What is interesting is that Multai also is included in this area, Multai being the source of the Tapti river in the central

Indian hills. In a sense, this heralds the formation of a political unit in Khandesh; Elichpur or Achalpur being a core point of Khandesh. Both Multai and Betul lie on a road which links the Nagpur/Vidarbha area with the Hosangabad sector on the Narmada of Madhya Pradesh, and from the Betul area there is also a route to the Achalpur area.

The Deccan and Vidarbha-Khandesh of this period seems to have witnessed the formation of several dynastic lineages, with fast-changing foci of power. The post-Ikshvaku dynasty scenario of Andhra seems to begin with the Ananda-*gotra* or Ananda family group of kings who seem to have ruled from Kandarapura or Chezarla in the Guntur district. They possibly curtailed the supremacy of the Pallavas of Kanchipuram in the Amaravati area, the centre of Pallava power in Andhra. The scholarly opinion regarding their chronology varies but is unlikely to be later than the second half of the fourth century.

Further to the east, between the Krishna and the Godavari, the Salankayana dynasty came into existence with their centre at Vengi or Peddavegi near modern Ellore (the Godavari district). Samudragupta defeated one of the Vengi kings, and he must have belonged to the Salankayana dynasty. The Pallavas seem to have extended their power to this area by the close of the AD fifth century. The Vishnukundins came next in this area.

The Vishnukundins themselves were centred at Vinukonda, east of the Srisaila hill of Kurnool. Their importance lies in the fact that they established control all over the Andhra coast from Visakhapatnam to Nellore between the beginning of the AD sixth and the mid-seventh centuries. An early king, Madhavavarman I, claims to have advanced beyond the Godavari and subdued the capital city Trivara of the Panduvamsi rulers of south Kosala. The Chalukyas of Badami put an end to the Vishnukundin supremacy in the Andhra coast in the first part of the seventh century.

In this general period of the fifth-sixth centuries and later, Kalinga also showed a succession of, or confrontation between, a number of dynasties beginning with the Pitribhaktas who ruled from Simhapura (said to be modern Singupuram near Chicacole/Srikakulam) and whose seals bear the term '*Pitribhakta*' as a dynastic designation. The Matharas ruled from Pithapuram (Pishtapura) further south. Some find-spots of their grants, which fall in the Pitribhakta territory suggests that the Matharas usurped the power of the Pitribhaktas. Pithapuram was also the capital of another Kalinga dynasty, the Vasishthas. It has been suggested that the Vasishthas originally ruled in central Kalinga and later subdued the Matharas of Pithapuram and transferred their capital there.

In the sixth and seventh centuries, the power of Kalinga was shared between the eastern Gangas whose core area lay in the Ganjam and Srikakulam districts, and the Chalukya rulers of Badami. The eastern Gangas had their capital at Mukhalingam with a secondary centre at Dantavruktanagara near Srikakulam. They also ruled the Ganjam region. A minor branch of the eastern Gangas ruled from Svetaka which is identified with Chikati of the Ganjam district.

South Kosala of the period came first under the Sarabhapuriya kings who ruled from Sarabhapura or modern Sirpur, beginning in the early AD sixth century. Their focus was entirely in this region where they were supplanted by the Pamduvamsi kings around the middle or third quarter of the AD sixth century. The Pamduvamsis were possibly based in the Chanda region of Vidarbha from where they moved eastwards to south Kosala. In the Mekala region around the Amarkantak plateau there was another group of Pamduvamsi kings about the fifth century. The Pamduvamsis as a whole were a long-lived power in the eastern part of Vidarbha, the jungle country around Amarkantak and the adjacent forested tract of Shadol, and south Kosala.

From the middle of the sixth to the middle of the eighth centuries, Badami in the modern Bijapur area of Karnataka or south Deccan was the stronghold of the Chalukyas known as the Early Western Chalukyas. Their first major king was Pulakesin I (c. AD 535–66), and by the time of his son Kirtivarman I (c. AD 566/567–597/598) the kingdom took in parts of the Konkan coast, as the Chiplun grant of this king implies. This is also suggested by the Aihole inscription of his son Pulakesin II that he defeated the Nalas, Mauryas, and Kadambas, the last two being limited to the Konkan coast. The Nalas in this case could belong to the Bellary-Kurnool area. The Mauryas in this case could mean the successors of a Mauryan governor of the area. The Kadambas had their capital at Banavasi in north Kanara. Kirtivarman was followed by his younger brother or half-brother Mangalesa (c. AD 597/598–610/611) who gained victory over the Kalachuris and conquered Revatidvipa. The victory over the Kalachuris gave him possession of northern Maharashtra whereas Revatidvipa has been identified with the promontory of Redi to the south of Vengurla in the Ratnagiri district. Mangalesa was followed after a civil war between him and Pulakesin II (the son of Kirtivarman I) by Pulakesin II (c. AD 610/611–642). First, he consolidated himself in the Bijapur territory which was then threatened by two kings, Appayika and Govinda, possibly both from the neighbouring areas across the Bhima. The *Aihole Prasasti* composed by the poet Ravikirti is the most important source of knowledge regarding his rule and conquests. He subjugated the Kadambas of Banavasi and along with them, the western Gangas of south Mysore and the Alupas of Humcha of the Shimoga district of north-west Mysore or Karnataka. He then conquered Gharapuri, the capital of the Maurya kings of the area which has been identified with Elephanta near Bombay or Rajpuri near Janjira. The next thrust was towards the Gujarat coast and the adjoining sections of Malwa. The Badami Chalukyas under Pulakesin thus established themselves in a compact area—Karnataka including the southern Konkan coast, northern Maharashtra including the north Konkan coast, southern section of the mainland Gujarat coast, and the adjoining section of Malwa. This brought him into confrontation with the ambition of Harshavardhana in Gujarat and Malwa. Pulakesin defeated him.

Pulakesin II next turned his attention to the east, proceeding up to south Kosala and Kalinga. Possibly he went straight across Vidarbha to south Kosala and then went from south Kosala to Kalinga. He then followed the Andhra coast to the south, uprooting the rulers of the Pithapuram and Ellore areas. By setting up a governorship in this part of the Andhra coast under one of his brothers, he initiated something which later on led to the formation of the eastern Chalukyan dynasty. In the south, he first laid siege to the Pallava capital Kanchipuram, and then crossed the Kaveri to establish relationships with the Cholas, Pandyas, and Cheras. The battle with the Pallavas seemed to have been inconclusive, with both sides claiming victory.

By any standard, Pulakesin II's expansion of the Badami-based Chalukyan power was remarkable, showing a clear perception of the interlinkage of the territories he was keen to control. His success against the western Gangas of south Mysore and against the Kadambas and Alupas elsewhere in Mysore brought him face to face with the Pallavas. Eventually, it is the Pallavas under Narasimhavarman I, son of Mahendravarman I during whose reign Pulakesin II attacked the Pallavas, who destroyed Pulakesin and conquered his capital Badami in AD 642. However, it appears that the Chalukyan power northwards remained unimpaired and they recouped under Vikramaditya I (c. AD 655–81) who defeated the Pallavas and possibly humbled the other south Indian kings of the Cholas, Pandyas, and Cheras. In the north, in the Navsari region of Gujarat, his younger brother who was the governor there defeated a king of the Maitraka dynasty between the Mahi and the Narmada.

The struggle with the Pallavas and the other southern kings continued with varying degrees of success and failure under his successors such as Vikramaditya II (*c.* AD 733/734–744/745) who eventually conquered Kanchi and triumphed over the other southern powers. It was also during his reign that an invasion of the Arabs was repulsed by his northern viceroy *Avanijanasraya* Pulakesin. However, around the middle of the eighth century the power of the western Chalukyas was usurped by the Rashtrakutas. At its height, the western Chalukyan power extended from Nellore to Navsari-Broach, but its prolonged conflict with the Pallavas wore it down and made possible for the growth of various regional powers within the kingdom, the Rashtrakutas being one of them.

The power of the eastern Chalukyas lay in the Andhra coast and was initiated by Pulakesin II's conquest of the area. He installed his brother Vishnuvardhana as its viceroy who assumed the role of an independent king soon afterwards. This took place around AD 631. The distribution of his grants in the Vizagapatam district in the north and the Guntur district in the south shows the extent of Vishnuvardhana I's kingdom in Andhra. The capital was possibly shifted from Pithapuram to Vengi and eventually in the tenth century, from Vengi to Rajamahendri on the Godavari. The kingdom continued to extend to Guntur and possibly the northern section of Nellore. The Nellore part was apparently annexed by the Pallavas around the middle of the AD eighth century. Once the Rashtrakutas appeared on the scene, the tussle for political power in the Andhra coast took place between them and the eastern Chalukyas.[6]

South India and the Deccan till the Eighth Century

In south India the major dynastic sequence begins with the Pallavas of Kanchi. They are known to exist since the middle of the AD third century, and in the beginning of the fourth century, the king Sivaskandavarman established the Pallava power between the Krishna and the south Penner or Ponnaiyar, including a large part of south Karnataka up to Bellary. This is a vast area but to some extent this orbit lies to the north of the three traditional kingdoms of south

India—the Cholas, Pandyas, and Cheras. Also, this looks more to the north and north-east—south Karnataka and the Andhra coast—than to the south. From this point of view, the Pallava domain forms a kind of bridge between the Deccan and the Andhra coast and the Kaveri belt. The great age of the Pallavas begins towards the end of the AD sixth century. Under Simhavishnu of this period they conquered Cholamandalam or the Chola territory, which would mean the region based on the lower Kaveri. He established his power up to Kumbhakonam, which lies at the entrance to Thanjavur. The control up to the Kaveri was maintained under his successor Mahendravarman I (c. AD 600–30) and possibly extended to Tiruchirapalli where he left behind his inscriptions. In the north, he faced the hostility of Pulakesin II of the Chalukyas of Badami and possibly lost some areas in that direction. It is not a great distance from Badami to Bellary which was under the Pallava control, and it was absolutely natural that the Pallavas would come in the way of Pulakesin II's ambitions. The Pallava-Chalukya battle of this phase took place at Pullalur or Palur near Kanchipuram. Mahendravarman's son was Narasimhavarman I (c. AD 630–68) under whom the Pallavas became victorious against the Chalukyas, defeating Pulakesin II in three battles including the one at Manimangalam near Kanchipuram. After Pulakesin II's death which weakened the Chalukyas, the Pallavas possessed Badami for a number of years, bringing the title *Vatapikonda* (captor of Badami) to Narasimhavarman I. Apart from subduing the Chalukyas, he sent a naval expedition to Sri Lanka to re-instate the Sri Lankan prince Manavarma in his kingdom. The first expedition resulted in failure but the second expedition which sailed from Mahabalipuram was successful.

The struggle with the Chalukyas continued under Narasimhavarman I's grandson, Paramesvaravarman I (c. AD 670–95). Pulakesin II's son Vikramaditya I captured Kanchi and camped at Uraiyur (modern Tiruchirapalli) on the Kaveri. Eventually, Paramesvaravarman triumphed in the battle of Peruvalanallur in the Tiruchirapalli area, and the Chalukyas left the area. His successor Narasimhavarman II (c. AD 695–722) sent an embassy to China in AD 720. The reign of the next king Paramesvaravarman II (c. AD 722–30) is not noticeable except that there was another Chalukyan invasion towards the end of his reign. The next king Nandivarman II Pallavamalla (c. AD 730–95) lost Kanchi briefly to Vikramaditya II of Badami, and this was likely to have happened around AD 740. However, Kanchi was re-possessed soon afterwards by the Pallavas. The Pallava possession of the lower Kaveri brought them face to face with the Pandyas of Madura and the Pandya king of the time, Rajasimha I defeated Nandivarman near Thanjavur. Eventually, the Pandya-Pallava struggle went in favour of the Pallavas, but meanwhile, with the waning of the Chalukyan power, the Rashtrakutas appeared on the scene. The founder of the Rashtrakuta power Dantidurga captured Kanchi but gave his daughter in marriage to Nandivarman II. There was also a struggle between Nandivarman II and the western Gangas of Karnataka.

For a long time the Kaveri area was in the Pallava possession. This implies that this traditional Chola territory was not under the Cholas any more. It is probable that they continued to survive in the area as feudatories of the Pallavas during this period. The Cholas do not become prominent till the ninth century. From the AD fifth century onwards we also get the evidence of the presence of the Kalabhras in the Chola territory. In the fifth century there was a Kalabhra king, Achchutavikranta who ruled over the Chola territory from Kaveripattinam. Why a port town should be the capital of the Chola region at this point is not understood. Of all the proposed identifications of the Kalabhras, the most satisfactory one is that they belonged to the Vellala community of warriors of the Pudukottai area and were possibly once the feudatories of the Cholas and the Pallavas. The Kalabhra power in the area declined after the Pallavas and the Pandyas became powerful and began to administer the Chola territory.

During the Kalabhra occupation of the Chola country some Chola princes are likely to have migrated to Karnataka and elsewhere, and in the Renandu area of the modern Cuddapah, Anantapur, and Kurnool districts, there are copper-plates of the AD seventh century testifying to the presence of Chola rulers, or Chola feudatories under the Pallavas or Chalukyas, in that area.

The Pandyan territory also was under the Kalabhra occupation but towards the close of the AD sixth century it was free under the Pandyan kings Kadungon (c. AD 590–620) and his successor Maravarman Avantisulaman (c. AD 620–45). It appears that the main struggle of the Pandyas of this period was with the Cheras. The Cheras were defeated by Sendan (c. AD 645–70) but more successful in this regard was Arikesari Parankusa Maravarman (c. AD 610–70) who won a major victory against them at Nelveli or possibly modern Tirunelveli. He also won success in the coastal region and elsewhere in the perimeter of the Pandya territory. His successor Kochhadaiyan Ranadhira (*c.* AD 710–40) fought again in the Tirunelveli region, the battle having taken place at Ambasamudram. More importantly, he turned his attention to the Coimbatore region or Kongu country which then was possibly under the Cheras and subjugated it. From this base he moved towards the west coast, moving up to Mangalapuram or modern Mangalore, overthrowing the power of the Maharathas in that area. The next king Maravarman Rajasimha I (*c.* AD 740–65) was also a powerful ruler and retained the Pandya grip over the Kongu country. He also defeated the Pallavas in the Kaveri sector, that is, the Chola area, and was also successful against the Badami Chalukyas, first by making an alliance with the western Gangas at their boundary. The Velvikudi grant of his successor Nedunjadaiyan (*c.* AD 765–815) mentions that he renovated the forts and palaces at Madura, the Pandyan capital, Vanji, the Chera capital, and Uraiyur, the Chola capital. The pattern of his kingdom is clear from this reference.

The western Gangas were based in the Kolar region of Karnataka. Kongunivarman or Madhava I (*c.* AD 350–400), the founder of the western Ganga line, had his capital at Kolar. The capital shifted under Harivarman (*c.* AD 450–60) to Talakad or Talkad (Talavanapura) on the bank of the Kaveri near Sivasamudram. In the beginning, the western Ganga kings seem to have been the feudatories of the Pallavas. The western Ganga king who seems to have thrown away the Pallava suzerainty was Durvinita (*c.* AD 540–600) who conquered Punnad in southern Karnataka, Kongu country, and maintained a good relation with the Badami Chalukyas but not with the Pallavas. The next important king of this line was Sripurusha (*c.* AD 725–88) during whose reign the Rashtrakutas under Krishna I invaded the western Gangas. He shifted his capital from Talakad to Manyapura or Manne near Bangalore.

The founder of the Kadamba power at Banavasi in north Kanara district of Karnataka was Mayurasarman of the AD mid-fourth century. The Kuntala territory, of which this was the centre, came under the attention of all the major powers of the region, including the Badami Chalukyas and even the distant powers such as the Vakatakas. From time to time, the Kadambas tried to expand their power over the hilly tract up to the Srisailam area of Kurnool and they possibly controlled the contiguous territory in Karnataka as far as Halebid where, in the late fifth century, there was a separate branch of the Kadambas

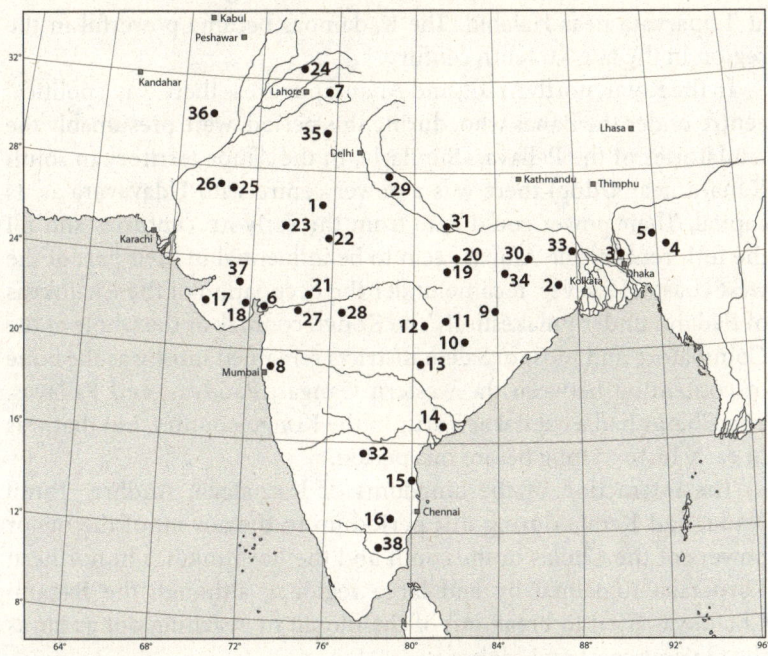

1. Pawayya
2. Susunia
3. Samatata
4. Davaka
5. Kamarupa
6. Broach
7. Katripura
8. Thana
9. Sambalpur
10. Raipur
11. Dandakaranya
12. Durg
13. Bhawani Patna
14. Peddavegi
15. Nellore
16. Kanchipuram
17. Girnar
18. Valabhi
19. Satna

20. Kalinjar
21. Mahismati
22. Eran
23. Mandasore
24. Sialkot
25. Mandore
26. Merta
27. Nanded (Rajpipla)
28. Burhanpur
29. Kanauj
30. Aphsad
31. Prayag
32. Badami
33. Karnasuvarna
34. Rohtasgarh
35. Thaneswar
36. Gomal valley area
37. Anahilapataka/Patan
38. Gangaikondacholapuram

Map 4.1   Location of Some Major Sites and Areas Mentioned in
             Chapter 4

at Triparvata near Halebid. The Kadambas became powerful in the region in the late AD tenth century.

In the Kolar, north Arcot, and Anantapur areas there was a political centre under the Banas who, during this period, were presumably the feudatories of the Pallavas. Similarly, in the Alupa territory in south Kanara near Udupi there was a power centre with Udayavara as its capital. Their power could date from the early AD centuries and till the fifth century the Alupas seem to be influential in their part of the west coast. However, it came under the occupation of the Chalukyas of Badami under Pulakesin II. The Kongu country or the whole of the Coimbatore and most of Salem districts remained mostly as the bone of contention between the western Gangas, Pandyas, and Pallavas. The Cheras had a capital at Karur in the Kongu country, but that was in early history, long before this period.

The interaction of the kingdoms of Karnataka, Andhra, Tamil Nadu, and Kerala during this period up to the advent of the major powers of the Cholas in the south and the Rashtrakutas in northern Karnataka remained by and large regional, although the Badami Chalukyas tried to break out of the mould by reaching out as far as the Gujarat coast and Malwa.[7]

Notes

1. Majumdar (1954a: 4).
2. Majumdar (1954b: 9).
3. Majumdar (1954c: 44).
4. Majumdar (1954d: 118).
5. Majumdar (1954e).
6. Sircar (1954a, 1954b).
7. Sathianathaiyer (1954).

5

The Supra-regional Orbits of the North and the South

c. AD *800* to c. AD *1000*

The Extent and Interaction of the Rashtrakuta Power, c. Eight–Tenth Centuries

The history of the Deccan remained basically the history of the Rashtrakutas for more than 200 years between AD 753 when Dantidurga defeated the Chalukyan king Kirtivarman II and became the master of the whole of Maharashtra, and AD 975 when they lost the Deccan to Taila. During Dantidurga's time, the family which originally belonged to the Osmanabad area in southern Maharashtra was based in Ellichpur or Achalpur in Khandesh (western part of Vidarbha) and had been a feudatory family of the Western Chalukyas for some time. Before he overthrew the Chalukya sovereignty, he fought, along with the Chalukyan Vikramaditya II and the Chalukyan feudatory in Gujarat Pulakesin, against an Arab invasion of Gujarat in AD 738. He also participated in the Chalukyan campaign against Kanchipuram in AD 743. After the death of Vikramaditya II in AD 747, he conquered the Gurjara power of Nanded (near Broach) and became the overlord of both western and eastern Malwa. These successes brought him into conflict with the Chalukya sovereign Kirtivarman II whom he defeated in AD 753 and assumed the title *Maharajadhiraja Paramesvara Paramabhattaraka*. He died in AD 758. Under Dantidurga's successor Krishna I, the Chalukyan attempt to regroup ended in failure and thus the western Chalukyas completely moved out of the scene. Krishna I then captured the western Ganga capital Manyapuram and proceeded along the Andhra coast to capture Vengi or Peddavegi from the eastern Chalukyas. He also captured southern Konkan. The whole of the Deccan, Malwa, Andhra coast, and south Konkan seem to have acknowledged the overlordship of Krishna I. He died around AD 773 and after a brief reign of Govinda, the Rashtrakuta power came to rest on Dhruva who came to the throne about AD 780. The western Ganga kingdom was annexed to the Rashtrakuta kingdom which thus now extended up to the upper reaches of the Kaveri. Having assured the submission of the Pallavas he overran the eastern Chalukyas of Vengi. The political condition of north India then drew his attention. Kanauj became the focus of struggle for power between the Gurjara-Pratihara king Vatsaraja and the Pala dynastic king of eastern India, Dharmapala. Vatsaraja installed Indrayudha as his puppet king at Kanauj. This drew Dharmapala to the scene but he was defeated by Vatsaraja. However, the enmity between the Gurjara-Pratiharas and the Palas did not end, and when Dhruva decided to intervene, the Gurjara-Pratihara and the Pala armies were on their way to battle. When Dhruva crossed Malwa and decided to proceed to Kanauj, the Gurjara-Pratihara army met his force somewhere near Jhansi in Bundelkhand and was routed. Dhruva marched ahead and defeated Dharmapala as well. Kanauj was for him to take, but for a power based south of the Narmada, it was too far from the base. Dhruva returned to his base in AD 790.

Dhruva's successor was Govinda III who ascended the throne in AD 793. He had to defeat and control the western Gangas and the eastern Chalukyas of Vengi again, but having secured his position in this sector, he decided to intervene in the power struggle between the Gurjara-Pratiharas and the Palas over Kanauj. The Gurjara-Pratihara king Nagabhata was defeated in Bundelkhand and Chakrayudha, Indrayudha's successor at Kanauj, surrendered to the Rashtrakuta king who also received the admission of defeat from Dharmapala. At this point of time, the Rashtrakutas were the undisputed masters of northern India. Govinda III received the submission of other north Indian kings, proceeding up to the Himalayas. He then returned to the south of the Narmada. The eastern Chalukyas of Vengi had to be submitted again, and a confederation of the Gangas, Pandyas, Pallavas, and Keralas defeated. The Rashtrakuta forces now occupied Kanchi and the contemporary king of Sri Lanka seems to have sent him tributes.

Govinda III's successor Amoghavarsha who came to the throne in AD 814 did not also receive any respite from the eastern Chalukyas. The struggle with them was a protracted one and eventually the Rashtrakutas lost much of the eastern Chalukyan territory. The western Gangas put up resistance too, but after the marriage of a Rashtrakuta princess to a Ganga prince in AD 860, the hostilities ended. Some inscriptions record that Amoghavarsha received the submission of the rulers of Anga, Vanga, Magadha, Malava, and Vengi. Malava and Vengi were within the Rashtrakuta orbit but Anga, Vanga, and Magadha were far out of this orbit and the claim is true only in a general sense that the east Indian power of the Palas who then ruled these areas admitted defeat before Amoghavarsha in the battle for Kanauj.

It was Amoghavarsha who shifted the Rashtrakuta capital to Manyakhet which lies near Gulbarga in the southern Deccan. The location of the earlier capital of the Rashtrakutas is undetermined. It could be in the Achalpur sector which was once their home territory or it could be in the area of Nasik or in the area of Ellora caves where the famous Kailasa temple was built at the order of Krishna I. It appears that with the shifting of his capital to Manyakhet (modern Malkhed) Amoghavarsha visualized a situation when the southern sector of his dominion would come in for primary attention. For the Malwa sector and also for ambitions in the Ganga plain, any of the three areas—the Achalpur area, the area around Nasik, and the area around Ellora—was a more suitable choice as the Rashtrakuta base.

Amoghavarsha died in AD 878, leaving the kingdom to Krishna II who had to fight mainly on two fronts. He and the Gujarat branch of the Rashtrakutas battled with the Gurjara-Pratihara king Bhoja to check his advance against Gujarat and Malwa. The conflict with the eastern Chalukyas proved more worrisome. The Vengi king attacked the Rashtrakuta feudatories, the Gangas and Nolambas in the south, and in the north he advanced up to Vidarbha, which he possibly did by marching either through Nizamabad or through Karimnagar and appearing straight in the heart of Vidarbha. The Rashtrakuta forces regrouped and defeated the Chalukyan forces in all directions. One of Krishna II's daughters was married to a Chola king but when he decided to intervene in Chola succession after the death of his son-in-law, he met defeat at the hands of the Cholas at Vallala or modern Tiruvallam in the north Arcot district.

Krishna II died in AD 914 leaving the throne to Indra III, the notable event of whose reign was to defeat the Gurjara-Pratihara king Mahipala. The Rashtrakuta army followed the Bundelkhand route via Jhansi and Kalpi and captured Kanauj. The war with the Vengi kings continued and was unsolved around AD 927 when Indra III died. He was succeeded by his son Amoghavarsha II who got killed by his younger brother Govinda IV. He, in turn, was removed from power by his uncle Amoghavarsha III around AD 936. He sent the crown-prince Krishna to maintain control over the Gangas and also sent him to Bundelkhand to capture Kalinjar and Chitrakut. One is not sure why he did that. The Kalinjar-Chitrakut area provides a straight access to the Allahabad area through Bundelkhand, especially the Satna area, and it appears that in the Rashtrakuta scheme of things the Ganga plain had continued to retain some importance.

Amoghavarsha III's crown-prince Krishna who became Krishna III after his accession to the throne in AD 939 led an expedition to the south, capturing Kanchipuram and Thanjavur around AD 943. He was repulsed by the Chola king Parantaka but retained control of the Arcot, Chingleput, and Vellore areas. In AD 949 the Chola army entered Arcot but was defeated in the battle of Takkolam. Krishna III then marched to Rameshwaram, set up a pillar of victory and came back to north Arcot. He was helped in this expedition by his Ganga ally. In AD 963 he led another expedition to northern India, receiving help again from the Gangas. He marched into Bundelkhand and later he went to Malwa capturing Ujjayini and defeating the Paramara ruler Siyaka. The struggle against Vengi was less successful, and the Rashtrakuta influence in that area ended.

The reigns of the two last Rashtrakuta kings, Khottiga and Karkka II, ended in disaster and the demise of the Rashtrakuta power. During the reign of Khottiga, the Paramara ruler Siyaka crossed the Narmada, passed across a large section of Maharashtra and captured the Rashtrakuta capital Manyakhet. The last king Karkka II had his power usurped by one of his feudatories in the Bijapur sector which is not far from Gulbarga, that is, the Manyakhet sector. The battle took place somewhere in north Karnataka and Karkka II retired to rule a small principality in the Mysore area of south Karnataka. The feudatory to whom Karkka III lost his power was Taila II, who defeated an attempt by the Gangas to re-capture power for the Rashtrakutas and became the overlord of the Deccan by AD 975.

There was war throughout the history of the Rashtrakuta dynasty. The feudatories were difficult to control and expeditions were frequent to the Gujarat coast, Malwa, Bundelkhand, and even the Ganga plain. But even then an equilibrium was maintained and they remained the most powerful monarchs of the subcontinent of their time. Under them, just as under the western Chalukyas before them, the Deccan and the adjoining regions like Malwa and the south assumed a distinctive importance of their own.[1]

The Gurjara-Pratiharas: Eastern Rajasthan, Gujarat, Malwa, and the Related Tracts Including the Ganga Plain, c. Eighth–Tenth Centuries

In the second quarter of the AD eighth century, the Gurjara-Pratiharas under Nagabhata I come into prominence. The Gurjara power had so long been confined to Jodhpur and Rajpipla (Nandipuri), but with Nagabhata the focus of the Gurjara confederacy fell on him. His base was in eastern Rajasthan and Malwa, and he shook off the suzerainty of the Jodhpur Gurjaras after successfully combining with the Rashtrakutas to defeat the Arabs. He is supposed to have ruled from c. AD 730 to c. 756. He was worsted in a battle by the Rashtrakuta king Dantidurga, but could keep his kingdom intact. There is no doubt that Malwa and parts of Rajasthan and Gujarat were within this kingdom.

After Nagabhata I, Vatsaraja who came to the throne around AD 778 was the important Pratihara king. His ambitions in the Doab led him to control Kanauj and he defeated in that context the Pala king Dharmapala, only to be defeated in turn by the Rashtrakuta king Dhruva. Vatsaraja passes out of historical view after this defeat. It is said in an inscription found at Gwalior that Nagabhata II, Vatsaraja's son and successor, defeated the rulers of Andhra, Saindhava, Vidarbha, and Kalinga, and sieged the hill-forts located in the territories of Anartta, Malava, Kirata, Turushka, Vatsa, and Matsya. The inclusion of Malava in this list means that only parts of Malwa were then under Pratihara control and that Nagabhata II extended his influence in that area by capturing some hill-forts. Anartta means north Gujarat; the term Kirata suggests somewhere in the Himalayan belt, and the Turushkas can only mean the Arabs. Matsya or the Jaipur-Alwar area could be approached both from eastern Rajasthan where this territory is located and from Malwa. Vatsa or the Kausambi area lies somewhat out of the way. Approaching both Andhra and Kalinga from Malwa through Vidarbha was possible. The Saindhavas ruled in western Kathiawar. The list suggests that Nagabhata II's aim in any of these areas could not be the permanent possession of these territories. These were exclusively expeditionary exercises to exact tributes or alliances. More tangible success awaited him in the Doab where he and his three feudatories—the Pratihara family of Jodhpur, the Chalukyan family of southern Kathiawar, and the Guhilots of Chitor-Kota sector of Rajasthan—defeated the Pala king Dharmapala, proceeding as far east as Mungher in the heart of the Pala domain. However, the Pratihara power was defeated by the Rashtrakuta Govinda III, but it appears that 'Nagabhata II continued to exercise his sway over the greater part, if not the whole of Rajputana and Kathiawar Peninsula. In the east his sway extended up to Gwalior, and probably further east as to include Kanauj and Kalanjara'.[2] It appears that the Pratiharas lost a lot of their base in Malwa during this period, but if their control in the east extended up to Gwalior from Rajasthan and Kathiawar, that must have included a chunk of Malwa.

Whether the Pratihara capital was shifted to Kanauj under Nagabhata II is difficult to say but the most important Pratihara king after him and his grandson Bhoja certainly had his capital at Kanauj from where he issued a land-grant involving the Kalanjar area of Banda. This also suggests a change in the base of Pratihara power under Bhoja more to the east than their traditional domain in Rajasthan, Gujarat, and Malwa. Bhoja ascended the Pratihara throne around AD 836 and ruled till c. AD 885. It appears that the Jodhpur branch of the Pratiharas tried to be independent rulers in their own right after Nagabhata II, but by AD 843 Bhoja re-established his authority in central and eastern Rajasthan. The Guhilots of Rajasthan continued to be Pratihara feudatories. Bhoja's main struggle was with the Palas in the Ganga plain and with the Rashtrakutas. He was defeated by both, and also by the Kalachuris of the Jubbulpore area of central India. It appears that after he suffered these defeats the Jodhpur feudatory tried to disown his overlordship. However, Bhoja seems to have recouped soon afterwards and we find him undertaking, with the help of a ruler of the Gorakhpur area and his Guhilot feudatory, a successful campaign against the Pala king Narayanapala and annexing possibly some western territories of the Pala kingdom. Bhoja then undertook struggles with the Rashtrakutas, first winning Malwa and then taking possession of the Kaira area of mainland Gujarat. Whether the Rashtrakutas successfully won back Malwa is uncertain but Bhoja was later dislodged from Kaira. Considering the many successes and reversals of the Pratiharas under Bhoja, it is not easy to be sure of the outline of his kingdom which reputedly touched Panjab and included the whole of the Kathiawar peninsula and the whole of Oudh. Parts of Malwa were within his territory and the Chandellas of Bundelkhand and the rulers of the Gorakhpur area were his feudatories.

Bhoja's son and successor Mahendrapala maintained the Pratihara hold over these areas, possibly losing some territory in Panjab to the kings of Kashmir. His records have been found in south Bihar and north Bengal and this implies that he expanded his kingdom at the expense of the Palas in the east. His records have also been found in Kathiawar, eastern Panjab, Jhansi area, and Oudh. To claim that he ruled from the Himalayas to the Vindhyas would be an exaggeration but he certainly ruled the vast tract between Kathiawar and Bengal with Mahodaya or Kanauj as his capital.

Mahipala was the important Pratihara king after Mahendrapala. He ascended the throne in about AD 912. Between AD 915 and 918 his capital Kanauj was captured by the Rashtrakutas under Indra III who advanced up to Prayag. However, all was not lost, and there is evidence that in about AD 931 Mahipala was in possession of the area between Kathiawar and Banaras, and around AD 942–3 there is proof that he controlled the area of Chanderi at the entrance of Malwa from Bundelkhand. It appears that around AD 946 he was in possession of Malwa as well. The Rashtrakutas, however, continued to remain the Pratiharas' implacable enemies, and from a Rashtrakuta record of c. AD 940 one learns that they captured the Kalanjar and Chitrakut areas.

The Pratihara power went into decline after Mahipala. In c. AD 963 the Rashtrakutas under Krishna III dealt a severe blow to the Pratihara power. That they were truly victorious is suggested by the find of a record of Krishna III (written in Kannada) incised on a stone slab near Maihar. This suggests that the Rashtrakuta capture of Kalanjar and Chitrakut made it easy for them to attack the Ganga plain. Both Kalanjar and Chitrakut are easy to access (Maihar>Satna>Kalanjar/Chitrakut) from Maihar and the fact that there is a Rashtrakuta record from the Maihar area shows that the Rashtrakutas attacked the Ganga plain not through the usual Malwa>Jhansi>Kalpi route but through the corridor leading to Satna from the side of Jubbulpore.

By AD 960 the Pratiharas were on their way out, although they kept on ruling a small area around Kanauj where in AD 1027 there was a Pratihara king called Trilochanapala.

The ups and downs of the Pratihara dynasty need not blind anybody to the fact that their direct or indirect possessions in the Ganga plain covered at their height the entire area from eastern Panjab to south Bihar and north Bengal, and a broad swathe of land through Rajasthan and central India to Kathiawar.[3]

Eastern India including Orissa, c. Eighth–Tenth Centuries and Later

The first king of the Palas of Bengal, Gopala (AD 750–70), was succeeded by his son Dharmapala (c. AD 770–810) who is known for his struggles with the Gurjara-Pratiharas on the one hand and the Rashtrakutas on the other. The defeat of the Gurjara-Pratiharas at the hands of the Rashtrakutas served him in good stead, because by taking advantage of the Pratihara weakness he reputedly made himself, however temporarily, the suzerain of north India. The areas which came to consider him suzerain were Gandhara, Madra, Kira, Kuru, Matsya, Yavana, Yadu, Yavana, Avanti, and Bhoja. The position of Gandhara in the north-west is well-understood. Yavana may mean a Muslim principality lower down in the Indus valley. Madra will mean central Panjab and Kira will mean the Kangra valley. Kuru and Matsya will mean the head of the Doab and the Alwar-Jaipur-Bharatpur belt respectively. Avanti in this case denotes a part of western Malwa, which implies that eastern Malwa also came under purview. Yadu here need not suggest Gujarat; some parts of Panjab or Mathura are a better probability. The Bhojas were based in Vidarbha. If it is true that as per claim of his Khalimpur copper-plate inscription, Dharmapala had enjoyed suzerainty over all these areas, he was a remarkably successful king of his time. The entire sweep of the Indo-Gangetic plain from the north-west to Bengal with extensions into the Malwa corridor and Vidarbha formed reputedly his domain of influence. However, his core territory was Bihar and Bengal, itself a large area, and his interest in having a person of his own choice at Kanauj implies that the direct area of his influence in the Ganga valley possibly extended beyond Banaras. Kanauj lies between Kanpur and Farrukhabad, considerably upstream from Kanpur. Why should a power based in Bihar-Bengal aim to control Kanauj unless its territory stretches to somewhere near it?

Dharmapala's successor was Devapala (c. AD 810–50). His campaigns reputedly took him to Kambojas in the north-west and to the Vindhyas in the south. He defeated the kings of Kamarupa and Utkala, and received submission from the Hunas, Gurjaras, and Dravidas. The Hunas here possibly represent a Huna principality in the north-west. The Gurjaras mean the Gurjara-Pratiharas but one is not sure of the identity of the Dravidas. It has been assumed that this would refer to the Pandya king Sri-Mara Sri-Vallabha. Devapala's victory in Utkala must have made him aware of the Dravida kings further down the coast. It is possible that he made a quick thrust in that direction. Otherwise there cannot be any substance in the claim made in the Mungher copper-plate issued during his reign that he had his supremacy from the Himalayas to Setuvandha Ramesvaram.

It is obvious that under Dharmapala and Devapala the Palas whose home territory was northern Bengal or Varendri reached their zenith of power. As Majumdar puts it—'Never before, or since, till the advent of the British, did Bengal play such an important role in Indian politics'.[4]

The successors of Devapala were Vigrahapala and Narayanapala. Under Narayanapala the Palas lost south Bihar and even north Bengal, their home base. The Harjara kings of the Brahmaputra valley shook off their allegiance and so did the Sailodbhava kings of Orissa. Narayanapala managed to recover south Bihar and north Bengal before his death in 908. The kingdom was successively passed on to Rajyapala, Gopala II, and Vigrahapala II, covering in all about 80 years. The newly risen powers of the Chandellas and the Kalachuris of northern India claimed to have defeated the rulers of Gauda, Radha, Anga, and Vangala, suggesting that the Pala kingdom was then being broken into smaller principalities. One such principality went under the name of Kamboja whose record has been found in Dinajpur district, that is, in the Pala heartland of Varendri itself. Two other groups of kings represented those of Harikela in the Chattagram tract and the Chandras of the Comilla region. The Pala dynasty revived under Mahipala I who came to the throne in about AD 988.

In the ninth century, Kamarupa was ruled by the Salasthambha dynasty whose first important king Harjaravarman came to the throne in AD 829. His titles 'Maharajadhiraja Paramesvara Paramabhattaraka' indicate that Kamarupa no longer acknowledged the Palas as its suzerain. Nothing is known of his reign but his son and successor Vanamalavarman is known to have granted land to the west of the Trisrota or modern Tista. This shows that Kamarupa's traditional boundary extended into north Bengal. The Salasthambha dynasty of Kamarupa continued from *c.* AD 800 to *c.* 1000. Except its interaction with the Pala domain to the west, nothing is known about its interaction with the areas in other directions.

Orissa of this period saw the advent of a number of dynasties. The Bhaumakara dynasty rose in the middle of the AD eighth century. They were independent and powerful but there is no evidence that they exerted any major influence beyond their boundaries. However, one of them defeated the king of Radha, that is, a part of modern West Bengal, in the east, which is not surprising in view of the geographical contiguity between the two areas. Another inscription testifies that they had influence over the Kangoda territory of Kalinga. Around AD 860 the Bhaumakaras suffered reverses in the hands of the Pala king Devapala, after whose reign the Bhaumakara kings of Orissa came back into their own. Majumdar[5] points out that the names of the villages mentioned in the Bhaumakara land-grants give an idea of the extent of their kingdom in Orissa—Balasore, Cuttack, Puri, Angul, Hindol, Dhenkanal, Talcher, Pal Lahara, a part of Keonjhar, and the northern part of Ganjam. This shows that they were ensconced over a large tract of Orissa comprising both the coastal and inland forested territories. It is also interesting that all the land-grants of the dynasty were issued from Guhadeva-pataka or Guhesvara-pataka which no doubt was their capital but which regrettably remains unidentified. There is some support for the hypothesis that the Bhaumakara capital was located at Jajpur. This was the heart of the Odra country.

Among the other Orissan dynasties of the period were the Bhanja dynasties of Khinjali and of Khiching. The kingdom of Khinjali has been taken to correspond to Baudh and Sonpur and their immediate neighbourhood. The earliest inscription of the dynasty has been placed in the AD ninth century, which is more or less only a working hypothesis. The name of their first known king is Satrubhanja, who and his son Ranabhanja style themselves in their inscriptions as the 'lord of Khinjali'. These inscriptions were issued from Dhritipura whereas those of their successors were issued from Vijaya-vanjulvaka. The first inscriptions are in the context of Baudh and Sonpur whereas the latter inscriptions all mention places in Ganjam and Nayagadh. It appears that the later Bhanja rulers of Khinjali shifted their capital to Ganjam-Nayagadh. These kings possibly ruled till at least AD tenth–eleventh centuries.

The Bhanjas of Khiching or Khijjinga are better known, mainly because their location has been clearly identified in the present-day Mayurbhanj. The dynasty flourished roughly between AD 850 and 1000, and is possibly connected with the Bhanja family which was the ruling house of the princely state of Mayurbhanj in British India. As Majumdar writes:

This striking agreement in respect of the family name and tradition, the capital, and extent of the kingdom leaves no doubt that the modern ruling chiefs of Mayurbhanj are linked up with the old Bhanja rulers of Khijjinga; and makes it highly probable that they form one continuous royal line which has ruled for more than a thousand years in an uninterrupted line of succession. Such a phenomenon is very rare in Indian history, and the case of Mayurbhanj may be regarded as almost unique.[6]

There were other small dynasties in Orissa during this period. One was the Svetaka branch of the Gangas who were settled in Kalinga. The Tunga dynasty possibly ruled in parts of Talcher, Pal Lahara, and Keonjhar. The area was perhaps known as *Yamagarta-mandala*. There is another family called *Mayura-vamsa* which ruled in *Vanai-mandala*, which would mean the modern Bonai area. Among the other minor dynasties were the Sulkis who seem to have ruled in Talcher and Dhenkanal. Another dynasty was called the Nanda whose grants are issued from Jayapura which has been identified with Jaipur in the Dhenkanal area. They refer to the *Airavata-mandala* in the Cuttack district. There was another dynasty, the names of whose kings ended with 'dhavala'. Its only ancient ruler was known as Narendra-dhavala.

Most of these Orissan dynasties of the period were possibly nothing more than feudatories of more powerful royal branches, but on the whole they underline the factor of geographical complexity in Orissa. Northwards, beyond the coast, Orissa is a maze of hills, forests, and valleys, often with good agricultural lands. They offered the scope of formation of small states which in many cases must have derived benefit from the control of mineral and forest resources within their boundaries. The main political alignments lay along the coast and more or less left these smaller Orissan states alone. On the other hand, these states acquired the ideological appurtenances of their more famous and larger counterparts. They too had their share of land-grants and royal titles. From this point of view Orissa is unique. Nowhere else in eastern India do we have such a collection of inscriptions from such a large number of dynasties. The main reason must have something to do with the geography. Contrary to the general impression, the Brahmaputra valley is fairly open and does not permit arbitrary fragmentations. The same is generally true of Bengal as a whole where the dynasties which have historically figured have generally been dispersed in wide geographical units. Even the Chandra dynasty, whose evidence comes primarily from south-east Bengal has had its control over Sylhet which traditionally has belonged to lower Assam. The base of the Harikela kings lay in the Chattagram coast with clear thrust toward the Arakan area.[7]

The North Indian Dynasties, c. Eighth–Tenth Centuries: The Chandellas, Kalachuris, Paramaras, Hindu Shahis, and Others

The Chandella or Chandatreya kings of Bundelkhand were originally vassals of the Pratiharas and based at Kharjuravahaka or Khajuraho. The founder of the line was Nannuka in the beginning of the ninth century. He was followed by Vakpati who possibly fought battles within the periphery of the Vindhyan range. He had two sons, Jayasakti and Vijayasakti, both of whom took their turns to be kings. Jayasakti also bore the names Jejjaka and Jeja, and thus the territory ruled by the Chandellas came to be known as Jejakabhukti. In a Khajuraho inscription, Vijayasakti is supposed to have carried expeditions to the southernmost point of India; such claims had apparently no basis. He was followed by Rahilya, and as a tank near Mahoba or Mahotsavanagara bears the name Rahilyasagara, it is possible that the Chandellas had by then extended their power up to the Hamirpur area, which would mean that they had extended their kingdom considerably by then. Rahilya was followed by his son Harsha (c. AD 900–25) who seems to have helped his overlord Pratihara king of Kanauj to re-possess his capital after it was lost to the Rashtrakuta Indra III. Harsha's son Yasovarman, also known as Lakshmanavarman, took advantage of the weakness of the Pratiharas of the period and conquered Kalanjar fort, which gave him access to the Ganga-Yamuna valley. He then fought with the Kalachuris of the Chedi country near Jubbulpore and the Paramaras of Malwa and pushed his boundary in that direction. This brought him into conflict with the Somavamsi kings of south Kosala. According to his inscriptional record, he also invaded the Pala kingdom in the east, conquering Gauda and Mithila. This record also takes him to battle with the kings of Kashmir and Kuru. A battle with the Tomars who were then ruling the Kuru area is not an improbability but no credence can be given to the claim that he advanced as far north as the territory of the Kashmir kings.

During the time of Yasovarman's son and successor Dhanga (c. AD 954–1002), the Chandella kingdom extended up to Kalanjar in Banda, the Kalindi or the Yamuna, Bhilsa or Vidisa, the border of the Chedi territory of Jubbulpore, and Gwalior or Gopagiri. This seems to be a perfectly sensible boundary for a kingdom based in Bundelkhand. However, he lost Gwalior to the Kacchhapaghata king Vajradaman around AD 977. By this time, the Pratihara power of Kanauj got very weak, and Dhanga, after defeating the Pratiharas, began to rule up to the Yamuna. He advanced up to Banaras, and launched from there military campaigns against Anga and Radha. The Somavamsi kings of south Kosala are said to have come in conflict with him, but perhaps there is no truth in the claim that he fought the Andhras and Kuntalas as well. He is also known to have joined the confederacy of kings under Jayapala of Panjab against Sabuktagin of Ghazni in AD 989.[8]

The centre of the Kalachuri territory was Tripuri or modern Tewar between the modern Jubbulpore city and the Marble Rocks. The area was also known as *Dahala-mandala* which was a feudatory kingdom of the Rashtrakuta king Govinda III. The first known independent Kalachuri king of this area was Kokkalla I (accession to the throne in c. AD 845) who seems to have begun his reign by undertaking a successful expedition against the Pratiharas of Kanauj and their feudatories, Sankaragana of the Kalachuris of the trans-Sarayu area, Harsharaja of the Guhilots of Dharagarta or Dhod in the Mewar area of Rajasthan, and Guvaka II of the Chahamanas of Sakambhari. While in Rajasthan, he clashed with the Turushka or Muslim/Turkish soldiers in the employ of the Arab governors of Sindh. In the east he campaigned against Vanga or eastern Bengal. In the latter part of his reign he defeated the Rashtrakuta king Krishna II and invaded north Konkan, defeating Kapardin II of the Silaharas who were Rashtrakuta feudatories at that time. Kokkalla I was succeeded by his son Sankaragana sometime between AD 878 and 888. He first fought against the Somavamsi kings of south Kosala, conquering Pali from them. If Pali was captured by the Kalachuris of Tripuri, they must have travelled east up to the modern Bilhari/Katni area and moved south in the direction of Sarguja through the modern Umaria/Shahdol section.

From Sarguja the Ratanpur-Pali area of modern Chhattisgarh is easily accessible by following the Hasdo river. Sankaragana then combined with the Rashtrakuta king Krishna II against the eastern Chalukya king Vijayaditya III but was defeated in the battle which took place at Kiranpur in the Balaghat district which gave access to the Wainganga valley of Vidarbha and from there to the Andhra coast. Sankaragana, according to an inscription, invaded the Malaya country of the south, but possibly this has no basis. He was succeeded by Balaharsha who in turn was followed by Yuvaraja I who reigned in the second quarter of the tenth century. He attacked Gauda and Kalinga, both far from his home base. He apparently followed the Ganga till Rajmahal and from there entered Gauda and followed the Gauda-Orissa coast-Kalinga alignment. From Kalinga, he could come back through Chhattisgarh by following the Chhattisgarh>Vidarbha>Balaghat>Seoni>Jubbulpore alignment. This is a very long and circuitous way to move around with an army bent on conquest, but if there is any truth in the claim that the Kalachuris of Jubbulpore campaigned against Gauda and Kalinga, this had to be the route. Under Krishna III the Rashtrakutas attacked his kingdom and moved up to the Maihar area. They had already captured Kalanjar. However, the Kalachuris under Yuvaraja I soon drove out the Rashtrakutas and even claim to have invaded Karnataka, the Rashtrakuta home base, and southern Gujarat or Lata, also within the Rashtrakuta domain. His record also claims that he invaded Kashmir and the Himalayas, which is unlikely to have been the case.

It must be remembered that, although the Kalachuris of Chedi had their home base around Jubbulpore, they had within their core territory a large area of modern Rewa, which would mean that they controlled a large part of the central Indian forested tract and possibly the entire Vindhyan area in this sector overlooking the Ganga plain around Allahabad-Banaras. The distribution of the Saivite monasteries under their patronage is a good indication of this—Golaka-matha in *Dahala-mandala*, that is, the Jubbulpore area, the temple and the associated Saivite monastery at Chandrehe south of Rewa, the temple at Gurgi near Rewa, and the Siva temple at Bilhari.

In the third quarter of the tenth century, Yuvaraja II was succeeded by his son Lakshamanaraja who also raided Gauda and Vangala or eastern Bengal and advanced up to Orissa or Odra. He obtained from the Orissan king a bejewelled image of the *Kaliya damana*—form of Krishna. He subsequently fought with the kings of south Kosala. In the west, he successfully campaigned against Lata, the Gurjaras of Patan or Anahilapataka, the Abhiras of Junagadh, reaching eventually Somnath where he dedicated the *Kaliya* image obtained from Orissa to the god Somesvara. There cannot be any truth in the claim that he campaigned against Kashmir in the north and the Pandyas in the south.

Lakshamanaraja was followed successively by Sankaragana, Yuvaraja II, and Kokkalla II. Under Yuvaraja II, the Kalachuris were defeated both by the Chalukya king Taila II of the Deccan and the Paramaras of Malwa. The Paramaras captured Tripuri. However, under Kokkalla II, successful expeditions were undertaken against the Chalukya king Taila II in the Deccan, the Kuntala territory, and the Paramaras. He also advanced up to Gauda. Kokkalla ruled towards the end of the tenth and the beginning of the AD eleventh centuries.

Apart from the Kalachuris of Chedi, there was another group of Kalachuris who ruled in the trans-Sarayu area during this period. The first known king Rajaputra, who claims some success possibly against the Pala king Dharmapala in the east, reigned in the latter part of the AD eighth century. Another king of this dynasty in the second half of the AD ninth century, Gunambhodhideva, defeated the king of Gauda. It is possible that he participated in the Pratihara king Bhoja's expedition against Bengal.[9]

To the east of the Kalachuri kingdom in the Gorakhpur sector, there was a kingdom ruled by the Malayaketu dynasty which had its capital at Vijayapura (unidentified but possibly towards the present Nepal border, if not in the Nepalese tarai itself). The three known kings of this dynasty all seem to have ruled in the AD ninth century. The Kalachuri dynasty of the trans-Sarayu area continued till *c.* AD 1079 and somewhat later, and extended at its height from the Sarayu to the Gandak, comprising the Bahraich, Gonda, Basti, and Gorakhpur-Deoria areas. Maharajadhiraja Sodhadeva who ruled around AD 1079 is the last known king of this dynasty.

Dhar, in the heart of Malwa, was the centre of the Paramaras, at least of their main branch which emerged into prominence after the Rashtrakuta Govinda III defeated the Pratiharas in about AD 812 and handed over Malwa to them as his feudatories. He also asked another of his feudatories, Karkkaraja of south Gujarat to defend Malwa against any possible inroad by the Pratiharas. Upendra was possibly the name of the Rashtrakutas' Paramara feudatory. Of the two sons of Upendra, one ruled from Bagada in the Banswara-Dungarpur territory of Rajasthan, which geographically merges into Malwa. The first major king was Vakpati I who is credited with being the king of Avanti or western Malwa. It is probable that he accompanied the Rashtrakuta king Indra III on his expedition to Ujjain on the way to attack the Pratihara king Mahipala I. Vakpati I is also credited with leading his army to the banks of the Ganga, but of this there is no corroborative evidence. If he had gone there he had possibly done so by accompanying the Rashtrakuta army. Vakpati I was succeeded by Vairisimha II who could not resist the attack of the Pratiharas and their allies, the Kalachuris of the trans-Sarayu territory who came to control the territory up to the Narmada, including Dhar and Ujjain. This was around AD 939. Malwa was re-conquered by the Paramaras after AD 946 under Vairisimha II himself. He was followed by Siyaka II, also known as Harsha.

Taking advantage of the Rashtrakuta weakness, Siyaka II extended his territory up to the Sabarmati river and maintained good relations with the ruler of the Kaira area of southern Gujarat. On the bank of the Mahi river he defeated the Chalukyan ruler Avanivarman Yogaraja II of Saurashtra. There was a Huna kingdom to the north-west of Malwa, and Siyaka II defeated the Huna chief, although on the north-east he encountered defeat at the hands of the Chandella king Yasovarman who pushed his territory up to the Betwa river.

When Siyaka II decided to declare himself independent from the overlordship of the Rashtrakutas, the Rashtrakuta king Khottiga marched against him, but Siyaka II, assisted by the Banswara-Dungarpur branch of the Paramaras defeated him at Kalighatta on the bank of the Narmada. The Rashtrakuta army was pursued up to Manyakheta and the capital captured. This was in AD 972. Siyaka II could not hold on to the Rashtrakuta possessions in the Deccan but he extended his territory up to the Tapti, and on the north, he had his boundary with a state based in Jhalawar of Rajasthan. One does not know the location of Kalighatta, but if the Rashtrakuta army had proceeded from Manyakheta towards the Narmada, they were likely to have taken the present Gulbarga-Bijapur-Satara-Puna-Nasik alignment and crossed the Narmada somewhere near Thalghat which is the major crossing in modern times. When one remembers that Siyaka II had to undertake a similarly long thrust to Manyakheta, possibly following the same route, one is impressed.

Siyaka II was succeeded in *c.* AD 972/974 by Munja who was also known as Vakpatiraja II. With a view to expanding his kingdom, he first attacked, unsuccessfully, the Kalachuris. He could not annex any Kalachuri territory, but he plundered Tripuri. He then targeted various areas of Rajasthan, defeating first the king of Huna-*mandala*. The Guhilots of Mewar were attacked and the capital Aghata or Ahar plundered. The Mount Abu area and southern Jodhpur up to Barmer were wrested from the Chahamanas of Naddula or modern Nadol near Jodhpur. The Paramara princes were put in as governors of these Rajasthan territories where they and their successors ruled for many years. Munja then turned his attention to Lata or southern Gujarat and Anahilapataka or Patan near Ahmedabad. As these areas were once under the Rashtrakutas and as the Chalukya Taila II considered himself the successor of the Rashtrakuta territories, he sent his army to Lata and Malwa. The attacks were repeated and Munja thought he would push the war into the enemy territory. His crossing of the Godavari with this end in view was not successful and eventually he was killed by Taila. The date is between *c.* AD 993 and 998.

Under Munja's successor Sindhuraja, the Paramara territories which were surrendered to Taila were recovered. There is a textual reference to a tradition that Sindhuraja, aided by a Silahara chief of the Thana area in northern Maharashtra, intervened in a dispute between two kings of the Bastar and Chanda areas. This also brought him into conflict with the Somavamsi kings of south Kosala. He also fought against the Lata area of Gujarat and he is said to have conquered Aparanta or north Konkan, south of Lata. Although he tried to conquer Anahilapataka, he was not successful in that regard. His reign came to an end around AD 1000.

It is interesting to reflect that the Paramaras did not look towards the Ganga plain, their attention having been focused around basically western Malwa and the territories within its orbit—Rajasthan on the north, mainland Gujarat on the west, and the territories south of the Narmada. It appears that Gujarat had come to play a major role in their consideration. The fact that they had their capital at Dhar seems to suggest this. From Dhar, there is an open access to the Baroda area of Gujarat, and from here too the Narmada is easy of access, the first major point being Barwani.[10]

There were some other dynasties in central and west India during this period. The Saindhava dynasty (or the Jayadratha dynasty) with its capital at Bhutambilika or Bhumilika (modern Bhumili or Ghumli, 25 miles north-east of Porbandar and in a gorge of the Barda hills) was one such dynasty. It became visible in the second quarter of the AD eighth century, the first known king being Pushyadeva. He was defeated by the Rashtrakuta Dantidurga. Krishnaraja succeeded him and was followed by Agguka I who ruled in the last quarter of the AD eighth century. In the Saindhava inscriptions they are called *apara-samudradhipati* or 'master of the western sea'. The Arab rulers of Sindh cast their eyes on this kingdom and twice sent naval forces against them. Agguka I defeated them.

Agguka's successors were defeated by the Pratihara king Nagabhata II and also entered into a protracted war with the Chapas of Vardhamanapura at the mouth of the Saurashtra peninsula. The dynasty continued up to the early AD tenth century, possibly turning into feudatory chiefs later.

Contemporary with the Saindhavas there was a Chalukya dynasty in the Junagadh area. Although they are known in the latter part of the AD eighth century, their first major king was Vahukadhavala who ruled in the first quarter of the ninth century and was a feudatory of the Pratiharas of Kanauj who extended their supremacy to west India by this period. The subsequent history of the dynasty is essentially the story of struggles with their neighbours in Gujarat, mostly the Chapas of Vardhananapura. In the third quarter of the tenth century the Abhiras captured their territory.

In the second half of the tenth century, the Abhiras established their supremacy in southern and western Saurashtra under their king Graharipu. They ruled from Vamanasthali or Vanthali to the west of Junagadh. Supposedly a *mlechchha* (in this case, a Muslim chief) chief, antagonized his neighbour, Chalukya Mularaja of Anahilapataka, who attacked him. He was helped by the chief of Kachchha but that did not save him from defeat. His dynasty passes out of the scene after that.

In the early AD ninth century, there was a dynasty called the Varahas in the Wadhan corridor of Gujarat, which links the mainland Gujarat with Saurashtra. Only a couple of their kings are known.

There were two branches of the Chapa family of Gujarat. One ruled from Vardhamanapura and the other from Anahilapataka. The former comes into view in the early ninth century and spent most of its known existence in fights with the Saindhavas and later against the Chalukyas who captured Anahilapataka. They lost their territory to the Chalukyas. The Chapas based at Anahilapataka are known from the middle of the AD ninth century but lost their kingdom, after an uneventful history, to the Chalukyas who came to the throne of Anahilapataka in AD 941-2.

It is said that three branches of the Chalukya family are known. The oldest of them ruled from Mattamayura in central India, possibly in the area of Rewa. Only three of them are known and the last of them ruled till the last quarter of the ninth century. The second branch was based at Anahilapataka and founded by Mularaja I who was busy establishing his supremacy mainly in Saurashtra and Kutch. His kingdom was invaded by the Chahamanas of Rajasthan with whom he concluded a treaty. The Lata king Barappa also fought against him but was ousted. He suffered defeat at the hands of the Paramara Munja and the Kalachuri Lakshmana. It is said that Mularaja's kingdom extended up to Sanchor in Rajasthan and the Sabarmati river in Gujarat. His reign possibly came to an end around AD 995. His successors could not hold their own for a long time.

The third branch of the Chalukyas ruled in Lata but lost to the Anahilapataka branch.[11]

The Chahamanas also were divided into several branches. The branch which ruled Lata in the middle of the eighth century is least known. A much better known branch established itself at Sakambhari or modern Sambhar near Jaipur and is known from the seventh century. By the latter half of the ninth century, the Chahamana dominion was included in the Pratihara territory which extended from western Malwa to Didwana in the Jodhpur sector. The Pratihara Nagabhata II had the help of their Chahamana feudatory in his battle against the Arabs in Sindh. The first Chahamana king of Sakambhari, who assumed the title 'maharajadhiraja' and was not anybody's feudatory, was Simharaja in the mid-tenth century. By this time they had their base extended up to Sikar. His successor Vigraharaja (c. AD 973, date of accession) successfully invaded Gujarat and carried on expedition up to the Narmada. His kingdom extended up to Parbatsar near Jodhpur. It has been pointed out that towards the end of the tenth century, the Sakambhari Chahamanas ruled up to Sikar on the north, Jaipur on the east, Pushkar (Ajmer) on the south, and Parbatsar (Jodhpur) on the west.

There was a Chahamana family at Naddula or Nadol near Jodhpur. They were powerful in the area of Jalor, Mount Abu, and Bhinmal. There were two other Chahamana branches in Rajasthan, one in Dholpur as a Pratihara feudatory in the ninth century and another at Partabgarh in southern Rajasthan, also as a Pratihara feudatory.

The Guhilas ruled in two branches in Rajasthan—the Guhilas of Mewar and the Guhilas of Dhod. A king of the Mewar branch, Bhartripatta, calls himself 'maharajadhiraja' in an inscription of AD 943 found at Aghata or Ahar in the outskirts of Udaipur. The kingdom was also known as Medapata with Aghata as its capital. Aghata is said to have been a great centre of commerce during this period with links with Karnataka, south Gujarat, Madhyadesa or north India in general, and Takka or the Panjab foothills adjoining the Chenab. Another king, Saktikumara, has also left behind inscriptions which suggest that the Guhila kingdom of the Mewar branch ruled basically in the Udaipur area. It was also during this time that Aghata was destroyed by the Paramara king Munja.

The north-eastern part of Udaipur belonged to the Guhilas of Dhod or ancient Dhavagarta. Initially, they were the feudatories of the Pratihara kings of Kanauj and participated in that capacity in the Pratihara expeditions in eastern India and in the Deccan. It seems that Chitrakuta or modern Chitor was their capital. It is interesting that some silver coins of one of their kings, Guhila II, bearing the legend *Sri-Guhila* have been found at Agra.

The Tomars ruled parts of Haryana or eastern segment of the former eastern Panjab with their capital at Dhillika or Delhi. They emerged as a ruling but feudatory group in the first half of the eighth century. Basically, they were the feudatories of the Pratiharas and known to have established temples at Prithudaka or Pehowa near Kurukshetra in Haryana. In the tenth century, they developed conflicts with the Chahamanas of Sakambhari with fluctuating results. Chahamana Vigraharaja III Visaladeva overthrew the Tomars in the middle of the twelfth century. Till then they ruled the Delhi-Haryana area.

In early tenth century, the possessions of the Pratiharas in Panjab were taken away by the Kashmir king Sankaravarman who gave them to the Thakkiya family, one of his feudatories. In the latter part of the tenth century, a king of this family, Satrughnadeva, ruled from Tribhandapura or modern Bhatinda.[12]

The Hindu Shahi kingdom was established by Kallar in the second half of the AD ninth century, taking it from the Turkish Shahiya family who ruled in the Kabul valley and Gandhara. When it became difficult for him to hold on to the Kabul valley, he made Udabhanda or modern Hund on the Indus, east of Peshawar, his capital. Under Bhima, who flourished in the tenth century, they successfully defended their kingdom, especially against the kings of Kashmir. An inscription of Bhima describes him as *Maharajadhiraja Paramesvara Shahi Sri-Bhimadeva*, thus fully establishing his independent royal identity. Bhima was succeeded by Jayapala who was possibly the most powerful king of the dynasty. In his Bari Kot inscription from upper Swat he is called *Paramabhattaraka Maharajadhiraja Sri-Jayapaladeva*. His kingdom included western Panjab, north-western Frontier region including possibly the hills and valleys, and eastern Afghanistan.

The Karkota dynasty of Kashmir came to an end in the AD mid-ninth century, and after Lalitaditya Muktapida, its most famous king was Jayapida who is known principally for his legendary travels in the east including Prayaga and Gauda. The Utpala dynasty which came next was founded by Avantivarman. The dynasty ended about AD 939. The dynasties which followed it—those of Yasaskara and Parvagupta—ended at the start of the eleventh century, leaving Kashmir to the Lohara dynasty. The Kashmir kings of this period were more keen on retaining their power in the valley and its peripheries in Panjab than on undertaking any grand scheme of expansion.

There were small states in the Panjab hills in the areas of Rajauri or Rajapuri, Darbabhisara (unidentified but somewhere in the foothills of Kashmir), Jalandhar or Trigarta, Kangra or Kira, Chamba, Kulu or Kuluta, and so on. Of these, the history of Chamba is known in some detail from its inscriptions. The Mushana dynasty of Chamba with its capital at Brahmapura or Bharmour came into existence as early as the sixth century and is known principally from its conflict with the neighbouring Kangra region. The capital was shifted to modern Chamba possibly not earlier than the AD ninth century. One of the kings, Sahillavarman, joined the Shahi kings in their battle against the Muslims in the tenth century. We find his successors ruling Chamba in the eleventh century.

In the Almorah area of modern Uttaranchal, two copperplate grants of AD sixth century were issued from a place called Brahmapura (unidentified) and refer to the king Dyutivarman and his ancestry. The grants were made to the temple of the god Viranesvara, a form of Vishnu, at Brahmapura itself.

The other major copperplate grants of the Kumayun-Garhwal region were issued from the city of Karttikeyapura or modern Baijnath or Vaidyanatha on the road to Kausani from Almorah. These are essentially AD ninth century charters.[13]

The Southern Areas, c. Eighth–Tenth Centuries

The eastern Chalukyas of Vengi lived under the shadow of the Rashtrakuta power for a long time in the eighth century, but in the beginning of the ninth century their king Vijayaditya II (c. AD 799–847) fought against the Rashtrakutas, overrunning at one point the Rashtrakuta dominions and reaching as far as Cambay (or Stambha) in Gujarat and destroying it. The success was short-lived and the Rashtrakutas under Amoghavarsha I defeated him in the battle of Vingavalli. Vijayaditya III (c. AD 848–92), the grandson of Vijayaditya II, defeated the Pallavas of Kanchi and took away the Nellore territory from them. He defeated the Pandya kings of Madura and developed a good relationship with the Chola kings. He defeated the Nolambas and Gangas of the Mysore area. He defeated the combined force of the Rashtrakuta king Krishna II and the Kalachuri king (of Tripuri) Sankaragana in the battle of Kiranpur in the Balaghat district. He overran the Rashtrakuta kingdom up to Ellichpur. He also turned his attention, with some degree of success, towards Bastar and the Gangas of Orissa. The struggle with the Rashtrakutas continued, generally not with any abiding success; the Rashtrakutas also took sides in the royal succession of the eastern Chalukyas. The Chalukyan territory fell to Rajaraja Chola in AD 999.

It is somewhat intriguing that the battle against the combined army of the Rashtrakutas and the Kalachuris of Tripuri should take place in the Balaghat district. To access Balaghat from the eastern Chalukyan area of Vengi in the Andhra coast, one has to move down the coast to the Krishna valley and pass through the Warangal-Karimnagar-Chanda alignment to reach the Wainganga valley and then, from there, to Balaghat. Similarly, the Rashtrakutas had to join the Kalachuris somewhere north of Balaghat so that the combined force could come towards Balaghat where the battle took place. It is possible that the Rashtrakuta army went straight to the upper reaches of the Narmada where Tripuri, the Kalachuri capital is located, and from there they would follow the present Jubbulpore-Seoni alignment to Balaghat. Or, they could have come up to Ellichpur in Vidarbha and move up from there in the direction of modern Jubbulpore. In any case, what is implied is that the forested tracts of Madhya Pradesh were no obstacle to the movement of apparently large armies during this period.

Between the middle of the eighth and the start of the AD eleventh centuries, the history of the eastern Gangas of Kalinga seems for the most part to be no more than a list of kings who are mentioned in their inscriptions. During the tenth century, they were divided into a number of principalities. The rise of the Greater Gangas begins in AD 1038 when the grandfather of Anantavarman Chodaganga—Vajrahasta Anantavarman—was crowned. What is important is that the Kalinga area maintained through this period its geopolitical identity.

The Panduvamsi kings of south Kosala had their centre at Sirpur in Chhattisgarh which fell permanently to the Kalachuris in the eleventh century. Meanwhile, there was the rise of the Somavamsi kings of Orissa in the AD tenth century. They possibly partly succeeded in supplanting the Panduvamsis in south Kosala but were generally ousted from there by the Kalachuris of Tripuri, although they seem to have continued to retain some of their possessions in south Kosala. The first major king was Janamajeya Mahabhavagupta (c. AD 935–70) who has been called the king of Utkala or the Odra country. It appears that his son and successor Yayati Mahasivagupta (c. AD 970–1000) had developed conflicts with the Chedi Kalachuris. A number of the Somavamsi grants record villages in south Kosala and thus it may be inferred that the Kalachuri territory in south Kosala and the Somavamsi possessions in Orissa and south Kosala were overlapping.

The Pallavas of Kanchipuram remained a strong historical force in the south in the AD ninth century, although the Pandyas seem to have expanded their territory at the expense of the Pallavas under the rule of the Pallava Dantivarman in the first half of this century. Nandivarman III, his son, defeated the Pandyas in the battle of Tellaru, and generally extended his influence in the Kaveri region and the Coimbatore area. The chief cities of his kingdom were Kanchipuram, Mahabalipuram, and Mylapuram (Chennai). The inscriptions of Nripatungavarman, Nandivarman III's successor, have been found as far south as Pudukottai and he won a battle against the Pandyas at Kumbhakonam. Aparajita is the last major king of the Pallava dynasty of Kanchipuram. The Pandyas were again defeated, also near Kumbhakonam (at Sripurambiyam). Aparajita himself lost to Aditya I of the Cholas who till then were Pallava feudatories, in AD 983.

The Chola Vijayalaya (c. AD 850–71), a Pallava feudatory, became the master of Thanjavur and carved out a principality between the north and south Vellar rivers. His son, Aditya I, killed his Pallava

overlord Aparajita and added Kongudesa to his territory by defeating
the Pandyas and western Gangas. He seized Talakkad, the capital of
the western Gangas. Aditya I's territory now stretched from Kalahasti
to Pudukottai and included Talakkad and the Coimbatore-Salem area
or Kongudesa. He had the Chera king as an ally. Aditya I's successor
Parantaka I (c. AD 907–53) attacked the heart of the Pandyan territory
Madura and became victorious. The Pandyan king sought help from
the king of Sri Lanka but the Pandyas and the Sri Lankans were beaten
again in the battle of Vellur (south-west of Madura) which took place
in AD 915. Although the Pandyan king was ousted from his domain,
it took a long time to reduce the Pandyan territory to order, and in
his attempt to subdue Madura, he had the help of the Chera king and
chiefs of Kodumbalur (uncertain identification). In the general area
of the western Gangas, Parantaka first defeated the Banas in AD 915
and in the same year he defeated their allies, the Vaidumbas of the
Renandu area. He also inflicted a definitive defeat on the Rashtrakuta-
Pallava combine and extended his territory up to Nellore, which led
to the formation of a Chola kingdom from the North Pennar river
to Cape Comorin. This was bordered on the west by the Chera and
Western Ganga dominions. However, the Rashtrakuta king Krishna
III combined with Butuga II of the Western Gangas to defeat in
AD 949 the Cholas at the battle of Takkolam. The Cholas lost both the
Pallava and Pandya domains. Tondaimandalam or the Kanchipuram
sector went to the Rashtrakutas.

The Chola power re-surfaced with the accession of Rajaraja
Chola in AD 985. Between the death of Parantaka I in AD 953 and
the accession of Rajaraja, a Chola king, Parantaka II (AD 957–73)
campaigned against the Pandyas and also undertook an expedition to
Sri Lanka. In both cases the results were indecisive.

If one moves from the areas of the Pallavas and the Cholas to
the area of the Pandyas during this general period, one goes back
to the reign of the Pandya king Nedunjadaiyan (c. AD 765–815).
His predecessors rescued the area from the Kalabhras and defeated
the Chera kings, pushing up to Mangalore. He himself obtained
victory against the Pallavas at Pennagadam near Thanjavur and also
crushed the Ayo-vel, the ruler of the hilly land between Tirunelveli
and Travancore. Nedunjadaiyan further defeated the Adigamans or
Atiyamans of Tagadur in Dharampuri and brought Kongudesa under
his control. He annexed Venad in southern Travancore and fortified
Karavandapuram in the Tirunelveli district.

His successor Srimara Srivallabha (*c.* AD 815–62) continued the policy of subjugating the enemies of the Pandyas. First, the Kerala or Chera king was defeated at Vilinam and then at Kumbhakonam a great victory was obtained against a coalition of the Gangas, Pallavas, Cholas, Kalingas, and Magadhas. The fact that even the Kalingas and Magadhas were coming down to fight against the Pandyas at Kumbhakonam shows that the movements of armies became rapid and long-ranging during this period. Srimara was subsequently defeated twice by the Pallavas, once at Tellaru by Nandivarman III, and for a second time at Arichit by Nripatungavarman, also of the Pallavas.

Srimara's successor Varagunavarman II (*c.* AD 862–80) was roundly defeated by an alliance of the Pallavas, Cholas, and western Gangas at Sripurambiyan. Parantaka Viranarayana (*c.* AD 880–900) who succeeded him obtained some success against the Pandyas' traditional enemies and also tried to possess Kongudesa. Parantaka Chola's capture of Madura took place during the reign of Viranarayana's successor Rajasimha II who, being defeated, took shelter in Sri Lanka.

The Chola authority in the Pandya kingdom was overthrown as the aftermath of the Chola defeat at Takkolam at the hands of the Pandyas under Vira Pandya. He himself was defeated by the Cholas in the battle of Chevur. The Pandyan authority, however, did not immediately die out but lasted till Rajaraja I put the whole of the Pandyan territory under the Chola control.

The western Gangas always remained pressed between the ambitions of the Rashtrakutas in the north and the Pallavas in the south. In AD 768 it was occupied by the Rashtrakuta Krishna I. What is curious is that Sivamara II (*c.* AD 788–812), the western Ganga king during whose father's reign this occupation took place, somehow managed to keep his royal identity alive and even played a role in the succession struggle of the Rashtrakutas. Rajamalla I (*c.* AD 817–53) who was the successor of Sivamara II, allied with his northern neighbours, the Nolambas, against the Rashtrakutas. Rajamalla's successor Nitimarga (*c.* AD 853–70) was victorious over the Banas of the Kolar area and the Rashtrakuta power itself. The western Ganga power continued to persist in this area, interacting on a purely regional level and setting up an alliance with the Rashtrakutas. In AD 1004, the Cholas captured the western Ganga capital Talakkad, and the western Ganga kings acknowledged the Cholas as their overlords. As has been pointed out, the story of the Gangas does not end here. In the twelfth century, a Ganga king was the minister

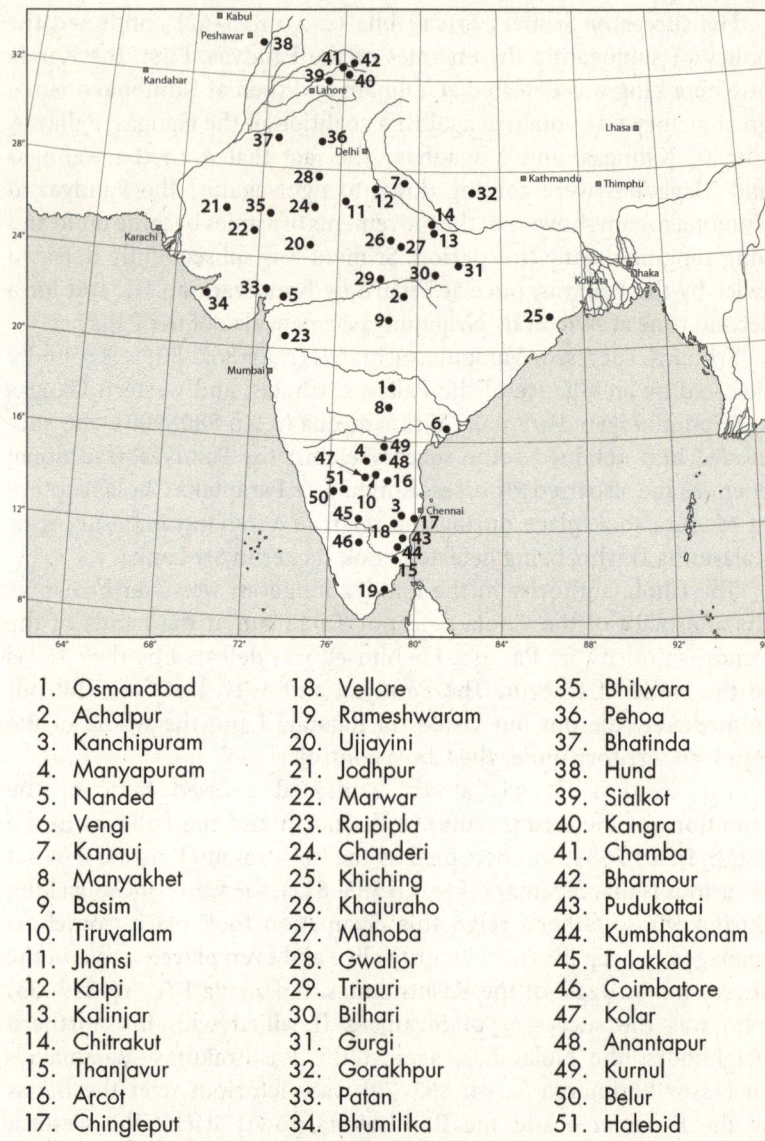

Map 5.1   Location of Some Major Sites and Areas Mentioned in
          Chapter 5

1. Osmanabad	18. Vellore	35. Bhilwara
2. Achalpur	19. Rameshwaram	36. Pehoa
3. Kanchipuram	20. Ujjayini	37. Bhatinda
4. Manyapuram	21. Jodhpur	38. Hund
5. Nanded	22. Marwar	39. Sialkot
6. Vengi	23. Rajpipla	40. Kangra
7. Kanauj	24. Chanderi	41. Chamba
8. Manyakhet	25. Khiching	42. Bharmour
9. Basim	26. Khajuraho	43. Pudukottai
10. Tiruvallam	27. Mahoba	44. Kumbhakonam
11. Jhansi	28. Gwalior	45. Talakkad
12. Kalpi	29. Tripuri	46. Coimbatore
13. Kalinjar	30. Bilhari	47. Kolar
14. Chitrakut	31. Gurgi	48. Anantapur
15. Thanjavur	32. Gorakhpur	49. Kurnul
16. Arcot	33. Patan	50. Belur
17. Chingleput	34. Bhumilika	51. Halebid

of the Hoyasala king Vishnuvardhana, and another Ganga king of
Sivasamudram defied the power of Krishnadeva Raya of Vijayanagara
in the sixteenth century.

The Banas ruled in the Kolar-Anantapur sector and had on their north, successively, the Renandus and Vaidambas. North-west of the Vaidumbas lay the western Ganga territory, and to the south-west of the Banas was the western Ganga kingdom. In AD 878, in the battle of Soremati or Soremadi in the Anantapur district, they and the Vaidumbas defeated the western Gangas and Nolambas. In AD 892–3, they in their turn were defeated by the Nolambas. The Banas eventually fell to the power of the Cholas, but late as the sixteenth century they were the governors of Madura under the Vijayanagara kings. The Nolambas had their base in modern Chitaldurg, with three principal cities at Uchchangi (unidentified), Hemavati (unidentified), and Chitaldurg. They were roundly defeated by the western Gangas in the tenth century. The Vaidumbas who are likely to have had their base in Kurnool were feudatories of the Banas. Eventually, they became vassals of the Cholas.

In south Kanara, the Aluvas or Alupa was ruled by Chitravahana II (c. AD 800) and his successors till the kingdom was incorporated in the Hoyasala kingdom in the fourteenth century. Kongudesa came to form a part of the Chola domain. In Kerala, the power in the eighth/ninth century belonged to the Perumal family which is reputed to have converted to Islam or Christianity. Bhaskara Ravivarman (c. AD 978–1036) in his charter written in Tamil, records the donation of lands and privileges to a Jew, Joseph Rabban, in the area of modern Cranganore.[14]

Notes

1. For the Rashtrakutas, see Altekar (1955).
2. Majumdar (1955a: 27).
3. Ibid., pp. 19–43.
4. Majumdar (1955b: 52).
5. Majumdar (1955c: 68).
6. Ibid., p. 76.
7. For the Harikela kings, see Chakrabarti (2001: 166–70).
8. For this section, see Ganguly (1955: 82–131).
9. Ibid.
10. For this route, see Chakrabarti (2005).
11. Ganguly (1955: 82–131)
12. Ibid.
13. Ibid.
14. For this section, see Sathianathaiyer (1955).

6

The Thrusts and Counter-thrusts of Power
c. AD *1000 to* c. AD *1300*

North India, c. Eleventh–Thirteenth Centuries

In east India, the close of the tenth century was a bad period for the
Pala dynasty. Mahipala (*c.* AD 988–1038) who succeeded Vigrahapala
II faced a situation in which the Palas lost their ancestral kingdom in
Bengal. There are indications that north and West Bengal were then
ruled by the Kamboja family (of unidentified origin) and that south
and east Bengal were then under the rule of the Chandra dynasty.
It appears that the Pala rule was then confined only to Magadha.
Mahipala began by recovering the Pala possessions in Bengal and
elsewhere. One does not know the extent of his success in Bengal
but his records in the Tripura district of east Bengal and Bangarh in
north Bengal suggest some success in that direction. His records have
also been found in north Bihar, which means that the area was in his
possession. An inscription dated AD 1026 from Banaras shows that
he was involved in renovating structures at Sarnath, and it may be
inferred that his kingdom extended at least up to Banaras.

Rajendra Chola's invasion of Bengal in AD 1021 happened
during Mahipal's reign. His record mentions that he defeated in
this connection Dharmapala of Dandabhukti, Ranasura of southern
Radha, Govindachandra of Vanga, and Mahipala of the Palas. It
appears that northern Radha was won from the Palas. Dandabhukti
means the Danton area of south-west Midnapur and the adjoining

area. Southern Radha means the tract south of the Damodar and north of the coastal area of Midnapur, whereas north Radha means the area to the north of the Damodar. It is interesting that the present western section of West Bengal had all these political units during this period. The Chola invasion was short-lived, but more problematic was the Pala struggle with the Kalachuri king Gangeyadeva. It is apparent that this struggle stemmed from the fact that the Palas had their area of control up to Banaras, and from the other side, the Kalachuris were interested in expanding their base from the direction of Tripuri to the middle Ganga valley. The Tripuri-Banaras route is Tripuri>Satna area>Rewa>Mirzapur>Banaras.

The Pala-Kalachuri conflict took place on a protracted basis under the Kalachuri Gangeyadeva's successor Karna and Mahipala's successors Nayapala (c. AD 1038–55) and Vigrahapala (c. AD 1055–70). The Kalachuri army advanced as far east as Uddandapura (or Odantipuri/Bihar Sharif) in Magadha. The battle led to a treaty, and as a reward for his help in this battle, the Gaya area or Gaya-*mandala* was given by Nayapala to the care of a feudatory. It also has to be noted that Mahasivagupta Yayati, a Somavamsi king of south Kosala in the second quarter of the eleventh century attacked Gauda and Radha. Again, it was a long-ranging raid. The south Kosala army is likely to have come through the Chhotanagpur plateau, first to the Radha area and then from Radha to Gauda. It is likely to have followed the modern railway alignment from Kharagpur to Bilaspur. During Vigrahapala's time, the Kalachuri Karna invaded the Pala territory once again, which led to a treaty and matrimonial alliance between the two families. Around AD 1068, the Pala territory was attacked by the Chalukyas of the Deccan, which would mean the western Chalukyas.

Vigrahapala was succeeded by Mahipala II whose reign was short-lived and noted for the rebellion of two of his feudatories, one of the Gaya area and the other of the Burdwan-Birbhum area. The latter was known as Isvaraghosha of Dhekkari. Soon afterwards, the Palas lost Varendri to Divya, a person of Kaivarta (fisherman) caste. The Pala kingdom became limited only to northern and central Bihar and was represented by Ramapala (c. AD 1077). In his attempt to wrest Varendri from Divya's successor Bhima, Ramapala enlisted the help of a large number of feudatories—Bhimayasas of Pithi (also called 'lord of Magadha'), Viraguna, king of Kotatavi, Jayasimha, king of Dandabhukti, Lakshmisura, the king of Apara-Mandara and the 'head jewel of the circle of feudatories of the forest, Surapala, ruler of Kujavati, Rudrasikhara, ruler of Tailakampa, Bhaskara, king of Ucchhala, Pratapasimha, king of Dhekkariya, Narasimharjuna, king of Kayangala-*mandala*, Chandarjuna of Sankatagrama, Vijayaraja of Nidravali, Dvorapavardhana, ruler of Kausambi, and Soma of Paduvanva. Only a few of these areas can be identified—Kotatavi (possibly the forested tract of Midnapur), Dandabhukti, Apara-Mandara (Garh-Mandaran area near Arambagh), Tailakampa (Purulia), Dhekkariya or Dhekkari, and Kayangala. The references to Magadha and Kausambi in this regard are confusing, although it is possible that Ramapala received help from these directions. However, it appears from this list that there was a large concentration of small states all over the forested tracts of West Bengal. One notes the expression 'the circle of feudatories of the forest'. This is in the context of Apara-Mandara. In fact, Apara-Mandara is near the extensive forests around Vishnupur, and the forested tract of West Bengal begins in this sector. From this reference one understands that by the eleventh century there were large-scale formations of small states all over West Bengal.

Ramapala won back Varendri and turned his attention to east Bengal and Kamarupa, entering a kind of alliance with the former and conquering the latter. His attempt to subdue the Gahadavalas of Kanauj did not succeed. His attempt to put a person of his choice on the throne of Utkala did not also succeed in the long run. Anantavarman Chodaganga put a person of his choice on Utkala's throne. Ramapala is reputed to have undertaken an expedition as far as Bastar where he captured its capital Chakrakotta. Ramapala died in AD 1120 and at the time of his death the Pala kingdom comprised a large part of Bengal, Bihar, and Assam.

Ramapala's successors soon faced opposition from many sides. During the reign of Kumarapala, his immediate successor, the feudatories of Gaya, Magadha, and Mithila turned rebellious, and the area up to the Danapore area of Patna was annexed by the Gahadavala Govindachandra (*c.* AD 1124). The Kalachuris of Tummana (Tuman in Bilaspur district) were the allies of Govindachandra in the Gahadavala fight against the Palas. Anantavarman Chodaganga invaded south and west Bengal in about this period. There was also rebellion in Kamarupa. Anantavarman Chodaganga annexed the area up to the Bhagirathi and had as his ally the Senas who were then ruling as feudatories in Radha. Kumarapala ruled till AD 1125 and his successor Gopala III till AD 1144. The Gahadavalas advanced up to Mungher (AD 1146) but the new Pala king Madanapala wrested back the territory with the help of the feudatory in Anga. He also fought against the advances of Anantavarman Chodaganga, but eventually the most serious danger came from the Senas with whom he fought a battle on the bank of the Kalindi river in the Maldaha district and eventually lost Varendri to them. Madanapala was left only with Anga where he ruled till AD 1161. The line of Gopala and Dharmapala ended with him.[1]

The Sena dynasty emerged in the limelight when the Pala kings were under attack from various quarters including their own feudatories and there was no difficulty in consolidating their home base in Radha. The most important king of this dynasty, Vijayasena (c. AD 1095–1158) defeated his rivals in the western part of modern West Bengal and led a naval expedition along the Ganga against the Gahadaval king Govindachandra who then was influential in Bihar. He also claims to have defeated Nanyadeva, the king of Mithila. The most important thing was that he got control of Varendri from the Palas and also of the Vikrampur region of Dhaka from its king Bhojavarman. On the whole, his rule was secure in Radha, Gauda (including Varendri), and Vanga. His venture in Kamarupa was not successful in the long run, and he also invaded Kalinga, defeating the Chodaganga kings. His successor Lakshmanasena possibly added Mithila to the Sena domain. He fought against the expansion of the Gahadavala power as far as Bodh Gaya in the east. He defeated the king of Kamarupa and possibly had a victory over Kalinga as well. In AD 1202, his possessions in central and western Bengal fell to the Muslims. He survived till AD 1205 in the Vikrampur region of eastern Bengal where there were Sena dynasty kings till the middle of the thirteenth century.[2]

Eastern Bengal had power centres of its own. In the eleventh century, the most important area was south-east Bengal stretching from Tripura to Chattagram. Its capital was Pattikera (the Mainamati area near Comilla). This kingdom bordered Myanmar and a king named Harikaladeva Ranavankamalla ruled till AD 1219. The kings of Pattikera had their successors in the Deva dynasty in the same region which passed into Muslim control in the latter part of the thirteenth century.

Further east, in Assam, a dynasty whose kings bore names ending with *Pala* came to the fore towards the close of the AD tenth century and continued to rule the Brahmaputra valley without any major disruption, although there were pressures from the Bengal side. In the first half of the thirteenth century, the Muslim power in Bengal tried unsuccessfully to expand towards Assam. However, in the middle of the thirteenth century, there was a movement of the Ahoms of upper Myanmar across the Patkoi route between Assam and Myanmar, and slowly they came to control the Brahmaputra valley. By this time, there was a kingdom in modern Kachhar and its adjoining areas. It is possible that the Kachhari kingdom emerged earlier but it was in the thireenth century that this is visible in the historical record. It has been pointed out that in the eleventh and twelfth centuries, there was a ruling family of kings in Sylhet or Srihatta, who had their names ending with *Deva*.[3]

The focus of the history of Bihar in the eleventh and twelfth centuries is on Mithila, where the Karnataka dynasty under Nanyadeva established its supremacy in AD 1097. This dynasty had its capital at Simran or ancient Simaramapura in the Nepalese territory north of Champaran. The history of this dynasty is essentially the history of conflicts with the Palas and Senas of Bengal and the rulers of Nepal. Mithila or Tirhut was taken by the Muslims in the early fourteenth century, which was also the time when the ruler of Mithila, Harisimha, undertook a conquest of Nepal and began to rule from Bhatgaon.

More interestingly, there were at least three small kingdoms during this period in different parts of Bihar. The first one was at Jayapura or modern Jayanagar near Lakhisarai, where in the twelfth century, there was a dynasty whose kings bore the name *Gupta*. They were swept away by the Muslim invasion. At Pithi in the Gaya area, two kings with *Sena* in their names are known in the second half of the thirteenth century. At Japila in the Shahabad area, the Khayaravala dynasty ruled throughout the twelfth century.[4]

A dynasty of Rashtrakuta origin figures in the history of the upper Ganga plain after the demise of the Pratiharas in about AD 1019. Some names are known and they seem to have survived at Kanauj and in possibly parts of Panchala till the advent of the Muslims. More significant in the history of Kanauj region is the Gahadavala dynasty which appears in the region in the AD eleventh century. By the end of this century, a Gahadavala king Chandradeva was in possession of Banaras, Ayodhya, and Kanauj. Govindachandra (*c.* AD 1114–54) was the most important king of this dynasty and a large number of his inscriptions have been found in the areas of Banaras, Fatehpur,

Kanpur, Kanauj, Gonda, Gorakhpur, and Danapur (near Patna).
It is basically the area between Kanauj and Patna with extensions
in the trans-Sarayu area. Another important Gahadavala king
was Jayachandra (*c.* AD 1170–93?) who basically maintained the
Gahadavala kingdom till he was defeated by the Muslims in the battle
of Chandawar in the Etawah district in AD 1193.

In the Mathura-Bharatpur area a dynasty called Yaduvamsi
dynasty ruled from Bayana (ancient Sripatha) in the eleventh and
twelfth centuries, with its kings bearing the name *Pala*. They seem to
have survived till the end of the AD thirteenth century.[5]

The Kachchapaghata kings established their independence in the
Gwalior and the adjacent areas of Dubkund and Narwar in the second
half of the AD tenth century at the expense of the rulers of Kanauj and
Malwa. Gwalior or ancient Gopadri finally went to the Muslims in
the AD mid-thirteenth century after a seesaw struggle of more than
100 years. Dubkund is about 120 km south-west of Gwalior, and
Narwar also is in that direction on a major route to Malwa. Gwalior
lies at the apex of this territory. Chahadeva of Narwar is said to be
the most important king of the region, whose coins bear the dates
between AD 1237 and 1254.

In the beginning of the eleventh century, the Chandella kings of
the Khajuraho area had to bear with the invasion of Kalanjara by
Mahmud of Ghazni in 1019 and 1022. The Chandella king of the
time was Vidyadhara. His and his successors' main struggle was
directed against the Kalachuri kings of Tripuri and the Paramaras of
Malwa. They were also interested in the Ganga-Yamuna belt which
adjoined their territory. This struggle was conducted with varying
success but under Madanavarman (*c.* AD 1129–63), the Chandella
kingdom included Bhilsa, Mau in Jhansi, Ajaigarh (to the south-
west of Kalanjar), Khajuraho/Chhatarpur, Mahoba in Hamirpur,
and Kalanjar. This is a fairly compact territory with large stretches
of forest and hills, and on two sides they could have had easy access
to the other areas. On the side of Ajaigarh and Kalanjar, they could
have had access to the Ganga-Yamuna belt, and Bhilsa gave them a
foothold in Malwa. From Khajuraho, they could also pass through
Panna to the area near Satna, which would give them easy access to
the Kalachuri heartland of Tripuri.

In 1202, Kalanjar was attacked again by the Muslims but they
could not hold it for a long time because of their defeat at the hands
of the Chandella king Trailokyavarman (*c.* AD 1205–41) who annexed

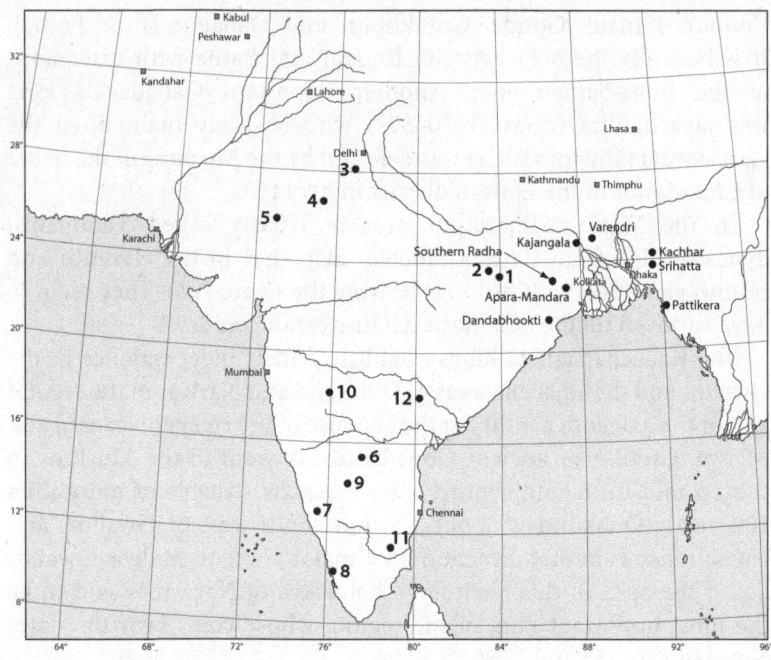

1. Odantapuri
2. Gaya
3. Bayana
4. Narwar
5. Chitor
6. Kalyani
7. Shimoga
8. Quilon
9. Chitaldurg
10. Devagiri
11. Gangaikondacholapuram
12. Warangal

Map 6.1   Location of Some Major Sites and Areas Mentioned in Chapter 6

Rewah to the Chandella territory. The Chandella kings are noted till early AD fourteenth century when the Muslims made their appearance in this central Indian heartland.[6]

In the beginning of the eleventh century, Gangeyadeva was the Kalachuri king at Tripuri. He allied with Rajandra Chola and Bhoja, the Paramara king of Malwa to attack, unsuccessfully, the Chalukyas of the Deccan. He obtained success in south Kosala where he defeated the Somavamsi kings and then conquered Utkala with the help of the Kalachuris of Tummana in the Bilaspur area. He did not fare well against his former ally, the Paramaras or against Bundelkhand, but he conquered Banaras and attacked on the east the Pala territory up to Anga. In 1034, however, Banaras was looted by the Muslims. For some reason, Gangeyadeva conducted an expedition in the Kangra area and possibly the adjacent parts of Panjab.

The Tripuri Kalachuri power was apparently at its height under Gangeyadeva's successor Karna who came to the throne sometime between AD 1034 and 1042. He advanced as far east as Radha, which he seems to have occupied, and even Vanga which lay further east. He ran expeditions against Odra and Kalinga and moved down the coast, overrunning Nolamvadi, Kongudesa, the Malabar coast, Madura, and even Kuntala. This must be considered a remarkable military manoeuvre. The entry to the coast was through south Kosala, moving through the Raipur area and proceeding along the Andhra coast up to Anantapur-Kurnool and entering Coimbatore-Salem from where the road to both Madura and the Malabar coast was open. Once in Karnataka, reaching Kuntala in its south-west section was not difficult. He combined with the Chalukyas of Gujarat to attack Malwa and the adjoining territories but was not successful in the long run. He was not successful against Bundelkhand either. Thus, despite his far-ranging military expeditions, Karna was not successful in the peripheries of his own kingdom and could possibly add only the Prayag territory to it. An expedition to Champaran in north Bihar was conducted under his successor Yasahkarna and another to Andhra, although he met repeated defeats at the hands of the Gahadavalas, Paramaras, and Chandellas. The Tripuri Kalachuris were involved in regional power-struggles with them and the Chalukyas of Gujarat till the early part of the thirteenth century when they died out.

The Kalachuris of Tummana were established in that area in early eleventh century, interacting mainly with Orissa, Bastar, and the Andhra area. One of their kings Jajalladeva (early AD twelfth century) claimed to have received tributes from the chiefs of the *mandalas* (administrative sub-divisions) of south Kosala, Andhra, Khimdi (Ganjam district), Vairagara (Wairagarh in Chanda), Lanjika (Lanji in Balaghat), Bhanara (Bhandara?), Talahari (unidentified), Dandakapura (Bastar section?), Nandavali (unidentified), and Kukkkuta (unidentified). Although some of these places cannot be identified, the list gives an idea of the area where the Kalachuris of Tummana (and later Ratanpur) were active. The history of these Kalachuris can be traced up to the beginning of the AD thirteenth century.[7]

In the beginning of the eleventh century, the Paramaras of Malwa were powerful under Bhoja whose kingdom included Chitor,

Banswara, Dungarpur, Bhilsa, Khandesh, Konkan, and the upper course of the Godavari. Considering that the Paramara core area is western Malwa, this configuration suggests spread towards south-east Rajasthan, eastern Malwa, Khandesh or eastern Vidarbha, Nasik area of Maharashtra, and the adjacent north Konkan. This is a compact territory. Long range, he attacked south Deccan and the Mukhalingam sector of Kalinga. He conquered Konkan from the Silaharas but did not succeed against Bundelkhand, the Gwalior area, Kanauj and the Chahamanas of Sakambhari, and Nadol (in Marwar). Bhoja also fought against the Chalukyas of Gujarat, once sacking their capital Anahilapataka. He died in 1055, leaving the kingdom to Jayasimha who combined with the western Chalukyan power to go up to Vengi, but otherwise the political forces involved in Malwa remained the same—the Chalukyas of Gujarat and the Kalachuris of Tripuri in the main, with additional involvements of the miscellaneous powers from Rajasthan and Bundelkhand. Under Lakshamanadeva in the early twelfth century, the Paramaras raided Gauda, Anga, and Kalinga, repulsed a Muslim attack on Ujjain, and even carried out an attack against the Kangra valley. The southern part of the Paramara kingdom at this point possibly comprised the Yeotmal district of Berar and the Adilabad district of Andhra, giving them ready access to the affairs in that region. Throughout the twelfth century, it appears that the Chalukyas of Gujarat were the Paramara's determined enemy, driving them out of Malwa and making it a part of their kingdom. However, the Paramaras under Vindhyavarman won back Malwa in the 1170s and invaded, around 1190, the Hoyasala territory in Karnataka. It was Gujarat which continued to loom large in the Paramaras' scheme of power, and they fought for different areas in Gujarat, occasionally being successful and occasionally being driven out. The Chahamanas of Rajasthan also began to play a major role in the fate of Malwa. In the early fourteenth century it was lost to the Muslims.

The Paramaras left behind a few minor power-centres in Rajasthan—Mount Abu (capital Chandravati), Vagada (Banswara and Dungarpur, capital Utthunaka or Arthuna in Banswara), Jalor (ancient Jabalipura), and Bhinmal. All these centres grew basically in the eleventh century and were tied up with the affairs of Malwa and Gujarat.[8]

In the early part of the eleventh century, the Chalukyas were firmly settled at Anahilapataka in Gujarat. Their location gave them easy access to Rajasthan and Malwa outside Gujarat, and they were deeply involved in the power struggle in these areas. This did not always bring them success but Mount Abu and the Marwar area came closely within their orbit. The kingdom of Jayasimha (c. AD 1094–1143?) of this dynasty gives us an idea of what the kings of this dynasty were trying to control—Bali in Jodhpur and Sambhar in Jaipur in the north, Bhilsa in the east, and Kathiawar and Kutch in the west. The southern boundary possibly included Lata, the southern part of the mainland Gujarat coast. Involved deeply in the regional power-struggles virtually all over east and west Rajasthan, Malwa, and Gujarat, the Chalukyas could not always hold their own and had also witnessed Muslim inroads on a number of occasions. Gujarat passed into the Muslim hands in the early fourteenth century.[9]

Towards the end of the tenth century, the Chahamanas of Sakambhari were a rising power, but it was in the early eleventh century that they began their programme of aggrandizement. Under Ajayaraja in the early twelfth century, they attacked Ujjain in Malwa and founded the city of Ajayameru (modern Ajmer). Under Vigraharaja who flourished around the middle of the twelfth century, their kingdom possibly reached its zenith—Delhi, Hansi, Pali, Jalor, Nadol, Siwalik hill in the Saharanpur sector of Uttar Pradesh, Udaipur, and Ajmer. This means that they had a grip of Rajasthan and ruled the Delhi-Haryana region with extension up to the Sivaliks beyond Saharanpur. This is a vast kingdom, tying up the whole of Rajasthan-Delhi-Haryana belt. Their main adversaries naturally included the Gujarat Chalukyas with their own ambitions in Rajasthan, and the Muslims of Panjab were at the doorstep of this Chahamana kingdom which kept them at bay for a long time.

The Chahamanas of Ranasthambhapura or modern Ranthambore, a collateral branch of the Ajmer branch of the Chahamanas, came into prominence in the thirteenth century. The area near Sawai Madhopur at the entry to the plain of Malwa received the attention of the Muslim power of Delhi of this period almost right from the beginning, and was annexed to the Muslim territories in the very beginning of the fourteenth century. The Chahamanas of Nadol in the Jodhpur segment of western Rajasthan looked more to the Chalukyan orbit of Gujarat and the Paramara area of Malwa. This is also true of the Chahamanas of Jabalipura or Jalor. There were two other branches of the Chahamanas in the Jodhpur segment, one at Satyapura or Sanchor and the other at Devada. In the early thirteenth century, the Guhilots of Mewar were powerful, having set up their capital at Chitor, but apart from the inter-regional wars in Rajasthan they were involved in protracted struggles with the Gujarat Chalukyas on the one hand and the Muslims on the other.[10]

Kashmir came under the First Lohara dynasty in the early eleventh century, and it appears that the main aim of this dynasty was to increase power at the expense of the regional hill-states including Chamba. The policy did not change under the Second Lohara dynasty which came to power in the beginning of the AD twelfth century, but the fact that Kashmir during this period was not a completely isolated area is shown by the fact that Gahadavala kings of the Ganga-Yamuna plain and the Silahara kings of Konkan sent representatives to the Kashmir court. In the early fourteenth century, a large army consisting of Tajiks and other Central Asian Muslims in general overran Kashmir. Soon afterwards, there was a Muslim on Kashmir's throne.[11]

The last major focal point of the ancient Indian dynasties in north India was the reign of Prithviraja III of the Chahamanas who, in the last quarter of the twelfth century, was the king of a large kingdom. This is how D.C. Ganguly describes it:

He inherited from his predecessors a kingdom which extended up to Hissar and Sirhind, in Patiala, on the north-west, and Delhi on the north. It was bounded on the south by the kingdom of the Guhilas of Mewar, and the territories of the Chahamanas of Nadol, who were vassals of the Chalukya Bhima II; on the east by the kingdoms of the Yaduvamsis of Bayana-Sripatha, the Kachchhapaghatas of Gwalior and the Gahadavalas of Kanauj; and on the northwest by the kingdom of the Yaminis of Lahore.[12]

The major danger came from the Muslim annexation of western Panjab in about 1186, with Multan as its capital. The first battle was fought at Tarain near Thaneswar in 1190–91, which the Muslims lost, but in the second battle at the same place they won.

The Southern Dynasties, c. Tenth–Thirteenth Centuries

In south Deccan, in the Bijapur-Gulbarga area, the person who filled the power vacuum left by the end of the Imperial Rashtrakutas was Taila II (c. AD 973–97) who initiated the line of the Later Chalukyas of Kalyani. Originally a Rashtrakuta feudatory, Taila II's home base was Tardavadi or Taddewadi on the south bank of the Bhima in the Bijapur district. Having usurped the Rashtrakuta power, he turned his attention to the western Gangas who, under Panchaladeva at that point, had a kingdom stretching from Dharwar to the Krishna. Taila II's victory over him in AD 977 brought him the area up to northern Mysore area, which in turn put him in conflict with Uttama Chola of the Cholas, with the result going in his favour. The Silaharas of south Konkan were then brought under his control. The Silaharas of this area had their capital at Valipattana. In the next stage, the Yadavas of *Seuna-desa* or the area around Daulatabad near Aurangabad acknowledged his supremacy, thus securing his base in north Deccan. He could easily launch an attack on Lata in south Gujarat from this base, which he successfully did. However, this brought him face to face with the Gurjaras who could not be dislodged. He was more successful in Malwa where he defeated the Paramara king Munja, but it is doubtful if Malwa was brought directly within his control.

Taila II was a worthy successor of the Rashtrakutas. The core area of his kingdom comprised the Shimoga, Chitradurg, and Bellary districts, the southern part of the Konkan coast, and the territory up to the upper Godavari, if not up to the Narmada. Virtually the whole of south Karnataka was ruled by him and his feudatories.

Satyasraya (*c.* AD 997–1008), Taila II's successor, was defeated by the Paramaras in the beginning of his reign, and he thus lost whatever advantage Taila II got in Malwa. It appears likely that the Banavasi area was attacked by the Kalachuris of Tripuri during this time. The Silaharas of north Konkan, who remained outside Taila II's control, now submitted to Satyasraya who burnt down their capital Amsunagara and exacted tributes from them. The danger to Satyasraya came from the south. Rajaraja Chola, Uttama Chola's son, advanced up to Bijapur, conquering all the territories of south Karnataka on the way. Eventually he was defeated by Satyasraya and went back to Thanjavur. This gave Satyasraya an opportunity to extend his influence in the south and he took advantage of this by taking possession of the territories up to Kurnool and Guntur.

Vikramaditya V (*c.* AD 1008–14) claims to have defeated the Somavamsi king of south Kosala, although the south Kosala king claims that the king of Karnataka was defeated. It is possible that south Kosala was approached from the Later Chalukyan base in Guntur. Jayasimha II (*c.* AD 1015–43) faced danger from a confederacy of the Kalachuris, Paramaras, and Cholas against him. The Paramaras annexed north Konkan to their kingdom, ousting the Chalukyan feudatories, the Silaharas. Rajendra Chola worsted the Chalukya forces in the battle of Musangi or Maski, but in the end was driven out of the Chalukyan kingdom. Jayasimha II pursued Rajendra Chola up to the western Ganga territory and the Chera kingdom and attacked Dvarasamudram (Halebid) and some parts of the Malabar coast. North Konkan was re-conquered. The focus of Jayasimha II's kingdom was on the Shimoga, Tumkur, Anantapur, and Cuddapah districts in the south, and in the north it extended beyond Kulpak, about 70 km north-east of modern Hyderabad. The Chalukyan capital was shifted sometime after AD 993 from Manyakheta to Kalyana/Kalyani near Bidar. His feudatories ruled the Banavasi and Santalige areas from the capital Balipuram which is in the Shimoga district. Another sector was governed from Kampili or modern Kampli in Hospet.

The main problem before the next king of the Later Chalukyas, Somesvara I (c. AD 1043–68), was the Cholas under Rajadhiraja I. In his first campaign which took place soon after Somesvara I's accession, the Chola king was opposed at Pundi in the Bellary district but without success. Somesvara I then put up a major resistance at Koluru on the bank of the Bhima near Chitapur. The Cholas won, entered Kalyani, and plundered it. The next battle took place at Kollippakkai and again Somesvara I was defeated. The second Chola invasion of the Later Chalukyan territory took place in 1047 and the places which fell to the Cholas were Kampili, Pundur, and Mannandippai. However, the Cholas were driven out in AD 1047 itself. The Cholas attacked for the third time in AD 1051–2, first seizing Kollapuram. The major battle took place at Koppam (possibly modern Kopbal on the bank of the Hirehalla, a tributary of the Tungabhadra, near Lingsugur), and although the Chola king Rajadhiraja I died in the battle, his brother Rajendra II who was present with him won it. Rajendra II went back to the Chola country after this victory without annexing any part of the Chalukyan territory.

Somesvara I himself had ambitions in the south. He is reputed to have invaded Kanchipuram and in AD 1058–9 he attacked the Chola kingdom. The battle took place at Mudakaru (modern Mudukakere on the bank of the Tunga in the Channagiri area of the Shimoga district). Somesvara I was defeated. The struggle with the Cholas intensified after Rajendra II's successor Virarajendra came to the Chola throne. He claims to have defeated the Later Chalukyan king five times, the first of which was at Gangavadi in central Mysore. The later Chalukyas were pushed back to the bank of the Tungabhadra.

The scene then shifted to the Vengi area of Andhra. The Cholas obtained a decisive victory at Kudal where, sometime before AD 1049,

Somesvara I asserted his sovereignty over the ruling eastern Chalukyan king Rajaraja whose successor Vijayaditya VII sought the help of the Chola Virarajendra against him. Virarajendra marched to Vengi and defeated the Later Chalukyas. Virarajendra met the Later Chalukyan army again at Kudal where there was a Sangamesvara temple. This temple is in the Singapalle village in the Rayadurg area of Bellary. The Cholas won decisively, but that did not prevent Somesvara I from leading an expedition against the Cholas in AD 1063–4, which also he lost. This battle took place at Mudukakere on the bank of the Tunga in the Shimoga district. The Cholas spent some time in chasing the Later Chalukyan army, overrunning Rattapadi and planting a pillar of victory on the Tungabhadra. They then turned their attention to Vengi in Andhra where the Later Chalukyas had recouped their power. The Later Chalukyans were defeated on the bank of the Krishna near Vijayawada. Interestingly, this long chain of defeats at the hands of the Cholas was no obstacle to a Later Chalukyan sacking of the Chola capital Gangaikondacholapuram in 1067–8.

Somesvara I fought in many other directions, beginning with his fight to re-exert sovereignty over north Konkan and following it up by marching against Lata, Gujarat, and even Malwa where he plundered Mandu, Ujjayini, and Dhar. In AD 1055, when the Kalachuris of Tripuri and the Chalukyas of Gujarat tried to extend their hegemony over Malwa, Somesvara I defeated them, restoring the Bhoja Jayasimha to power. In the east coast, along with his Kakatiya feudatory Prola, he entered Kalinga and also Bastar and south Kosala. He also attacked the Malabar coast and the south Kanara territory of Alupa. It is unlikely that he, as some of his inscriptions claim, attacked far-off places like Vanga, Magadha, Kanauj, Sri Lanka, and so on. There is no doubt that in the south his kingdom included the Shimoga, Chitaldrug, Anantapur, and Kurnul districts.

After Somesvara I, there was a struggle for power between his two sons, which is interesting because of the role played by the Chola monarch Virarajendra in this. Somesvara I was succeeded by a son who on accession became known as Somesvara II (c. AD 1068–76). The contending son Vikramaditya was the son-in-law of the Chola king, which shows that despite a long history of war between the two dynasties, matrimonial relationship between the two was possible. In any case, Virarajendra in his desire to put his son-in-law on the Later Chalukya throne attacked Somesvara II's territory. He sacked the city of Kampili and set up a pillar of victory at Karadikal or Karadi in the Lingsugur area of the Raichur district. However, Somesvara II defeated him, and the contending brother began, as Vikramaditya VI, to rule a part of his kingdom—Bellary, Anantapur, Chitaldurg, and Dharwar districts—as a feudatory of Somesvara II. This feudatory was strong enough to intervene in the Chola succession after Virarajendra, placing Virarajendra's son Adhirajendra on the throne. When Kulottunga I usurped the Chola throne, Vikramaditya VI's campaign against him was not successful. An inscription of Kulottunga I, dated AD 1080, states that he fought with Vikramaditya VI between Nangili in the Kolar district and the Tungabhadra and captured the two areas of Gangamandalam and Singanam. Four years before that, Vikramaditya VI (c. AD 1076–1126) succeeded Somesvara VI.

Sometime before AD 1085, Vikramaditya captured Kanchipuram which was in the Chola territory. Between AD 1091 and AD 1093, he captured Vengi and retained it till AD 1099 when Kulottunga I re-captured it. Vikramaditya VI re-possessed Vengi towards the end of Kulottunga's reign. He also fought against the Hoyasalas and brought them under control. The Kadambas of Goa acknowledged his suzerainty, despite phases of hostility. The Silaharas of southern Maharashtra (Kolhapur-Satara area) were his vassals too. Around AD 1088, he crossed the Narmada and carried raids into the Lata and Gurjara territories. The boundaries of his kingdom were no doubt shifting and fluid, but it has been claimed[13] that in the south, his kingdom comprised the Hassan and Tumkur districts, Khammam and Godavari districts in the east and south-east, and the Narmada in the north. The Hoyasalas of Halebid/Dvarasamudra, the Kadambas of Goa, the Pandyas of Nolambavadi, the Santaras of Patti-Pomburcha (Humcha in the Nagar area of Shimoga), the Sindas of Erambarage, the Yadavas of the Aurangabad area, and the Kakatiyas of Warangal in Telangana were his feudatories.

The reigns of Vikramaditya VI's successors—Somesvara III (c. AD 1126–38), Jagadekamalla (c. AD 1138–51), and Taila III (c. AD 1151–6)—were spent primarily in keeping the Hoyasalas as a feudatory and contending pressure from the Cholas. The Kakatiyas of Telangana also turned out to be problematic. Taila III was defeated by the Kakatiyas and after his death, the Later Chalukyan throne was occupied by Bijjala, a scion of one of the many branches of the Kalachuris which were flourishing in the Deccan and elsewhere as feudatories of the ruling kings. Bijjala was the feudatory ruling the southern part of Taila III's kingdom.

Bijjala and his successors ruled till AD 1181 when the Later Chalukyas under Somesvara IV re-captured power, although the history of the Later Chalukyan dynasty came to an end shortly afterwards, in c. AD 1189. Bijjala spent the early part of his reign by trying to establish order in the south, fighting in the Banavasi area and in Anantapur. He also fought against the Cheras of Kerala and the Cholas. The kings of Andhra and Kalinga, and the Chalukyas of Gujarat were also struggled with, although much of all these struggles was indecisive. The pattern continued under his successors too. Somesvara IV, the last Later Chalukya king, had within his kingdom Shimoga, Chitaldurg, Bellary, and Bijapur and still retained the Hoyasalas, the ruler of Banavasi, the Pandyas of Nolamvadi, and the Kadambas of Goa as his feudatories. The Yadava king Bhillama deprived him of his sovereignty in about AD 1189.

The Silahara kings of north Konkan, south Konkan, and south Maharashtra (Kolhapur, Miraj, and Karhad) come to the fore in Konkan in the AD ninth century, and in south Maharashtra in the AD tenth century. They ruled mostly as independent or semi-independent kings owing suzerainty to overlords like the Rashtrakutas, Later Chalukyas, and others. Their kingdoms were finally annexed to the Yadava kingdom.

The kings of the Yadava dynasty flourished as vassals of the Rashtrakutas of Manyakheta and the Chalukyas of Kalyana for centuries before they became independent. Their core area was western Vidarbha or Khandesh and the Nasik and Ahmadnagar districts of the Maharashtra heartland. In the first half of the ninth century, Dridhaprahara, a king of the dynasty, established his capital at Chandradityapura (Chandor) in the Nasik district. His successor Seunachandra I founded a city and named it Seunapura and the kingdom itself *Seuna-desa* or *Sevuna-desa*. It was located in the area of modern Daulatabad in the Aurangabad district. The first independent king of the dynasty, Bhillama V (c. AD 1185–93) wrested from Somesvara IV of the Later Chalukyas their capital Kalyan, Kisku-nad (capital Erambarage or modern Yelburga in Lingsugur), Tardavadi-nad (the Mutgi area in the Bagewadi area of Bijapur), Belvola (Gadag in Dharwar), and the adjoining territories including Mangalaveshtaka (modern Mangalvedha) in Sangli. From this base in southern Deccan, Bhillama attacked the Hoyasala territory, reaching Seringapatnam, and even the Chola territory beyond. Kulottanga III of the Cholas was defeated by him. The Hoyasalas under Ballala II defeated the Yadavas in 1188-9 at Ingalaguppe (Ingalakupe) in Seringapatnam and made them withdraw from the Hoyasala territory. In Vidarbha, Bhillama captured the city of Srivardhana near Nagpur. The city seems to be unidentified but it was captured from a chief known as Antala. He also tried to make forays in Gujarat and Malwa but were not successful. His main struggle was with the Hoyasalas. Ballala II attacked him at Hangal, Gutti, Rattapalli, Soratur (near Gadag), and Lokkundi (near Gadag) and captured the forts at these places. Ballala II then captured Erambarage and the adjoining areas, advancing up to the Krishna. There is, however, no doubt that the Yadavas of Devagiri (the city founded by Bhillama V) carved out a kingdom from western Vidarbha to south Deccan.

Jaitugi (c. AD 1193-1200), Bhillama V's successor, continued the policy of expansion at the expense of the Hoyasalas but was not much successful. He annexed parts of Kurnul and this brought him in touch with the Kakatiyas of Warangal who were defeated. After the triumph over the Kakatiyas, he fought Anangabhima II of the Ganga dynasty of Orissa and Kulottunga III of the Cholas. In the north, Gujarat and Malwa received his attention but nothing much could be achieved in that sector.

Jaitugi's successor Singhana (c. AD 1200-47) began by recovering the territories lost to Ballala II of the Hoyasalas, which brought him close to the northern border of Banavasi, the capital of which was then at Balligrama (modern Belgami) in Shimoga. Singhana made a successful attack against Balligrama, capturing the whole of Banavasi and its adjacent area of Santalige and reaching the banks of the Tunga river. He advanced against Dvarasamudra, the heartland of the Hoyasalas, and reached the Kaveri. However, he had finally to accept the Tunga river as his southern border. In the Konkan coast, Singhana accepted the suzerainty of the Kadambas of Goa and the Ratta family of Venugrama or Belgaum which was the capital of the Kundi country. The Silahara family in the Kolhapur area, which ruled from Panhala, was overthrown. The ruler of Bhambhagiri (Pimpalner area of west Khandesh) submitted to him, but it appears that the Silaharas of north Konkan were left undisturbed. He conquered a large part of Anantapur, possibly with the aim of extending his supremacy in the Kakatiya territory but that was not successful. In east Vidarbha, he conquered the Chanda district and the chief of a territory which had its capital at Parnakheta (unidentified). Singhana also targeted southern Gujarat, crossing the Tapti and attacking the area repeatedly. He won every time but could not make much headway against the Gurjara territory under the Chalukyas. His final attempt to march against the Chalukyas ended in defeat.

Singhana's empire extended from Khandesh up to the Shimoga and Anantapur districts, and from the western coast (excluding northern Konkan) up to the eastern parts of Hyderabad and Berar. Nikumbha family of Durgapura (Khandesh), Rattas of Venugrama, Kadambas of Goa, and the Sindas of Embarage ruled their territories as his vassals. Dennayaka, whose headquarters were at Ambadapura, modern Amrapur in the Buldana district, was his governor of Berar. His officer for the administration of the Sindavadi country was Jagadala Soma Nayaka. He appointed Vankuva Ravuta the viceroy of the southern countries, Belvola, Huligere, Banavasi and Bassavura. Mallideva, governor of Belvola, the Guttas of Guttal, and the Sindas of Banavasi were placed under his supervision.[14]

Singhana's successor was his grandson Krishna (c. AD 1247–61) who was busy controlling the territory which abutted the Hoyasala kingdom. The control over Bellary and Chitaldurg concerned him most. The Silaharas of north Konkan ruled Thana, Alibag, Ratnagiri, and the southern part of Surat. Krishna's victory over them did not result in any territorial annexation. He also attacked south Kosala (Bilaspur and Raipur sector) and possibly came into conflict with the Kakatiyas as well. Malwa and Gujarat continued receiving his attention, although without any specific result except minor victories. It has been pointed out that Krishna's inscriptions have been found in Shimoga, Chitaldurg, Bellary, Dharwar, and Belgaum, giving a clear indication of the southern boundary of the Yadava kingdom which had as its heartland northern Maharashtra.

Under Mahadeva (c. AD 1261–70/71), the Yadavas struggled to retain their possessions at the southern border but their major success came against the Silaharas of north Konkan. Their territory was annexed to the Yadava kingdom which also launched successful attacks against Malwa and the Kakatiya territory of Telangana. Interestingly, the Silahara king died in a naval engagement with the Yadavas.

Ramachandra who obtained the Devagiri throne after a civil war overran the Belavadi or Belur area of Hasan and laid siege to Dvarasamudra. The campaign ended in failure, and similarly his campaign against Gujarat ended in failure too. He was successful in his conflicts with the chiefs of the Jubbulpore area, Bhandara, and Wairagarh (in Chanda), and possibly with the other minor chiefs of this eastern sector. His inscriptions show that his rule extended up to Nagpur and Balaghat. In 1294, Devagiri was successfully attacked by Alauddin Khalji who came by Ellichpur. In the early fourteenth century, the Kakatiyas pushed their territory up to Medak and Raichur and the Hoyasalas seem to have pushed the Yadavas out of Shimoga and Chitaldurg after the battle at Sirise. In the early fourteenth century again, Ramachandra helped the Muslims in their invasions of the Kakatiya and Hoyasala territories. The Muslims took possession of the Yadava kingdom in about AD 1317.[15]

For long the feudatories of the Later Chalukyas of Kalyani, the Kakatiyas came into their own after the death of the Chalukya Vikramaditya VI in AD 1126 when the Chalukya kingdom began to disintegrate. Pola II who was then the ruling chief of the Kakatiyas tried to gain power at the expense of the other Chalukyan feudatories in Telangana and Andhra coastal districts. The Chalukya king of the time Tailapa II tried successfully to subjugate him. Rudra I who came to the Kakatiya throne in AD 1158 after Pola II, attacked Tailapa II, which led to his death and saw the consolidation of the Kakatiya power in the Kurnul, Guntur, Krishna, and Godavari districts. The notable Kakatiya king of the period was Ganapati who ascended the throne in AD 1198. From his inscriptions found in the Warangal, Nalgonda, Mahbubnagar, Godavari, Krishna, Kurnul, Nellore, Cuddapah, Chittur, and Chingleput districts, it may be inferred that his kingdom extended from the Godavari district to Chingleput and from the north of Telangana to the sea. The Chola power was in serious decline during this period and was subdued by the Pandyas who, in view of the southward extension of the Kakatiya power, conquered Kanchipuram and Nellurapura or Nellore. The Pandya-Kakatiya battle took place at Mudugur on the bank of the Peraru river. The Kakatiya capital was established at Ekasilanagari or modern Warangal by Ganapati whose last known date is AD 1261. Prataparudradeva came to power in AD 1290, and began by re-capturing Nellore. In 1309–10, he fought but eventually succumbed to the army of Malik Kafur, Alauddin Khalji's general. After the departure of the Muslim army he turned his attention again to the south, capturing all the areas up to Tiruchirapalli. His inscriptions have been found in the areas of Tiruchirapalli, Chingleput, Cuddapah, Kurnul, Nellore, Guntur, Krishna, Godavari, Nalganda, Warangal, Raichur, and Medak, showing that under Prataparudra the Kakatiya kingdom extended from the Godavari to Trichy and from Medak to the sea. However, in

1322 the Muslims attacked Warangal again and defeated him. His last known date is AD 1326.[16]

The eastern Chalukyas with their capital at Vengi had long been linked to the Imperial Chola fortunes. In AD 1076, Kulottunga Chola annexed the eastern Chalukyan territory to the Chola kingdom, thus maintaining a grip over virtually the whole stretch of the Tamil Nadu and Andhra coast and making the eastern Chalukyan power irrelevant.

The eastern Chalukyas were bordered up the coast by the eastern Gangas of Kalinga with their capital at Kalinganagara. When Kulottunga Chola annexed the eastern Chalukyan territory, the Kalinga king on the throne was Rajaraja I Devendravarman who repulsed Kulottunga's attack on his kingdom. His successor was Anantavarman Chodaganga (c. AD 1078–1150) who was possibly the most important of the eastern Ganga kings. In the early part of his reign, the Cholas captured the Vishakhapatnam area and pushed further up the coast. The lost territory was subsequently recovered by Anantavarman who also pushed the Ganga boundary up to the Godavari, although he eventually had to cede this to the Cholas. He was more successful in the east, in Orissa, the whole of which was annexed to his kingdom before AD 1118. Taking advantage of the slow disintegration of the Pala power during this period, Anantavarman moved as far east as Mandara or the modern Arambagh area in West Bengal and thus established his rule up to the Bhagirathi/Ganga. The Kalachuris of south Kosala and the Paramaras of Malwa did not permit him to move northward from Orissa.

Under Anantavarman's successors attempts were made from to time to extend the Ganga supremacy up to the Godavari, but more importantly, they repulsed a Muslim attack from Bengal in the first quarter of the thirteenth century. In 1244, the ruling Ganga king Narasimha I defeated the Muslims and captured the Radha tract. The Muslims re-captured the Radha tract towards the end of AD 1255.[17]

The history of the Somavamsi kings from the eleventh century onward is somewhat jumbled up. The Somavamsi king in the beginning of the eleventh century was Bhimaratha Mahabhavagupta II, one of whose feudatories was the Mathara chief Punja of Bamandapati or modern Bamragarh. It is interesting that this feudatory described himself in an inscription as the owner of 15 small villages. It is apparent that small feudatory states were cropping up in various parts of Orissa during this time. The Somavamsis were basically the rulers of south Kosala which is geographically closely linked with Utkala. Under Uddyotakesari Mahabhavagupta IV (c. AD 1055–80) Utkala was brought under the Somavamsi rule. In Utkala, the Somavamsi capital was at Jajpur in Cuttack. The Somavamsis lost south Kosala to the Kalachuris and in Orissa their power was usurped by the Gangas.

In the AD eleventh to the thirteenth centuries, there are inscriptions of a number of other dynasties ruling in Bastar and the northern areas of Orissa. The dynasty which is mentioned in the context of Bastar is the Chhindaka dynasty whose capital seems to be Chakrakuta or Chakrakotta. Their location on a major route from Kalinga to south Kosala ensured their importance and involvements with the rulers of Kalinga, northern Orissa, and south Kosala. The dynasty seems to persist up to the beginning of the fourteenth century. In the same south Kosala, Bastar, and north Orissan area, one finds inscriptions of the Telegu-Choda kings who apparently descended from the Cholas and sought fortunes in this region. Similarly, in the same region, there are inscriptions showing the existence of kings bearing Rashtrakuta lineage. An inscription found in the Ganjam district and dated in the AD eleventh–twelfth century, mentions a feudatory ruler who claims descent from *Tailapa* lineage (*Tailapavamsi*), which would mean a western Chalukyan lineage.[18]

The Hoyasala territory lay between the territories of the Cholas and Chalukyas and was thus subject to pressure from both sides. Originally allied with the Chalukyas, they carved out a feudatory principality for themselves, and when the Chalukyas declined, they became independent successors to the Chalukya rule in the southern part of their border. The feudatory who took a step in this direction was Vinayaditya who seems to have ruled the territory of Gangavadi or the area of the modern districts of Mysore, Chamrajnagar, Tumkur, Kolar, Mandya, and Bangalore in Karnataka. In fact, the Gangavadi and the Nolambavadi (modern Chitaldrug sector) sectors of Karnataka and the adjacent areas seem to be the main focus of the Hoyasala kingdom. However, the founder of the Hoyasala power was Bittiga or Vishnuvardhana (c. AD 1106–52/56), although he did not assume independence. He ruled virtually the whole of the Mysore area with considerable portions outside to the north. Ballala II (c. AD 1173–1220) made the Hoyasala kingdom secure by fighting other Chalukya feudatories such as the Kadambas and declared himself independent. Meanwhile, the Pandyas of Madura were pressing hard on the Cholas, and much of the Hoyasala Narasimha II's reign (*c.* AD 1120–34) was spent in coming to the aid of the Cholas against the Pandyas and setting up a southern capital north of Srirangam in Trichy. The struggle seems to have ended in favour of the Pandyas. In the north, the Hoyasalas resisted successfully the pressure of the Yadavas of north Deccan. In early fourteenth century, they had to face the onslaught of Alauddin Khalji and after him the power of the Tughluk dynasty of Delhi. After the Tughluk dynasty fell, there was a Muslim power enclave at Madura, and it appears that this power obtained a decisive victory against the Hoyasalas, bringing about its virtual end. Throughout their struggle both as Chalukya feudatories and independent kings, the Hoyasalas remained exclusively a regional power trying to find a place between the Chalukyas with their base in north Karnataka and the Cholas and Pandyas in the south.[19]

The major phase of Chola history begins with the accession of Rajaraja I (*c.* AD 985–1014) who first attacked the Cheras of Kerala and defeated them in a naval battle at Kandalur or Tiruvananthapuram. Kollam or Quilon was attacked along with another place called Vilinum. He then possessed the Pandyan territory of Madura, and the area of modern Coorg. He also led an expedition to Sri Lanka, destroying Anuradhapura and making Polonnaruva his capital. It appears that the northern part of Sri Lanka was captured by him and made a part of the Chola kingdom. The Gangavadoi-Nolambavadi area or the area of the western Gangas fell to him in about AD 991 and remained in Chola possession till AD 1117. The Chalukyas further north were attacked but not with lasting success. The Cholas had to fall back to the south of the Tungabhadra. A matrimonial alliance with the Eastern Chalukyas of Vengi, in whose battle for succession he intervened, brought the area under his control and facilitated his conquest of Kalinga. He also conquered the Maldives. The kingdom established by Rajaraja I incorporated the northern part of Sri Lanka, the Maldive islands, and the whole of south India up to the Tungabhadra, and the south-eastern coast up to Kalinga.

The list of the territories conquered by his successor Rajendra I (*c.* AD 1012–44) included the Raichur doab, Banavasi, Kulpak near Hyderabad, Manyakheta in north Karnataka, Sri Lanka, Maldives, an island called Sandimattivu in the Arabian sea, the western Chalukyan territory, Maski, places in Bastar, Madura, Orissa, south Kosala, Jajnagar in Orissa, Dandabhukti in Midnapur in West Bengal, and the territories of the kings Dharmapala, Ranasura, and Govindachandra of West Bengal, and the territory of the Pala king Mahipala I. In 1018,

Sri Lanka was completely conquered and ruled as a province. He also captured the Pandya territory in 1018, converting it into another province to which he later added the Chera kingdom. He was not completely successful against the western Chalukyas who, sometime after their defeat at Maski, re-established their authority up to the Tungabhadra, if not up to Bellary. The expedition to Bengal was not conducted as a thoughtless raid. The coast up to Kalinga was under his control, and the diversion from Kalinga to south Kosala through Bastar was under his control too. The Chola army, with its flank protected, marched up the Orissa coast, entered Bengal, defeated the kings of the Radha tract (both north and south Radha), crossed the Bhagirathi/Ganga, defeated the Pala king Mahipala and came back. Getting the water of the Ganga and pouring it in the irrigation tank of the new Chola capital Gangaikondacholapuram gave this long raid a ritualistic colour. In about AD 1025, Rajendra I sent his naval expedition against Sumatra and the Malayan peninsula. The places attacked during this expedition have been listed in the relevant inscription—Srivijaya kingdom of Sumatra, Pannai which was on the east coast of the same island, Malaiyur, also in Sumatra, Mayirudingam near Ligor in Malaya, Ilangasoka south of Ligor, and Mappapalam near the Isthmus of Kra, two places—Mevilimbangam and Valaippandur—which remain unidentified, Talaittakkolam or Takkola in this isthmus, Madamalingam near the Bay of Bandon in Malaya, Ilamuridesam or modern Lamri in northern Sumatra, Manakkavaram or the Nicobar islands, and Kadaram or modern Kedah near Penang. It is apparent that this expedition which covered a large part of South-East Asia, especially the section which looked west across the Indian ocean and involved a full-fledged naval force, was envisaged to maintain the Chola stronghold over the commerce emanating from that region. It is interesting to reflect that the Srivijaya king against whom Rajendra undertook his expedition was the successor of Mara-Vijayatunga-varman at whose request Rajaraja granted the revenue of a village for the upkeep of a Buddhist monastery founded in 1006 by the Srivijaya king at Negapatam. The grant of this village—Anaimangalam—was also renewed by Rajendra in the beginning of his reign. The relation of the Cholas with the Srivijaya king had obviously deteriorated greatly in the intervening years.

Sri Lanka grew restive in 1029, and there was unrest in the Pandya and Chera areas too. Towards the end of his reign, the territory of the western Chalukyas was attacked and victory won at Pundi on the Krishna. The western Chalukyan capital Kalyani was ravaged.

Rajendra's successor was Rajadhiraja who independently ruled between 1044 and 1052. The rebellion in Sri Lanka was subdued but in the battle of Koppam against the western Chalukyas he lost his life and the throne went to Rajendra II who became victorious and pushed north up to Kolhapur. There were further battles with the western Chalukyas but despite repeated victories, the Cholas failed to annex the western Chalukyan territory permanently. The western Chalukyas also proved hostile to the stability of the eastern Chalukyan kingdom of Vengi with which the Cholas were matrimonially linked. Rajendra II's successor, Virarajendra I (c. AD 1063–70) defeated them at Vijayawada. He also defeated a rebellion in Sri Lanka and in about AD 1069 sent an expedition to Kadaram/Keddah to install a ruler of his choice on its throne.

Virarajendra's son Adhirajendra died soon after his father's death, and the Chola throne went to Kulottunga I (c. AD 1070–1120) who belonged to the eastern Chalukyas of Vengi but was a great-grandson of Rajaraja I. Kulottunga I represented the Chalukya-Chola line. In AD 1073, the Kalachuris of south Kosala attacked Vengi, although without success. Vijayavahu of Sri Lanka captured Polonnaruva in AD 1070 and declared himself king of Sri Lanka in AD 1073 and independent of the Cholas. In 1088, Kulottunga made peace with him by giving his daughter in marriage to him. The Chola authority was reasserted in the Pandya and Chera areas where the Chola military colonies were established, leaving the internal administration to them. Kulottunga also claimed to have destroyed Kadaram but in AD 1090, at the request of the Kadaram king, he renewed the grant of the village sanctioned by his Chola predecessors for the upkeep of the Negapatam Buddhist monastery. Kulottunga twice invaded Kalinga (AD 1096, AD 1110) but this did not lead to any annexation. He maintained a friendly relation with the Gahadavalas of Kanauj but the Gahadavala kingdom was far from his territory. Towards the end of his reign the Gangavadi and Nolambavadi areas came to be possessed by the Hoyasalas who raided the Chola territory up to Rameshwaram, and the western Chalukyas won Vengi.

Vikrama Chola became the sole Chola ruler after the death of Kulottunga in AD 1120 and ruled till AD 1135. He recovered the Kolar area and some other parts of Gangavadi from the western Chalukyas.

His reign and that of his son Kulottunga II, who ruled till AD 1150, was uneventful.

Rajaraja II came to the throne in AD 1146 and ruled till AD 1173 and his successor Rajadhiraja II carried on till AD 1179. The main feature of this period was a war between two factions of the Pandyas, one of which sought the intervention of Sri Lankan king Parakramabahu, necessitating the intervention of the Cholas in favour of their rival faction. This resulted in protracted warfare which was not resolved till *c.* AD 1177 during the reign of Rajadhiraja II (*c.* AD 1163–79).

Kulottunga III (*c.* AD 1178–1216) succeeded Rajadhiraja II. The Pandya problem re-surfaced during his reign, with one of the contending parties, Vira Pandya, taking the help of Sri Lankan forces. Kulottunga III dethroned him and gave the Pandya throne to his rival Vikrama Pandya. Vira Pandya took the help of the Cheras but was defeated and took shelter in Quilon in the Chera territory. The Sri Lankan king Nihsankamalla proved troublesome, repeatedly invading the Pandya country and sieging Rameshwaram. Between AD 1190 and 1194, the Chola authority was restored in Kongudesa, and Kanchipuram was taken in AD 1196 from the Telegu-Chola feudatory kings who controlled the area between north Arcot and Nellore. In *c.* AD 1205, another expedition was sent to the Pandya territory which, however, did not come under his control. In *c.* 1208 there was an expedition to Andhra.

Rajaraja III (*c.* AD 1216–46) and Rajendra III (*c.* AD 1246–79) were the two last Chola monarchs. The Pandyas inflicted a definitive defeat on Rajaraja III and captured the Chola capital. Meanwhile, one of the Chola feudatories, Kop-Perunjinga, imprisoned Rajaraja III at Sendamangalam in the south Arcot district. This brought about the intervention of the Hoyasala king Narasimha II on behalf of the Chola king who was freed from his imprisonment by Kop-Perunjinga. This led to the establishment of a firm Hoyasala hold over the Chola kingdom, and Narasimha's son Somesvara (*c.* AD 1234–63) established himself near Trichy. The Kakatiyas captured Kanchipuram. Rajendra III tried to augment the Chola power with the help of the Telegu-Cholas and possibly defeated the Pandyan king Maravarman Sundara Pandya, but the Pandyas rallied under his successor Jatavarman Sundara Pandya who brought about a significant change in the political configuration of south India. The Hoyasalas were defeated and the Cholas subdued. The Kakatiyas were driven out of Kanchipuram and Nellore captured. The Telegu-Cholas also were defeated. From *c.* 1258 to 1279, Rajendra III's position was that of a Pandyan feudatory. Kop-Perunjinga who defeated Rajaraja III in AD 1231 at Tellaru near Wandiwash and imprisoned him at Sendamandalam was reduced to vassalage by the Pandya Jatavarman. His inscriptions have been found largely in north Arcot, south Arcot, and Chingleput, and to a lesser extent in Thanjavur, Kurnul, and Godavari districts. It is apparent that the first three districts formed the core of his political power.[20]

Right through the tenth, eleventh, and twelfth centuries, the Pandyas were under the shadow of their northern neighbours, the Cholas, and it is only after the Chola decline that the Pandyas re-asserted themselves. Maravarman Sundara Pandya (*c.* AD 1216–38) reduced the Chola king Rajaraja III to vassalage, burning Uraiyur and Thanjavur, and moving as far north as Chidambaram. The Hoyasala support saved the Cholas who could maintain intact their core territory. Sundara Pandya remained powerful and annexed parts of Trichy and Pudukottai. Jatavarman Sundara Pandya I (*c.* AD 1251–68) was the most powerful king of the Pandyas of this period. He defeated the Chera king Udayamartanda, drove out the Hoyasalas from the Chola belt by defeating them at Kannanur near Trichy, and proceeded victoriously to Sendamandalam in the Namakkal area. Between 1254 and 1256, he reduced northern Sri Lanka to vassalage. He captured Kanchipuram, defeated the Kakatiyas and possessed Nellore. He also annexed Kongudesa, defeating the Hoyasalas. Maravarman Kulasekhara Pandya ruled from *c.* AD 1268 to 1310 and re-asserted the Pandya control over Kerala, Kongudesa, Chola territory, Tondamandalam or the Kanchipuram sector, and Sri Lanka. The tooth relic of the Buddha was brought to Madura around 1284 by his general who led the expedition to Sri Lanka. The Sri Lankan king Parakramabahu III (*c.* AD 1302–10) took it back by peaceful negotiations after visiting Madura. In the early fourteenth century, the Pandya territory was invaded by Muslims.[21]

Notes

1. For this section, see Ganguly (1957a: 24–45)
2. Ibid.
3. Ibid., p. 44.
4. Ibid., pp. 47–9.
5. Ibid., pp. 55–9.
6. Ibid., pp. 58–60.
7. Ibid., pp. 61–6.

8. Ganguly (1957a: pp. 66–74).
9. Ibid., pp. 81–9.
10. Ibid., pp. 74–81.
11. Ibid., pp. 7–103.
12. Ganguly (1957b: 109).
13. Ganguly (1957c: 191).
14. Ibid., p. 196.
15. Ganguly (1957d: 198–203).
16. Ibid., pp. 203–9.
17. Ibid., pp. 207–8.
18. Sircar (1957: 214–18).
19. For the Hoyasalas, see Majumdar (1957: 226–33).
20. For the Cholas, see Sathianathaiyer (1957a); Sastri (1935–7).
21. For the Later Pandyas, see Sathianathaiyer (1957b: 256–60).

7

The Emerging Historical–Geographical Pattern of India's Ancient Political History

This volume is based on the belief that without trying to group the different physiographic components of the subcontinent into a neat hierarchical order of historical importance, as some earlier scholars had done, it will perhaps be more indicative of the geopolitical forces operative in Indian history if the various geographical orbits within which the political forces or dynasties of the various periods interacted could be highlighted showing their recurrent patterns. In the long run, this will have the effect of demonstrating that regions in Indian history, as elsewhere, had never any immutable historical shape or identity but were fluid both in their interactions and outlines. If the earlier approach is reminiscent of geographical determinism, the second approach examines closely the range of geographical possibilities of the regional power centres of various periods and the extent to which they operated within that frame. What is important about the geographical frames of ancient Indian political history is not that its course is frequently characterized by regional political units of limited dimensions but the web of inter-regional interaction which they created for themselves within the overarching limits of the geography of the subcontinent. This web was not limited to a particular set of regions but had a pan-Indian ramification in the sense that at any particular point of time it was composed of the circles of various regional interactions which had in turn inter-regional linkages of their own, eventually ensuring that none of the regions could politically thrive in isolation.

The Mythical Domain

Even the first political canvas which belongs entirely to the domain of tradition is not devoid of geopolitical realty. The five sons of the king Yayati of the mythical Lunar dynasty shared between themselves the lower Doab, the upper Doab, Baghelkhand, Bundelkhand, and the modern Gwalior tract. The kings of the equally mythical Solar dynasty controlled the area from Ayodhya to Vaisali, with Mithila as an important geographic point of their control. A vast area of northern India is left out in this canvas. What is shown is only the sweep of the Ganga-Yamuna plain from the western Uttar Pradesh to the eastern segment of north Bihar, and roughly the area from Gwalior to Rewa to its west. From the Gwalior-Rewa stretch it is possible to be in touch with the Narmada and Gujarat, and Haryana-Panjab is easily accessed from western Uttar Pradesh. The Puranic literature depicts this canvas as the core area of political geography, and it does so possibly for the simple reason that this was the area the compilers of the puranic tradition were acquainted with.

The Kings Mentioned in both the Puranic Literature and the Later Vedic Literature

When one moves away from the mythical kings and dynasties to the consideration of specific states mentioned both in the Puranas and the later Vedic literature, one finds that the textual orbit of Indian political geography now includes the whole of the alluvial corridor from Gandhara in the north-west to Kosala, and possibly Magadha and Anga, in the east, the uplands which border this alluvial zone on the west, Vidarbha, northern Deccan, Kalinga, and apparently large sections of Andhra. Those who compiled this literature had no clear idea of what lay further south, east, or even west, but over a very large part of northern India and the Deccan, they could think of specific states and groups of people. No claim can be made on this basis that these states and political units were the only such early political formations in the subcontinent. However, their enumerations represent the general range of geographical knowledge of the concerned texts.

The Sixteen *Mahajanapadas*

The same is possibly true of the notion of 'sixteen major principalities'. These principalities do not cover all the areas of the subcontinent, and yet there is no reason why during the time of the Buddha there could not be major principalities in the areas which remained unmentioned in the Buddhist and Jaina sources. For instance, south Kosala is not mentioned as a *Mahajanapada* and neither is Odra or Orissa. However, if one takes into consideration the early historical date and sheer massiveness of their principal sites—Malhar in the case of south Kosala and Radhanagar in the case of Odra—it becomes very difficult to argue that they were not *Mahajanapada* period settlements. The mention of a few principalities in the Jaina list, which are not mentioned in the Buddhist list, also suggests that not all the major principalities of the period were considered while drawing up these lists. The notion that the Jaina list is later than the Buddhist list is only an unfounded assumption. Because the Jaina list contains names which do not occur in the Buddhist list, the former is automatically considered to be later in date.

Whatever it is, the geographical configuration of the recorded major principalities is the following—a straight open sweep from the north-west to Magadha, a second sweep from Anga to Avanti or western Malwa, and a third sweep from the area of Kasi to the Deccan. We feel that these three sweeps were all important in their own ways. The importance of the alluvial corridor from Gandhara to Magadha needs no special emphasis. The Buddhist sources are replete with references to movements along this corridor. For instance, Jivaka, the physician, travels from Rajagriha to Taxila to learn medicine, and he comes back after completing his studies there. The journey from Anga to Avanti is well understood too. The route will pass through the kingdom of Vatsa, and again, one of the major themes of the early Buddhist literature is the hostility between Avanti and Vatsa. Similarly, there is no problem of travelling from Kasi to the Deccan through a complex of routes which took people across the hills and jungles of central India or the open plateau of Malwa. In combination, these three sweeps form possibly the earliest historical geopolitical configuration of Indian history, with its roots deep in the legendary or traditional domain. Or, they can be visualized as the first clearly visible three interlinked but separate orbits of the Indian history.

In the matter of interaction between these states, the texts principally mention the power tussle between Kasi, Kosala, and Magadha, and between Magadha and Anga. Initially, it was Kasi which was powerful, deriving its strength not merely from its rich agriculture, crafts, and river trade but also from its importance as one of the most important communication nodes of India. Kosala had certain advantages too. Geographically it covered a larger area than Kasi and had also a major route—the one to north Bihar from the upper Ganga valley—passing through it. It also had access to the Nepalese tarai belt and beyond. Anga is basically lineally arranged along the Ganga and backed by the Kharagpur hills and the Rajmahal hills. Communication-wise, it controls both riverine and overland connections with the lower part of the Ganga-Bhagirathi plain.

The Expansion of the Magadhan Power

What matters most is that Magadha became powerful not merely at the expense of these three states in its peripheries but also at the expense of many other states of north India. One cannot say that the picture of Magadhan expansion or the way in which it attained pan-Indian supremacy even before the Mauryas is at all clear in the historical sources. The consolidation of its power in Kasi, Kosala, north Bihar, and Anga was possibly already accomplished under the Haryanka dynasty or the dynasty represented by, among others, Bimbisara and Ajatasatru. The succeeding Sisunaga dynasty destroyed the power of Avanti which became strong after annexing the Vatsa kingdom. The Nanda dynasty which succeeded the Sisunagas continued the programme of Magadhan expansion, and as we have earlier noted, under Mahapadma Nanda they became hugely successful.

In the absence of a clear historical knowledge, one can make only assumptions regarding how Magadha under its various early dynasties expanded its power. One would assume that they initially took control of the belt from Anga to Avanti, making it the base of their movement into Gujarat and the Deccan. Possibly simultaneously they moved up the Ganga and established themselves in the Delhi-Haryana-Panjab sector. From their possession of Anga, it was also not difficult to take control of the region from Bengal to Orissa.

The expansion of Magadhan power in the pre-Mauryan phase is one of the imponderables of Indian history because its specific historical circumstances are virtually unknown. Comments such as that Magadha had access to more iron because it bordered the Chhotanagpur plateau are a bit juvenile in the sense that there were many other political groupings in India of that period, which had equally, if not greater, access to iron and other mineral sources. Kasi itself is a convenient example, located, as it is, in the neighbourhood of such early iron-producing sites as Malhar near Chakia and Raja Nal Ka Tila near Robertsganj.

It is unfortunate that the sources are silent about the details of the consolidation and expansion of Magadhan power. The Mauryans added the area from the Indus valley to the southern slope of the Hindukush to it, but the rest of the Mauryan territory was the result of the Magadhan might of the earlier 200 years. Spread over about 200 years, it was no doubt a slow process but in a sense it marked the logical culmination of the historical geographical picture that we see in the earlier period—an open sweep from the north-west to the eastern end of the Ganga plain with close links with the Malwa, western India, eastern coast, and the Deccan. The question why Magadha had come to enjoy a geopolitical edge over the other contemporary political units during this long period is not clear. There is absolutely no reason to infer that Magadha had any material advantage over her contemporaries but it was advantageously placed in relation to its neighbours in east India—its location on the Ganga along with an easy accessibility to the resources of the large Chhotanagpur plateau and the Kaimurs and the routes which passed through them and along the Ganga and the Son to Bengal and Orissa on the one hand and the Banaras region on the other. Once Magadha established its control over its eastern neighbours, it must have converted itself into a formidable military force because of its control of trade passing through the Bengal and Orissan littoral and its territorial possession of Banaras which was the terminal point of the trade coming from as number of directions including the Deccan, Malwa, and the areas up the Ganga. Whatever it is, the continuous rise in the power of Magadha for about 200 years before the Mauryas and the fact that this power remained stable and undisputed for roughly another 150 years under them must remain as a major imponderable of ancient Indian history. It was only partly matched in later years by the power of the Guptas, the Palas, and the brief flicker of the reign of Sher Shah Suri, but as a geopolitical force Magadha between the sixth and the second centuries BC remained unrivalled throughout the history of eastern India. Once the Mauryans came to power, they had control of most of the Konkan, Orissan, Bengal, and Andhra coasts, and through their possessions of southern Afghanistan, NWFP, Kashmir, and Nepal they fully controlled the Indian section of the contemporary trading world of West and Central Asia including the trans-Himalayan trade.

Needless to say, they had complete control of the mineral sources of the subcontinent except in its southernmost segment. We do not think that during the phase of pre-Mauryan Magadhan expansion, the geopolitical orbits which we enunciated earlier changed very much. Gujarat, the Deccan, Bengal, and Orissa must have moved into the orbit, but one can assume them to have been the extension of different sections of the earlier orbits.

The Achaemenids in the Indus-Oxus Orbit

The configuration of states that we have for India of the phase of 'sixteen major principalities' does not prepare us for the Achaemenid annexation of India up to the Indus valley. Of these states, only Gandhara and Kamboja are mentioned in the north-west but they mark only a relatively small part of the Indus valley and the territory to its north-east. The status of the areas lower down the valley in Panjab and Sindh during that period is unknown. In fact, the list and distribution of the political units as mentioned by the Buddhist and Jaina sources gives no indication of the role the Oxus-Indus orbit is going to play soon afterwards in Indian history.

The Achaemenid appearance is somewhat sudden in the historical record. Even the Achaemenid sources do not bear the details of how the region was annexed and if the annexation was done in view of any previous historical linkage with the area. Like the Magadhan expansion, this also remains a geopolitical enigma of ancient Indian history. At the same time, once it was annexed, the Achaemenids apparently took some care in integrating it with their overall administrative framework of the satrapies or administrative provinces. The tradition that Darius employed a Greek to explore the Indus shows that he was keen on fully exploring the geographical possibilities of the valley. As the Achaemenids were in control of the entire area between the Oxus and the Indus, they must have taken enough care to develop the linkages between its geographical components. One doubts if the Achaemenids suppressed the formation of small territorial units or groups of people in their Indian possessions because otherwise it was unlikely that the historians accompanying Alexander would have noticed so many territorial units all over the north-west, Panjab, and Sindh. That their geographical control over the annexed territory was clear and firm is also suggested by the sense of purpose and ease with which Alexander took his army successively from place to place. The area was not geographically unfamiliar.

We are not sure if we can look at the Oxus-Indus orbit in the subcontinent as a homogeneous geopolitical orbit. This is most unlikely to be the case because each of its components has its own geographical orientations. For example, if the hill valleys to the north-east of Peshawar were geared more to trade across the Pamirs with Central Asia, the area near Karachi would focus more on links with Iran and south Afghanistan across the Baluchistan valleys. For the region as a whole, the following alignments are clear. The valleys like Swat, Dir, Bajaur, and Buner are oriented towards Gilgit and Hunza on the one hand and towards Chitral on the other. The Gilgit-Hunza alignment will move across the Karakoram and the Pamirs. The Chitral alignment can also lead towards the Karakoram, but north-east Afghanistan is more easily and somewhat directly approachable from Chitral. Gilgit and Hunza also bring Kashmir within easy reach, and through Kashmir, Ladakh from where routes crossed the Karakoram or went to Tibet. In the Peshawar segment and in the entire hilly area below it including Kohat and Bannu, the focus is on keeping links with Afghanistan, which one can do through a host of passes. The same is true of Baluchistan which is separated from the Indus by the Suleiman-Kirthar hill rampart but there are gaps across this rampart, and from Sindh, movements to and from Afghanistan have never been a problem. While looking east, in the direction of the Indus and beyond, from the hilly border area, one line of movement would be across the Indus and the Rawalpindi area till the Salt range is crossed for the road to Lahore and Delhi. Another major line would emanate from the Gomal valley entrance from where the road would go past Multan and Bahawalpur to reach the Rajasthan-Haryana alignment to Delhi. From lower Sindh, one could cross the desert for Rajasthan or Gujarat or come up to Bahawalpur to join the Multan-Bahawalpur-Hissar alignment to Delhi. What we are trying to say is that the Oxus-Indus orbit within the territorial limit of the subcontinent had its sub-orbits whose importance fluctuated according to the historical forces affecting them. However, on the basis of the historical information that we have on this region in the early context, it is impossible to have any worthwhile information on these sub-orbits.

The Mauryan Domain

Possibly what has turned out to be somewhat detrimental to the Asokan studies is the propensity to read everything related to the Mauryan kingdom of his time in his inscriptions. These inscriptions had the specific purpose of preaching *Dhamma* to the people at large, and whatever historical information they contain is basically incidental. For instance, the fact that the Kalinga war deeply disturbed him does not necessarily imply that the Mauryan state ran itself on entirely peaceful lines before or after that. The geopolitical orbit which emerges with the very foundation of the Mauryan dynasty was the inner Indian orbit based in the Ganga plain, Central India, the Deccan, and the coastal tracts, which during this period has the added feature of incorporating the whole eastern chunk of the Oxus-Indus orbit up to the foot of the Hindukush and thus reversing the trend that we witnessed during the phase of Achaemenid and Greek occupations. It seems probable that Kalinga remained its only major gap, which Asoka had to fill up even at the cost of a major war. Previously we have pointed out that Kalinga was the meeting point of two routes going to the south along the east coast. Our assessment is that this vast orbit which emerged after the Mauryan victory in the Kalinga war not at the expense of smothering all regional identities within the kingdom. Asoka himself mentions groups of people with regional identities in his Rock Edicts (cf. RE V) and in his MRE I at Panguraria, he refers to the area as a geographical area having its own name—*Monema desa*. This denoted a small area, possibly not larger than the jungle area between the modern Bhopal area and the Narmada near Hosangabad. However, in the royal record this had a distinct name, and on the all-India level there must have been many small but recognized territories of this kind. The point is that the Mauryan grip over such diversely located territorial formations could not always be maintained peacefully. We have earlier argued that the south Afghanistan frontier and the frontier that lay at the edge of the Deccan plateau in Karnataka were unlikely to be entirely peaceful frontiers, and this is the reason why both these areas had more than their normal shares of edicts.

One of the questions we cannot even try to answer is why the Mauryan territory stopped expanding south of Chitradurg. The modern Mysore tract must have been the Mauryan frontier zone on this side. The edicts fully respect the separate political identities of the four southern states which between themselves cover the whole of the south up to the tip of the peninsula. It is possible that the shape of this frontier was laid down before the Mauryas, and after the Kalinga war, there was apparently no inclination on the part of Asoka to annex them by force.

Strictly speaking, it was during the Mauryan times that one can trace the already formed character of a separate geopolitical orbit in the south. It is quite interesting that the Sangam literature—whatever may be its date—consistently refers to the interaction between the four southern states only within this broad orbit and never outside it. It is also interesting that the area of modern Mysore and the southern Konkan coast does not quite lie within this orbit. Southern Konkan tends to get absorbed within the Deccanese influence whereas the Mysore tract seems to be a kind of 'divide' between the Deccan and the south. K.A.N. Sastri has tried to isolate a literary tradition which suggests that the Mauryas at one point tried to intercede in favour of a particular king contending for supremacy in the south. The tradition is embedded in the Sangam literature, and considering that the tradition is taken seriously by a scholar of the stature of K.A.N. Sastri, it may very well reflect a true event of history.

Further, our argument that the Brahmaputra valley and south-east Bengal up to the Chattagram coast were incorporated in the Mauryan territory is based purely on the geographical premise that with Mahasthangarh and the Pundra territory, of which it was the capital, under their control, there was absolutely nothing which would have prevented the Mauryan movement to the Brahmaputra valley, especially when the Karatoya, on the bank of which Mahasthangarh is located, is considered the traditional boundary of Assam. Similarly, the occupation of the Pundra territory would also have opened up for the Mauryas the entire south-eastern zone of Bengal.

Our argument is that the data on the political history of ancient India are far from being comprehensive and detailed—what we have basically on even the important dynasties is only a brief range of highly limited and fragmented evidence—and we are unlikely to come close to the historical reality unless we are ready to examine the geographical implications of the actual spread of this evidence.

Regarding Mauryan India we have also made a few other major geographical conclusions. We have tried to pinpoint the location of the battle of Kalinga in the light of our geographical perception of the situation in view of the later but somewhat similar march of Samudragupta along the Andhra coast to south India. Regarding the locations of Isila and Suvarnagiri we have pointed out the limitations of the present hypotheses regarding their locations and argued that Isila was possibly located at Chandravalli and that Sannati was Suvarnagiri.

Two other geographical implications of Mauryan India need high-lighting. There is no direct archaeological evidence but the Buddhist tradition records that Asoka sent missionaries of Buddhism both to Sri Lanka which is mentioned in one of his edicts as *Tamraparni* and the Malayan peninsula and the adjoining parts of modern Indonesia known in the early literature as *Suvarnabhumi*. Further, we feel that the location of Wari Bateswar at the mouth of the Brahmaputra river as early as *c*. 450 BC is partly explainable by its development as a port in relation to India's maritime trade with South-East Asia. The point is that in view of Asoka's sending of Buddhist missionaries to South-East Asia and Sri Lanka in the third century BC and the coming into existence of a port settlement in the Brahmaputra mouth as early as *c*. 450 BC, it is perfectly sensible to argue that India's contact with South-East Asia can be taken back to the period *c*. 500–*c*. 300 BC, if not somewhat earlier. On the other hand, the background of the Mauryan period of contact with Sri Lanka deserves some thought. How far back can one trace it in time? One would suggest that it should be as early as the beginning of the early historic period in south India, which, as has been argued elsewhere, is about 500 BC. We further suggest that the pearl fishery off the coast of the Gulf of Mannar could be one of the attractions for which the Mauryan India would be keen on maintaining contacts with that region, possibly even by sea. It is also possible that the Buddhist missionaries sent by Asoka to Sri Lanka went there by sea.

As we understand it, the cessation of violent warfare by the Mauryan state after the Kalinga war does not necessarily mean that the running of the state, especially on its borders, could be an entirely peaceful affair. We have argued that in the cases of south Afghanistan and south Karnataka this is unlikely to have been the case. Thoughts of the later history of both these areas suggest that these frontiers were likely to have been the grounds of constant political unrest as they have been through most of their documented history. We have suggested that the concentration of Asokan edicts in both these areas may imply some amount of unrest in these regions.

By no stretch of imagination can the Mauryan state be considered a weak state. Whatever historical evidence we have—a chain of edicts from one end of the kingdom to the other, the rigorous municipal administration of Pataliputra and the well-ordered general administration of the kingdom as evidenced by Megasthenes, the keenness to maintain an absolute royal control of the resources of the state in Kautilya's *Arthasastra*—suggests that the strength of the Mauryan kingdom was the result of a close understanding of the geography of the land. So the examination of the geographical nuances is quite important for its historical understanding.

The Interaction between the Gangetic and Indus-Oxus Orbits—from the Greeks and Indo-Greeks to the Kushanas

The Mauryan disintegration witnessed developments on a number of fronts. With the consolidation of the power of the Greeks and Indo-Greeks up to the entire stretch of the Indus valley, the Oxus-Indus orbit comes back very much into its own, but it may be noted that north Afghanistan drops out of this orbit during the phase of the Indo-Greeks just as it was not a part of this in relation to India during the Mauryan times. The Parthian intrusion seems to be too short to have any wider ramification, and the Scythians, after leading a brief political existence on their own, survive mainly in the shadow of the power of the Kushana kings, but in Gujarat, Malwa, and north Deccan they become powerful and independent after the Kushana power became weak. It is under the Kushanas that the Oxus-Indus orbit becomes important again almost in its entirety in Indian history. More than that, for the first three centuries AD this orbit seems to have controlled large chunks of the Gangetic valley.

It is important to note that the Gangetic orbit retained some individuality of its own even when it was being subjected to raids by the Greeks and Indo-Greeks or being territorially annexed by the Kushanas. Immediately after the Mauryan rule, the Ganga plain-Malwa segment falls in the lap of the Sungas and the Kanvas. Their control of the Deccan and Vidarbha as the inheritors of the Mauryan power does not seem to be clear, but in the inner orbit of the Ganga plain and Malwa they keep the old power structure alive. Further, as the large groupings of coins of pre-Christian and early Christian eras all over the Himalayan, Panjab, Rajasthan, Malwa, and the upper part of the Gangetic belt demonstrate, the minor territorial groupings of Gangetic India continued to survive in their own ways even in the shadow of the Kushanas and their Kshatrapas.

The centralized structure of the Kushana rule cannot, however, be doubted. From their base at Peshawar in the north-west they could control their possession of the entire Oxus-Indus orbit including Panjab and Sindh. At Mathura, they were conveniently placed to exert control in the eastern direction of the Ganga plain and also towards Rajasthan and Malwa. Gujarat was accessible both from Sindh and Malwa. It is not at all clear how in the shadow of such a well-defined paramountcy as that exercised by the Kushanas, local powers which were strong enough to issue coins in their names could lie dormant all over north India. These powers are in some cases thought to have come up in the wake of the Sunga decline. They lay dormant during the Kushana rule, but came back into their own after this rule became weak. It is also possible that they maintained their individualities even during the Kushana period. One of the possible explanations is that the Kushana paramountcy did not believe in interfering with the local forces as long as they did not interfere with the central structure of Kushana supremacy. Scholars usually put the powers which issued these coins under the rubric 'northern India after the Kushanas', but this is not strictly correct because a good many of them date in their earliest from the late centuries BC and continue to occur till the advent of the Guptas in the AD fourth century. The possibility that the coins issued in the names of the Kushana kings and those issued by the so-called 'tribal republics' and local kings were in circulation at the same time cannot be denied altogether.

The Emergence of Regional Political Foci—Orissa, the Deccan, Malwa, Gujarat, Sindh, and Parts of Rajasthan

The most distinctive aspect of the geo-politics of post-Mauryan India up to c. AD 300 is not the nature of interaction between the Oxus-Indus and Gangetic orbits but the emergence of Orissa, the Deccan, Malwa, Gujarat, Sindh, and parts of Rajasthan as distinct political foci. In Orissa, Kharavela carved out a kingdom whose outline makes good sense in geographical terms. In the Deccan, the Satavahanas satisfactorily filled the political void left by the Mauryas. In Gujarat, Sindh, and parts of Rajasthan, the Saka Satraps ruled on their own and fought with the Satavahanas for the control of Malwa and north Deccan. Except the rather brief but forceful expression of Orissa as a regional identity under Kharavela, this is basically Malwa-Gujarat-Deccan-Konkan coast orbit, with the adjacent tracts like Rajasthan added to it. This orbit seems to add a new dimension to the political fabric of ancient India. In various times there could be sub-orbits in this zone; we have cited the case of the Abhiras in northern Maharashtra during this period.

More importantly, with their ambitions in Malwa and Gujarat thwarted by the Sakas, the Satavahanas sought new grounds all over the Deccan (Maharashtra, Andhra, and Karnataka), Vidarbha, south Kosala, and the Konkan and Andhra coasts. In a sense, this is the southward and eastward extension of the Deccan-Malwa orbit. This is a vast orbit and it is natural that with time a few sub-orbits would emerge out of it. South Kosala, Vidarbha, Andhra coast, Bellary, north Kanara, Belgaum and Dharwar of Karnataka, the Konkan coast north of Karwar would all emerge as foci of regional powers in the late and post-Satavahana political scenario. What is important is that the geopolitical focus shifted considerably away from the Gangetic and Oxus-Indus orbits in the post-Mauryan political scene, and this happened primarily under the Satavahanas. The contrast between the Saka Satrapas of Gujarat-Malwa-Rajasthan orbit and the Satavahanas is that the Satavahanas, once their ambition towards the north was thwarted by the Sakas, fully exploited the geographical possibilities of Vidarbha, south Kosala, Konkan coast, Andhra coast, and the vast stretch of the Deccan plateau in Andhra, south Maharashtra, and Karnataka.

Although we have followed in our historical narrative D.C. Sircar's chronology for the Satavahanas, that is, they came up in the first century BC, we readily admit the possibility of their power being manifest immediately in the wake of the Maurya disintegration in the early second century BC. The argument is that the Sungas do not seem to have a clear presence either in Vidarbha or in the Deccan, and one has to envisage a kind of power vacuum in the immediately post-Mauryan phase in these regions unless we are ready to put the Satavahanas in the arena early in the second century BC. This date was championed by scholars like V.V. Mirashi and K. Gopalachari.

One would offer more or less the same argument for a second century BC dating for Kharavela. If he is put in the first century BC on a not very strongly argued palaeographic ground, we have a clear gap of more than a 100 years in Orissan political history after the end of the Mauryas. Whatever may be the verdict on Kharavela's conquest of Magadha—I would say that geographically, it might not have been easy for Kharavela to lead an army to Magadha across the Chhotanagpur plateau—but his thrusts down the coast to Andhra and across western Orissa to south Kosala and Vidarbha show his complete understanding of the geopolitical possibilities of the Orissan region.

It is not generally perceived that the Satavahana control, at the heyday of their power, of the whole area from Malwa to Bellary including the Andhra and Konkan coasts made them an uncommonly strong political power of the day in Indian history. This is one of the richest trading zones of the subcontinent and has in addition a lot of natural resources in the form of rocks, minerals, and timber. Simply by virtue of their position athwart the trade routes which passed through the area between south Kosala and the Konkan coast, they must have wielded a lot of influence on the contemporary economic history of the subcontinent.

The territory controlled by the Satavahanas develops geopolitical orbits of its own after the Satavahana break-up. Vidarbha is controlled by the Vakatakas who soon develop two power bases in the region, one around Nagpur and the other around Basim. South Kosala also falls under the Vakataka influence. The Krishna valley of Andhra goes to the Ikshvakus, and in the Machlipatnam area of Andhra one finds the Brihatphalayan dynasty. The Pallavas by the end of the AD third century extend their control up to Bellary in south Deccan. North Konkan comes to be ruled by the Abhiras and in south Konkan the Chutu Satavahanas establish themselves. South Maharashtra around Kolhapur develops a power base of its own. The once-homogeneous Satavahana scenario is now fragmented and highlights the sub-orbits which from now on will make repeated appearances in historical record.

The political history of India may seem to be unduly complex between c. 200 BC, the rough chronological point of the Mauryan downfall, and c. AD 300, the period before the Gupta dynasty's ascendancy. However, there are some clearly discernible geographical patterns in this otherwise complex history. Although we have summarized its broad trends in the previous section, it might be useful to highlight its points briefly once more.

The first of these patterns is the re-emergence of the Oxus to the Indus interaction zone. However, it did not take place in its pristine undivided character as it happened under the Achaemenids and Alexander. Its component units became important by themselves—Parthia or north-east Iran and its adjoining region under the Parthians, Seistan under the Scythians or the Sakas, and Bactria under the Greeks. Eventually the focus shifted to the Indo-Greeks of south Afghanistan and the Indus valley. However, under the Kushanas the region as a whole came into historical prominence. More than that, there was steady thrust towards, and grip of, a large section of the Ganga valley up to Banaras and even beyond. The earlier Greeks and Indo-Greeks, Parthians, and Scythians all tried to create wedges in the area abutting Panjab and Sindh, and especially in the Ganga plain, but they were not successful in doing so in the long run. The Kushanas were highly successful in this regard. Geopolitically they forced open all barriers between Central Asia and possibly the furthest end of the Ganga valley. This is something which did not happen before, and although short-lived, this created a vigorous political and economic world covering Central Asia, Afghanistan, Kashmir, the Pamirs, the Karakoram, the Indus valley as a whole, and the Ganga valley which was possibly ruled from Mathura or the Mathura-Banaras area. Malwa and Gujarat must also have been the parts of this network. What is also interesting is that the Saka satraps ruled on behalf of their Kushana overlords vast areas of the Ganga plain, Malwa, Gujarat, and Sindh. Even when the Kushanas were on the decline, these satraps retained their identity and political dominance.

This first pattern is well understood. What is not so clearly understood is the way in which some regional territorial formations continued to function, despite the existence of the supra-regional forces of the Kushanas and their satrapal representatives, in parts of the Ganga valley from Mathura to Ayodhya, and parts of Panjab-Haryana, Rajasthan, and Malwa. A clear understanding of this phenomenon will depend on a closely nuanced chronological framework of these areas, but on the whole, the trend of the evidence seems to be clear enough and lends strength to our hypotheses that the large orbits of interaction, as shown by the emergence of supra-regional political powers, are not the only foci of ancient Indian geo-politics and that these supra-regional foci are always held up by regional territorial formations.

Another feature of the political geography of post-Mauryan northern India is the ease with which the power of the Sunga dynasty lay confined to the middle and upper sections of the Ganga plain and eastern Malwa, repeating in a sense one of the earliest sweeps of political history of India—the Ganga plain and Malwa. It is a different matter that the Sungas could not withstand the repeated but short-lived thrusts of the Greeks and Indo-Greeks towards both Malwa (through Rajasthan) and the Ganga valley (Ayodhya and the Fatehpur area).

The Orissan coast and hinterlands emerge as a clear historical geographical entity during this period, and I, for one, find no special argument to put Kharavela in the first century BC, although the general scholarly consensus appears to support this date. One is not sure if there was a political vacuum in the region after the Mauryas; otherwise a date in the second century BC would suit Kharavela fine. It appears that the clear distinction between Kalinga and Odra disappears during this phase; Kharavela's styling himself 'lord of Kalinga' seems to be significant in this regard. However, his military movements towards Andhra (along the coast), Vidarbha (through the Raipur sector), and Magadha (possibly through the Chhotanagpur plateau or through the Gangetic West Bengal) defined the position of Orissa in the dynastic power struggles in the region.

There is also no particular reason why the beginning of the Satavahanas has to be put in the first century BC or even later, leaving a post-Mauryan political vacuum of more than a 100 years in the Deccan. With the induction of the Satavahanas in the scene, Malwa, Gujarat, and north Deccan became parts of a constantly interacting orbit, which came to incorporate the much larger area of Sindh, Gujarat, Malwa, east Rajasthan, parts of west Rajasthan, and north Maharashtra including the north Konkan coast in the first three centuries AD. This development was primarily due to the Saka satraps of Sindh, Gujarat, and western Malwa and in this sense its formation owed itself to the impact of the Oxus-Indus stretch where the Saka Satraps of Sindh originated in the first place. What is important to note is that this orbit is completely unrelated to the Gangetic orbit. We have also pointed out that this vast orbit developed in time a few sub-orbits of its own—north Maharashtra and Gujarat mainland, parts of south-east Rajasthan and west Rajasthan, and north Maharashtra itself.

The Sub-Orbits of the Satavahana Domain—Maharashtra, Andhra, and Karnataka

With the Satavahana ambition thwarted in the northern direction by the Saka satraps, they developed another vast non-Gangetic orbit of their own—Maharashtra (both Vidarbha and the Deccan including the coast), Andhra (both the coast and the Deccan hinterland), and Karnataka (the coast and southern Deccan). This is basically the Satavahana domain outside Malwa, and as I have pointed out, this basically defined the geopolitical identity of the Deccan and the related areas of Vidarbha, Chhattisgarh, and the Krishna-Godavari delta in the Satavahana and post-Satavahana contexts. Once the homogeneity of the Satavahana rule was over, this orbit as a whole had developed a number of sub-orbits, two of which—one identifying the Vakataka territory from Bundelkhand to Hyderabad, and the other identifying the Ikshvaku territory of the Krishna-Godavari delta—are important, in addition to a host of other lesser orbits in the Konkan coast (the Chutu and Kuntala territories), southern Maharashtra (the Kura territory around Kolhapur), south Kosala or Chhattisgarh (the Satavahana successors), northern Maharashtra (the territory of the Abhiras and the Bodhis), and so on.

By dominating the area from Bundelkhand to Vidarbha, and the Ajanta area, west of Vidarbha, the Vakatakas came to dominate a large part of the routes from the Ganga plain to the Deccan which came via Bundelkhand and reached Vidarbha on the way to Andhra on the one hand and the Ajanta-Aurangabad section on the other. The Vakataka domination of the region must have given it considerable geopolitical significance. Although on a lesser scale, the formation of the Abhira kingdom in the Nasik area of north Deccan was significant because the route which came to the Deccan from Malwa came first to north Deccan, with one of its branches going to the west coast ports. The geopolitical significance of the area was also reflected in the local formation of a new dynasty—the Bodhi dynasty—after the Abhiras. At the southern end of the Konkan coast, the Kuntala territory comprising north Kanara, Belgaum, and Dharwar controlled not merely the sea-borne trade of this area but also the trade which was going from the coast to the interior of the Deccan across the Western Ghats. The Kadambas come into limelight first in the Kuntala territory and later expanded up the Konkan coast to the Goa area and above, posing a threat to the power of the Abhiras further north.

Going by the distribution of their inscriptions, the Ikshvakus controlled the Krishna valley in Andhra, especially the Amaravati-Nagarjunakonda-Jaggayayapeta section which along with the coastline of the region was the most significant historical part of Andhra. The importance of the Ikshvakus no doubt derives from their control of this important trading zone. The commercial significance of this area is also the reason why the Pallavas wanted to extend their control up the Andhra coast to the Krishna valley from their admittedly inland base of Kanchipuram. When the Pallavas established their control in the Krishna valley by the early AD fourth century, they came to dominate the coastline from Mamallapuram to the Krishna mouth. When one thinks, along with this, the facts that they also extended their control up to Bellary in south Deccan and to the Kuntala territory, one realizes that the Pallavas dominated at one point a large part of the trade which came in and went out of the Deccan both by land and sea. In any case, the historical significance of the Machlipatan sector of the Andhra coast is also apparent from the fact that after the Ikshvakus a new dynasty—the Brihatphalayana dynasty—came up in the area.

When one looks at the geopolitical orbits of these post-Satavahana dynasties in the former Satavahana territory, one realizes that much of their significance derives from their locations on some major sections of the trade routes and trading zones, all of which basically developed during the Satavahana times and earlier. The very appearance of these dynasties in these areas is a geopolitical indication of the fact that the trade over this region had not declined after the Satavahanas.

The Gangetic-Malwa Orbit under the Guptas

The re-assertion of the Gangetic-Malwa orbit touching the Indus, Gujarat, and the Vindhyas under the Guptas must be considered something of a surprise too, because between the end of the Mauryas and the rise of the Guptas, that is, for about 500 years between c. 200 BC and c. AD 300, the Gangetic heartland and all its related areas were open to repeated thrusts and occupations by sundry powers based in the Oxus-Indus orbit—the Greeks, Indo-Greeks, Scythians, Parthians, and the Kushanas. They were no doubt Indianized to a large extent but the ease with which they could successfully attack and control even the eastern parts of the valley and all corners of the rich agricultural plain of Malwa is a poor reflection on the contemporary powers of inner India. That is why the expansion of Gupta dynastic power from Pataliputra to the border of south-east Bengal on the one hand and to the Indus, Gujarat, and the Vindhyas on the other, which took place basically in two reigns—those of Samudragupta and Chandragupta II—makes one wonder about the source of political and military strength Magadha of the AD fourth century. In a sense, this followed the pattern of the first Magadhan expansion—a sweep up the valley to the Delhi area and beyond, and another sweep through Malwa to Gujarat. The nine north Indian kings who figure in the Allahabad *Prasasti* composed by Harisena as the kings whose territories were annexed by the Guptas belong precisely to the upper Gangetic plain and Malwa. From this base, it was easy for Chandragupta II to extend the kingdom's limits to the Indus and Gujarat. Further, among the nine north Indian kings of the Allahabad *Prasasti*, Chandravarman has been identified with the king of the Pokharna area of modern Bankura. This was a kingdom in south-western Bengal and by annexing it, Samudragupta came to control the route to the Orissan coast through south-western Bengal.

What is not so clearly understandable is the reason of Samudragupta's long thrust towards the south. To send a conquering army from Pataliputra to Kanchipuram through south Kosala, Kalinga, and the entire Andhra coast was an incredible feat of arms and is in every sense reminiscent of the sending of Mauryan army to Kalinga. As the Gupta army did not stop in Kalinga but had to negotiate about 1000 km of the Andhra coast, defeating kings all the way to Kanchipuram, Samudragupta accomplished a more difficult feat of arms. We do not know why Samudragupta undertook such a campaign to the south because the Allahabad *Prasasti* is silent on the background of this campaign. The fact that the Gupta army followed an age-old trade route of the land to reach Kanchipuram from Pataliputra shows that by the AD fourth century, this route was so much open and understood that the king of Magadha had no hesitation to send his army along it. On the other hand, the very fact that such an army went up and down this route must have brought about a considerable rejuvenation of the trade links along this way. Raychaudhuri speculates why the Allahabad *Prasasti* does not mention the Vakatakas whom the Gupta army would have encountered if its route lay through Vidarbha. The point is that the Gupta army came first to south Kosala or the modern Chhattisgarh area and went straight to the Vizianagram area from there. It did not have to pass through the Vakataka territory. It is also possible that the campaign was undertaken to establish some Gupta control over the trade emanating from the long Kalinga and Andhra coast line. That the Gupta king was not completely ignorant of the importance of having maritime contacts is suggested by his relationship with the contemporary king Meghavarna of Sri Lanka and what has been called in the Allahabad *Prasasti* as 'all other dwellers in the islands'. These islands were in all probability the islands of South-East Asia. It is also obvious from this casual reference to 'all other dwellers in the islands' that the Gupta power, unlike the Cholas, Cheras, Pandyas, and even the Pallavas of the south, were exclusively land-based power. To undertake an active interest in the affairs of the sea and the lands beyond it was beyond their thought. The southern dynasties were unique among the Indian dynasties in the sense that all of them had actively interacted at least with Sri Lanka, and in the case of the Cholas this maritime orbit could extend up to South-East Asia.

If Samudragupta was satisfied with proceeding up to Vidisa in eastern Malwa, Chandragupta II wrested control of western Malwa and Gujarat from the Saka satraps and gave, so to speak, the Gupta possessions in central and west India their natural boundary. The claim of the Meherauli iron pillar inscription that Chandragupta proceeded victoriously as far as Bahlika or Bactria in north Afghanistan is apparently an exaggerated claim. The Gupta boundary during the time of Samudragupta came up to the Indus. To march from the Indus and travel across the Hindukush to north Afghanistan would hardly have served the Gupta king any purpose and possibly made it weaker. The strength of the Gupta kingdom is obvious from the fact that Skandagupta, Chandragupta II's grandson, could defeat the Hunas and keep them at bay.

It appears that the Malwa-Gujarat stretch was proving to be a difficult area for the Guptas to control after Skandagupta. It is precisely in this stretch that one can trace the existence of local powers by the end of the AD fifth century—the Maitrakas of Gujarat, and a few minor kings of the Vindhyan and Narmada belts—nothing serious except that the Gupta hold of the area was getting weak. The emergence of small powers in the modern Satna-Kalinjar-Banda segment is interesting and suggests the significance of this zone as a way of entry to the Ganga valley. The emergence of a local power around Mahishmati on the Narmada may underline the traditional significance of this zone as a major crossing point of the Narmada.

In the first part of the AD sixth century, the Hunas knocked at the door. Toramana, the Huna chief, controlled the territory from Panjab to Eran in east Malwa, and his son Mihirakula controlled possibly a larger area from Kashmir and Panjab to at least Gwalior. In a sense, the Oxus-Indus orbit enters the picture again in the form of the Hunas. It is interesting that the Huna thrust did not come down the Ganga-Yamuna corridor but followed the route to Malwa from Panjab through Rajasthan.

When the Maurya power disintegrated, the major new orbit that developed in inner India was the Deccanese orbit under the Satavahanas.

The Post-Gupta Scenario in North India, the Deccan, and the South up to c. Tenth Century

An inordinate amount of historical space is taken up in the post-Mauryan period by the Oxus-Indus orbit which came under a long line of powers ending with the Kushanas. In contrast, what we notice in the wake of the Gupta decline is the growth of a large number of major power centres all over the land. It is apparent that the economic framework of all these areas had become strong enough by this period to permit the local growth of powerful dynasties/states. Instead of a few major orbits we have now many more smaller but nonetheless powerful and interacting orbits. No political unit of the period was content to remain confined to its own nucleus. They interacted with a remarkable frequency and intensity which was not observable in the historical record before. In north India, the orbits which came up in the Gupta aftermath and lasted till roughly AD 800 are the following.

In Gujarat it was the Maitrakas in the Bhavnagar area, from where they could have a better access to the trade in the Gulf of Cambay and the entire stretch of the Kathiawar coast. This was also a position at the junction of Kathiawar with the Gujarat mainland, which was useful to make their power felt in both Gujarat and western Malwa. For the first time Gujarat develops an orbit of its own.

The same is true of the desert tract of Rajasthan around Jodhpur where the Gurjaras carved out a territory, possibly taking advantage of the trade routes which began to pass through the Rajasthan desert from Sindh around this time. The location of the second Gurjara base at Rajpipla may also have something to do both with the coastal trade and its location on the route from the coast to the Burhanpur area of Malwa. There are thus two Gurjara orbits, each with its own links.

In the middle Ganga plain, the Later Guptas had their base at Pataliputra and although the location of the Maukhari capital is uncertain, their main power base seems to be south Bihar. From the location of the Aphsad inscription of the Later Guptas, we infer that their power was oriented towards the modern Kiul-Bhagalpur territory including the Santal Parganas whereas the Maukharis had their base around Gaya. The Gangetic valley of this period was subjected to the attacks on Vanga, Anga, and Magadha by the Chalukyan king Kirtivarman who must have appeared in the region from his base at Badami in the Deccan part of Karnataka. In about this period, the Tibetan king Sron-btsan carried a raid in Bihar and Uttar Pradesh.

In east Bengal there were two small pockets, one around Comilla under Vainyagupta and the second around Kotalipara in Faridpur. In Bengal again, a major power centre developed at Karnasuvarna from where power was exerted as far west as Ganjam in Orissa and Rhotasgarh fort in Bihar. The Kamarupa kingdom of Assam becomes strongly visible during this period and had interacted with the powers based at Thaneswar and Karnasuvarna. It is also during this time that the Mana dynasty appears in the northern section of the Orissan coast and the Sailodbhavas between Chilka and Ganjam.

The upper Ganga plain including Kanauj fell under the domination of the Thaneswar-based power which extended its base not merely to east Panjab and Uttar Pradesh but also to Bihar, Bengal, and Orissa. In its ambition to control Malwa-Rajasthan zone it was checked by a defeat at the hands of the Chalukyan king Pulakesin II.

Looking at the picture as a whole, one is struck no doubt by the proliferation of both large and small power centres, but more than that, one sees the emergence of large geopolitical orbits. For instance, the orbit which was formed under the leadership of Harshavardhana in the first half of the seventh century, covering the entire Ganga valley corridor from Thaneswar and east Panjab to Bengal and then from Bengal to the Ganjam tip of the Orissan coast, may be the first orbit of its kind in Indian history. To begin with, it has a very asymmetrical geography—a broad sweep down the plain and then another sweep along the Orissan coast. More importantly, this was an orbit in which four far-flung powers were involved—the king of Kamarupa, the king of Gauda, the king of Kanauj/Thanewar, and the Chalukyan king of Badami in south Deccan. On the one hand, there is the growth of power centres at places where no power centre existed before, and on the other hand, there is the breaking down of the normal political frontiers. It may be interesting to reflect that none of the players involved in the power structure of the Ganga plain during this period belonged to the Gangetic heartland. Kanauj was not the original base of the kings of Thaneswar; they made it their capital later. All the concerned powers were based in the peripheries, with the Chalukyan power base being far away in the southern Deccan. A classic example of this kind in the eighth century is the tour of conquest of the Kashmir king Lalitaditya Muktapida whom the *Rajatarangini* credits with moving out of his base in Kashmir, Panjab, and the north-west, and undertaking a journey of conquest of virtually the whole of the subcontinent down to Karnataka. Whether true or not, one could have an ideal of venturing far away from one's borders during this time. In the earlier periods too, kings have ventured outside their borders, but by and large that meant stage by stage expansion, as it was in the case of the Mauryas or that of the Guptas.

In the eighth century, there was more proliferation of power centres in Gujarat and Rajasthan and even Bengal. The Gurjaras branch into different lines in Rajasthan, Gujarat, and Malwa. From their south Deccanese base, the Chalukyas moved up to the Lata area or the southern part of the Gujarat mainland coast. In Gujarat, the Chapotkatas set up a new power centre at Patan and in Rajasthan there were new power centres in Mewar, Jhalrapatan-Kota, and around Sakambhari, not far from Jaipur. In Bengal, one gets the name of the new dynasties like the Ratas and Chandras. This was also the period when the Muslim rule got consolidated in Sindh but remained confined broadly to that area for the next 300–400 odd years.

The Deccan between the AD sixth and eighth centuries offers more or less the same fragmented scenario in the sense that there were many new power centres, but, as in the north, it was accompanied by large interacting orbits. Here, the new power centres developed mainly in the ruins of the Vakataka power, which, from their base in Vidarbha controlled a huge territory extending up to south Kanara, Kalinga, and Andhra coasts, the Lata territory of Gujarat, north Konkan, and south Kosala. They were also influential in Bundelkhand. The states which grew up in its ruins were the Nalas of Bastar and south Kosala, the Sarabhapuriyas of south Kosala, the Panduvamsis of Mekala and south Kosala, the Bhojas of Goa, the Traikutakas of north Konkan, the Vishnukundins of Andhra, the eastern Gangas of Kalinga, the Kalachuris and the Chalukyas of south Deccan—to name only a few at random. The larger orbits of interaction were established by the kings like Pulakesin II of the Chalukyas of Badami. This zone took in the whole of modern Karnataka and its coast, Maharashtra and its coast, the southern Gujarat mainland coast, the adjoining areas of western Malwa, the Andhra coast, Kalinga, south Kosala, the Pallava territory, and the territories of the Cholas, Pandyas, and Cheras beyond the Kaveri. In a sense, this is an extraordinarily large orbit, full of diverse geographical configurations, and its significance becomes all the more heightened when one remembers that the political power over this orbit was attempted by a king sitting in south Deccan. On the whole, this set the pattern of subsequent expansions from the Bijapur-Gulbarga-Badami section of the Deccan.

The Pallavas aimed at controlling a more compact kingdom. They wanted the area up to the Kaveri in the south but towards the north they undertook thrusts as far north as Badami on the one hand and the Krishna valley on the other. The Pallava orbit of interaction is a smaller orbit than the one envisaged by the Badami Chalukyas, but it also included Sri Lanka to which they sent expeditions. The orbit of the southern dynasties during this period did not venture far north beyond the Pallava domain of Kanchipuram. Between the Pallavas and the Deccan, there were the western Gangas in the Kolar territory and the Banas in the adjacent area of Andhra.

With their first capital either at Achalpur in Khandesh or western Vidarbha or in the area of Ellora, the Rashtrakutas were advantageously placed to interfere in the affairs of both Malwa, Gujarat, and the Ganga plain. Krishna I cast the shadow of his control over Malwa, Gujarat, and the Konkan coast including its southern section. His successor Dhruva successfully participated in the power struggle between the Gurjara-Pratiharas and the Palas for suzerainty over the throne of Kanauj which by this time had come to symbolize the core area of the Ganga plain. The Rashtrakutas preserved their position in this sector under Dhruva's successor Govinda III who, however, had to contend for power in the Mysore tract (the western Gangas) and the Krishna valley in Andhra (the eastern Chalukyas of Vengi). The Rashtrakuta attempts to control these sectors did not invariably meet with success, but they persevered, and it is possibly because of this southward orientation that their capital was shifted under Amoghavarsha, Govinda's successor, to Manyakhet near Gulbarga. The principal centre of the Mauryas in the entire southern block was Sannati which also is located near Gulbarga.

The Rashtrakuta geopolitical orbit is worth pondering over. On the one hand, they fought repeatedly for the control of the Andhra coast, the territory of the western Gangas and the territories further south, and on the other they tried to keep under control the Gurjara-Pratihara ambitions in Malwa and Gujarat and exert powerful influence in the central Ganga plain around Kanauj. Their ambitions in the Ganga valley included their attempts to control access to it through Kalinjar and Chitrakut. It is a very large orbit but it is this which also excited the attention of the western Chalukyas of Badami, but they were not keen on maintaining a long-term hold in the Ganga valley. The Rashtrakuta concern with the Kalinjar-Banda-Chitrakut area is also striking because of the fact that they used the approach through Jhansi and Kalpi to attack the Ganga valley. The Rashtrakutas could not effectively retain their possessions of the Chola territory, but the significance of their march to Rameshwaram, and their possession of Arcot, Chingleput, and Vellore cannot be denied. This orbit came to be woven around a large complex of routes which linked the Ganga plain with the Deccan. The Gurjara-Pratihara orbit was confined to Gujarat, Malwa, eastern Rajasthan, the Ganga plain around Kanauj, and the approach to the plain through Satna, Kalinjar, and Chitrakut. Eventually their capital was shifted to Kanauj, and from there at least one of the Gurjara-Pratihara kings administered a kingdom which touched Panjab in the north-west, Kathiawar in the west, and possibly the whole of the Oudh territory (including the territory of their feudatories around Gorakhpur) in the east and north-east. They also exerted their power over the Pala territory in north Bengal and south Bihar, although these areas were not parts of their territorial possessions. The direct territorial possessions of the Gurjara-Pratiharas are basically the combined territories of a few *Mahajanapadas* of the sixth century BC India—Kosala, the larger part of Panchala, part of Vatsa, the whole of Akara-Avanti (that is, both eastern and western Malwa), and Saurashtra. At the height of their power under Dharmapala, the Palas of Bengal were paramount over a zone extending from Bengal (if not from Kamarupa) to Gandhara and Avanti.

Apart from these large orbits of power which were undoubtedly pan-Indian in scope, there were various regional orbits in various parts of India, which were built around the basic compulsions of the regional geography. In central India alone there were three such major principalities—the Chandellas of Bundelkhand, the Kalachuris of Tripuri, and the Paramaras of Dhar. The Bundelkhand Agency of British India covered broadly the areas of Hamirpur, Jalaun, Banda, Jhansi, Lalitpur, Chhatarpur, Panna, and Datia. Apart from the rather sparse agricultural tracts, the diamonds of Panna, and the iron ores scattered throughout the area, this hilly and forested zone saw a major route from the Deccan to the Ganga valley passing through it. Its Kalinjar-Ajaigarh-Banda section also gave ready access to the Ganga valley through Satna, Banda, and Chitrakut. The Chandellas had their capital here at Khajuraho and tried to be powerful mostly at the expense of the Kalachuris of Tripuri in the Jubbulpore section. Through Jhansi they could also move easily to eastern Malwa.

The Tripuri base of the Kalachuris gave them control over the Narmada in the sense that the valley up to the area of Hoshangabad is more or less open. Eastward, there is a long and reasonably wide corridor of movement up to Maihar, Satna, and Rewa, and thus to the Ganga valley. Northward, eastern Malwa is accessible through areas like Damoh and Sagar. Southward, there is an easy access to the areas of Mandla, Shahdol, Chhindwara, Seoni, and Balaghat, and thus to south Kosala, Vidarbha, and the adjacent areas. This outlines their interaction area and also explains why the Kalachuris could have a base in south Kosala at Ratanpur near Bilaspur and also why one of their groups could go easily as far east in the Ganga plain as Gorakhpur. The Kalachuris had a fort at Bandhogarh and patronized Saiva monasteries in Rewa, all carrying the implication that the entire jungle belt of central India was under their control.

The Paramaras with their centre at Dhar were quite centrally located in the west Malwa territory from where they could easily approach Gujarat, south-east Rajasthan, and Barwani on the Narmada (for the Deccan). The Paramara political history shows their concern mainly with this zone, that is, the Deccan, Gujarat, and Rajasthan. Among other things, the Paramaras were suitably placed to control the trade routes passing through west Malwa to the Deccan, Gujarat, and Rajasthan. Gujarat and Rajasthan also harbour a number of smaller territorial units during this period, that is, in the AD eighth–tenth centuries—the Saindhava dynasty near Porbandar in west Kathiawar, the Chapa dynasty at the mouth of the Kathiawar peninsula, the Abhiras in southern and western Kathiawar, the Varahas of the Wadhan corridor, the Chalukyas of Patan, and so on. Such a proliferation of Gujarati dynasties, especially in the Kathiawar segment, may connote fresh territorial formations in trade-rich pockets.

This was the time when the Rajasthan-Delhi-Haryana sector was getting divided between the Guhilots of Mewar, the Chahamanas of Sakambhari near Jaipur and various other Chahamana branches, and the Tomars of Delhi and Haryana. This seems to have formed an interaction zone covering the Delhi-Haryana-Rajasthan segment which had trade routes passing through the desertic west Rajasthan for Sindh, through east Rajasthan for Malwa, and through Haryana for Panjab and beyond. It also appears that the entire mineral-rich zone of the Aravalli belt of Rajasthan and the Salt lakes of west Rajasthan came under the control of these political powers.

In the north-west, the Hindu Shahi kingdom ruled both the Kabul valley and parts of Panjab, thus antedating Ranjit Singh's nineteenth century kingdom which flourished in the same area. The Hindu Shahi kingdom also covered the hills and valleys to the north-east of Peshawar and formed more or less a compact kingdom covering the north-western part of the subcontinent and eastern Afghanistan till the foot of the Hindukush. This gave this kingdom a pre-eminent position in the network of the subcontinent's north-western trade. Geopolitically, this also acted as a bulwark against the Muslim thrust in eastern Afghanistan and North Western Frontier for about 150-odd years from *c.* mid-ninth to early eleventh centuries.

The contemporary kings of Kashmir and the kingdoms which by then had been well established in the Himalayan belt from the Panjab hills (modern Himachal Pradesh hills) to the Almorah-Pithoragarh area were essentially confined to their own limited orbits. The trans-Himalayan trade and the trade between the hills and the plain, apart from the timber and mineral wealth of the Himalayan region, must have formed the mainstay of their wealth and power. The Kumaun-Garhwal hills are well known for their richness of copper and iron ores.

Turning to the Andhra coast in the AD ninth century, one finds the eastern Chalukyas of Vengi putting up occasionally successful struggles not merely against their better known contemporaries in the Deccan, the Rashtrakutas, but also against the Pallavas, the Pandyas, the western Gangas of Mysore, and the eastern Gangas of Orissa. What is striking is that at one point they fought against the combined Rashtrakuta-Kalachuri army in the Balaghat area, implying that the entire mass of land between the Narmada and the Andhra coast and Kalinga on the one hand and southern Deccan on the other was during this period one interacting orbit. The area itself can be divided into a large number of segments but at the level of army manoeuvres and struggles between powers the entire belt could be conceived as one unit. One is not sure of the source of the eastern Chalukyan strength. The location in the Andhra coast with easy access to the hinterlands and control over the route to south Kosala which began near Vizianagaram should at least partly be considered the reasons behind the strength of the eastern Chalukyas of Vengi. The eastern Gangas of Kalinga assumed significance only in the early AD eleventh century when Anantavarman Chodaganga came to the throne but till then Kalinga could maintain its distinct geopolitical identity. In south Kosala, the Panduvamsi kings were generally dispossessed of their kingdom by the Kalachuris. Meanwhile, the Somavamsi kings of Orissa controlled at least some parts of south Kosala. In fact, the south Kosala-Orissa zone forms a compact zone of interaction. One may remember that south Kosala had been in the sight of the kings of Orissa since the days of Kharavela.

Before the rise of the Cholas the main contending powers in the south were the Pallavas and the Pandyas. The resource-rich Kongudesa or the Coimbatore-Salem area must have been a major bone of contention, and one occasionally finds the Pallavas controlling territory as far south as Kumbhakonam. When around the middle of the ninth century the Cholas began to rise from their early principality between the north and south Vellar rivers, their main thrust was towards Coimbatore-Salem, and after that they advanced against the western Gangas who had their capital then at Talakkad. They also tried to wrest territory up to Nellore, thus creating a Chola power orbit between Nellore and Cape Comorin. At this stage the Chola ambition was thwarted by the combined strength of the Rashtrakutas and the Pallavas. The Pandyas defeated the Chera kings and pushed as far north-west as Mangalore and generally encountered the hostility of the other south Indian powers which include, somewhat curiously, even Kalinga which lies a great deal up the east coast from Tamil Nadu. One notes that in the territory adjacent to the western Ganga territory in Karnataka a few small territorial units developed during this period—the Nolambas, Banas, Renandus, and Vaidumbas. In south Kanara, the territorial nucleus was known as the territory of the Alupas. One is not sure how these small territorial units came about. In the case of the Alupas, the regional sea trade should have played a role and in the case of southern Deccan including parts of Karnataka and Andhra, their traditional position on the north-south routes may be one of the reasons.

The North and the South, c. Eleventh–Thirteenth Centuries

In the last couple of centuries before passing into the hands of the Muslims, there were some major conflicts in northern India. Apart from the invasion of Bengal by Rajendra Chola in AD 1021, which encountered a large number of political units in the western part of Bengal and thus implied a break-down of the Pala dynastic dominance in that sector, the Kalachuris of Tripuri and the Somavamsi kings of south Kosala had their eyes on the Pala kingdom which was also attacked at one point by the western Chalukyas. The deep south (the Cholas), southern Deccan (the western Chalukyas), the upper Narmada valley (the Kalachuris of Tripuri), and Chhattisgarh (the Somavamsis)—the armies could move from any of these quarters to Bengal. What is interesting is that it is not a question of operating within well-defined geographical orbits any more. It appears that on the dynastic level geographical parameters were getting very fluid during this period.

On the other hand, there was a fair degree of proliferation of small units on the local levels. While trying to win back north Bengal, the Palas had to depend on the help of a number of their feudatories from south Bihar to Hooghly (Bengal). The geographical names which one gets for these feudatories clearly suggest the ongoing process of territorial formations on the local level. It appears that this process is more markedly visible during this period. The combination of political powers is also interesting—the Kalachuris of Tummana or the Bilaspur area ally with the Gahadavalas of Kanauj against the Palas. The fact that Bilaspur and Kanauj are very widely separated was no obstacle to the formation of a political alliance between these two places, and that too against a power which during this phase in any case was based primarily in Bengal. The Sena kings, the successors of the Palas in Bengal, confined their manoeuvres only to north Bihar, Orissa, and Kamarupa, and in south-east Bengal by this time there was the growth of the kingdom of Pattikera. There could be smaller kingdoms elsewhere in east Bengal, such as Sylhet. Smaller principalities came up in Bihar as well, the records being obtained from Mithila, Lakhi sarai, Gaya, and Shahabad. Further north, the formation of the Gahadavala kingdom covering the Ganga plain from above Kanauj to Patna and parts of trans-Sarayu area was a major event, re-asserting the political significance of the Gangetic belt. The smaller kingdoms continued to develop and flourish, as in the Mathura-Bharatpur, Gwalior, and Dubkund-Narwar areas, all in the western fringe of the upper Ganga plain and all linked to the approach to Malwa. The Chandella kings of Bundelkhand were secure in their kingdom between east Malwa and the Panna-Banda sector, but the Kalachuris of Tripuri turned to be far more ambitious. Apart from their interest in Bengal and the territory controlled by the Palas in general, the Kalachuri king Gangeyadeva attacked, although unsuccessfully, the western Chalukyas of the Deccan, and carried inroads into south Kosala and Orissa. Travelling to Orissa through south Kosala from Tripuri was not difficult, even though one had to negotiate a lot of jungle country. Attacking the western Chalukyas of southern Deccan was geographically more ambitious. Equally ambitious was Gangeyadeva's expedition to Kangra. It is difficult to hypothesize about the reason but may have something to do with the possible fame of Kangra as a wealthy place, a fame which later on drew Mahmud of Ghazni to it. Gangeyadeva's successor Karna performed more amazingly, reaching south Kosala and marching down the coast till he could enter Tamil Nadu from the Andhra-Karnataka belt and march till Madura. From this area he also turned his attention to Kerala and south Kanara. In a sense, such army movements in the eleventh century are a clear indication of the fact that the interaction orbits are no longer static but acquired a fluidity of their own.

This is also somewhat true of what the Paramara king Bhoja tried to achieve from his core area in western Malwa. In his case, the ambition was directed principally at the geographically related areas such as northern Maharashtra, Gujarat, and east Rajasthan, but he also went as far as Mukhalingam in Kalinga and attacked south Deccan. One of his successors, Lakshmanadeva, in the twelfth century went to Anga, Gauda, and Kalinga, which was not a problem considering these areas lay one after another on a route by which the Gauda king Sasanka had extended his control up to Kalinga much earlier. However, he also led an expedition to the Kangra valley, in which case the motivation must have been purely of loot. That one of the Paramaras, Vindhyavarman, could attack the Hoyasalas in Karnataka towards the end of the twelfth century is equally amazing. In the wake of the Paramara supremacy in the Malwa-Gujarat-Rajasthan belt, there was a large-scale growth of political units throughout the belt up to Delhi-Haryana. In Gujarat, the Chalukyas of Anahilapataka or Patan proved to be powerful, and in Rajasthan, there were various groups of the Chahamanas, not merely at Sakambhari but also in places like Jodhpur, Jalor, Ajmer, and so on. This was the period when Kashmir extended its control over the Panjab hill-belt and had contacts with the Gahadavalas of the Ganga plain and, more interestingly, the Silaharas of north Deccan. The Chahamanas or the Chauhans with their kingdom in the Delhi-Haryana node gave way to the Muslims in the second battle of Tarain.

South India, c. AD Tenth–Thirteenth Centuries

The south Indian scenario between the AD tenth and thirteenth centuries is generally marked by the old and established power centres.

In south Deccan, which was earlier the base of western Chalukyan and Rashtrakuta powers, the power which emerged was that of the Later Chalukyas with their base at Kalyani. In the north, they interacted with the area up to Gujarat and Malwa. In the south, they tried to control the Mysore tract, and through its control, encountered the Cholas. In north Deccan, they encountered a new power in the shape of the Yadavas around modern Daulatabad near Aurangabad. The southern Konkan coast was an extension of their core area which extended in that direction up to Shimoga. Along the Andhra coast, they tried to extend control up to Vengi. These territorial ambitions naturally brought them into conflict with the Cholas, and although they fared badly in this conflict, they tried to make up for this by undertaking miscellaneous expeditions to Kalinga, the Bastar area, and south Kosala. Meanwhile, there was always a struggle to retain the control of the Konkan coast, especially the Alupa territory of south Kanara.

The Yadavas of Devagiri carved out a kingdom basically between western Vidarbha and south Deccan. Their ambitions further south led them to a conflict with the Hoyasalas in Mysore, and after they took over the Kurnool area of Andhra, they had to encounter resistance from the Kakatiyas of Warangal. After bringing the Kakatiyas to their control, they tried to move in the direction of Orissa. In the north, their forays against Malwa and Gujarat were not effective. In the Konkan coast, they had a fluctuating record of success. In the early fourteenth century, the Yadavas lost their kingdom to the Muslims.

The Kakatiyas ruled at their height a kingdom from the Godavari to the Kaveri and more or less the whole of the modern Andhra from the north to the sea. The location of their power base at Warangal is a clear indication of the fact that the kingdom grew up on the route which came through Vidarbha to the Krishna valley in Andhra. The eastern Gangas and the eastern Chalukyas had their base in Kalinga and the Vengi area respectively. The ambition of the Gangas in the direction of the Andhra coast was not successful but towards the east, under Anantavarman Chodaganga they ruled up to the Bhagirathi/Ganga. The Somavamsis of south Kosala, who came to Orissa after the Kalachuris of Tummana (Bilaspur sector) occupied their territory but gave way to the Gangas.

Throughout the Deccan and also in Bastar and the adjacent tracts there are references to various small principalities which were essentially feudatories of the principal ruling powers of their areas, but the fact that there were small territorial formations in this region during this period deserves notice. The Hoyasalas were pressed between the Chalukyas of south Deccan and the Cholas and Pandyas of the south, but they established themselves in the southern districts of Karnataka and maintained their regional identity well till the fourteenth century when there was a Muslim power at Madura and they were defeated by the Muslims.

The classic Chola kingdom under Rajaraja I ruled the entire south up to the Tungabhadra in the north, the east coast up to Kalinga, the northern part of Sri Lanka, and the Maldives. Under Rajendra I, the control of south India was complete with the complete annexation of the Pandya and Chera territories. In the north, the boundary went up to the Gulbarga area way beyond the Tungabhadra. In the Konkan coast, Banavasi in north Kanara was annexed and in Telangana, the Chola control extended up to Hyderabad. From Kalinga, south Kosala and Bastar could be brought under control, and from Kalinga again, his victorious army marched to Bengal, although without the intention of acquiring any territorial possession in that area. He added the whole of Sri Lanka and the Malaya and Sumatra sections of South-East Asia to the list of the Chola overseas conquests. None of the south Indian powers—the Pandyas, Cheras, and others—came nowhere the prowess of these two Chola kings who demonstrated to the full the geopolitical possibilities of a power based in the Kaveri delta. In contrast, the Pandyas at the height of their power under Sundara Pandya and Kulasekhara Pandya could proceed only up to Nellore and maintain control over the core Chola territory, Kerala, Kongudesa, Kanchipuram area, and Sri Lanka. The contrast with the Cholas at their heyday is striking. Whatever larger territorial ambitions the Hoyasalas had, that was seldom expressed except their trying to keep a hold in the core Chola belt.

Observations on the Ancient Indian Geopolitical Frames from the Early Historical Beginning to the Thirteenth Century

If one looks at the evolving geopolitical scenario of ancient India from its early historical beginning to the beginning of Muslim occupation of the Ganga plain in the AD thirteenth century, one comes away with a few general observations.

For the early period, the sources seldom highlight the areas outside the Ganga plain, but one does feel, even on the basis of rather brief and limited quantity of the textual sources, that the Malwa plateau, the North Western Frontier zone and Panjab, and the Deccan were linked closely with the fortunes of this plain. The story of political interaction is available only for a handful of kingdoms of this phase, but this should not hide the fact that the Deccan, the north-west, and the Malwa plateau were always parts of the early orbit. One remembers the *Suttanipata* reference to the sage Bavari who lived in a hermitage on the bank of the Godavari and asked some of his disciples to travel all the way to Sravasti (and then to Rajagriha) to find out about the Buddha, the new religious person who had then appeared on the scene. One hears of Jivaka, the Buddha's physician, learning his trade at Taxila and coming back to Rajagriha from there. One does not know if the kings were marching along these routes at this early period in search of territorial annexations, but as far as Malwa is concerned, political struggles between Avanti in western Malwa and Vatsa at the edge of the central Ganga plain cannot be denied. In a sense, this early orbit is a pan-India orbit, although the sources are silent on many of its components. The whole sweep of the alluvial corridor from the north-west to Magadha, if not to Pundra and Vanga, and the whole sweep from Anga and Magadha to Avanti, with knowledge of the Deccan—this is large enough to be dubbed a pan-India orbit. One is not sure if this orbit extended to the southern slope of the Hindukush. Gandhara is likely to have incorporated parts of south Afghanistan—possibly the Jalalabad area. The problem lies with the territory of Kamboja which has never been identified satisfactorily. The areas mentioned in this case have varied from Kafiristan in north-east Afghanistan to Rajouri in Kashmir. So, one has to leave this particular issue open.

The reason why the early pan-India orbit was replaced in the Indus valley and the area to its west up to the Hindukush by the orbit which covered the area from the southern part of Central Asia to the Indus valley is not clear either. The Achaemenid heartland was the Fars plain of Iran which is perfectly approachable from the Indian side through Baluchistan and Kirman. There is still traditional trade between the Kirman area and Sindh. It is possible that the Achaemenids took under their control the entire region from the Oxus valley to the Indus, mainly to ensure that this region which formed the hub of traditional trade affecting China, India, and the areas to the west, remained in their grip. The point to note is that the Oxus-Indus orbit took its first historical shape under the Achaemenids.

That trade had entered the geopolitics of the region is clear both from Achaemenid attempt to get the navigability of the Indus explored by Scylax of Caryanda and Alexander's subjugation of the valleys to the north-east of Peshawar. It has generally been supposed that Alexander conquered this area because he wanted to protect the rear of his army, so to speak. On the other hand, these valleys are the mainstay of the routes going across the Pamirs to Central Asia, and it is possible that Alexander focussed his attention on them to control the Indian side of the Central Asian trade.

One would think that the Mauryans did not change the picture, although they were looking at it from the Indian side and from within the Indian heartland. The Asokan inscription from Buner, and the locations of Shahbazgarhi and Mansera on the road to Gilgit and Hunza at the foot of the Pamirs testifies this. Besides, the references to a few kings around the Mediterranean in RE II and XIII clearly imply that the Mauryans were also concerned with the routes which went to the Mediterranean through West Asia. The Kandahar-Girishk-Herat route would put them in touch with the route going west through northern Iran, and access to the south Iranian route through Fars and across southern Iraq was possible through central and southern Baluchistan. In the study of Mauryan India, the Pushkalavati-Taxila alignment to the Ganga-Yamuna plain has received more attention than any other route to West and Central Asia. Both these places are well mentioned in both Classical and Indian sources and thus one can appreciate why this alignment has gained prominence. This has also to do with the fact that virtually nothing is known of the early historic phase in Sindh, from where easy access to south Baluchistan could have been obtained across Kohistan and the Hab valley. For central Baluchistan the entry point would have been the Sibi plain leading to the Bolan pass.

We believe that the study of two other external routes has been neglected in the context of Mauryan India. One of them led to Nepal through the Rampurwa section of Champaran in Bihar, and the significance of this route has been highlighted by the location of two Asokan pillars in the same locality. However, the details of this route—that is, how this route went to the Kathmandu valley and from there possibly to Tibet and beyond—still remains to be studied on the ground. The second route in all likelihood went from Pataliputra to Mahasthangarh and from Mahasthangarh to south China by following the north bank of the Brahmaputra and using a gap across the Patkoi range to reach Bhamo in north Myanmar for south China. The archaeology of this route is unknown beyond Mahasthangarh but between Pataliputra and Mahasthangarh, we have pointed out the location of the stump of an unmistakable Mauryan stone column in the context of a settlement with mud fortification at Banmankhi. It is also possible to suggest that another overland external route of Mauryan India went via south-east Bengal to Arakan, and from Arakan to the Srikshetra area of Myanmar. The early historic antiquity of south-east Bengal is clear from the finds from Wari-Bateshwar. Again, the archaeology of this route is generally unknown beyond Wari-Bateshwar. However, in view of the fact that the Arakan state of c. AD fifth century was using Sanskrit for its inscriptions and considering that Arakan is a straightforward extension of the Chattagram (Chittagong) coast of south-east Bengal, one can surmise that there was a traditional overland link between south-east Bengal and Arakan. The Mughal prince Shuja sought refuge in Andaman when he was chased by Aurangzeb's army, and we do know that he travelled overland. The route which he followed is still marked by large tanks at frequent intervals, which the local tradition associates with Shuja. There is a fair possibility that this route goes back to the early historic period, although its archaeology still remains uninvestigated in detail.

As a pan-Indian power, the Mauryan geopolitics could not ignore the areas through which India's external links—overland and maritime—were maintained. The inscriptions found at Sopara show the importance of this port in Mauryan India, but this does not mean that this was the only port area in which the Mauryan state was interested. The richness and variety of antiquities at the early historic sites in the Bhagirathi mouth and the Midnapur (Medinipur) coast implies a strong Mauryan presence in the region. Archaeologically there is no direct proof except that a stone object with Mauryan polish has been noted from Chandraketugarh. Both Tamluk and Chandraketugarh have to be considered flourishing ports of the Mauryan time. All that we are trying to argue is that the geopolitical frame of Mauryan India was strongly held up by a well-integrated network of overland and maritime routes. The evidence of archaeology is not always explicit in these cases, but even on the basis of what is archaeologically known, this inference can be made. In fact, we have argued that the whole purpose of the Kalinga war was to secure for the Mauryans control of an important junction of routes—the route which went along the Orissan coast to the south, and the route which came through Chhattisgarh and the Kalahandi-Bastar tract to the Andhra coast near Vizianagaram. The lure of control of maritime trade in this sector could also have played a role.

According to some scholars the Mauryans could establish their direct rule only in patches. There can be no objection to the idea of survival, continuation, and even the growth of political units on the local and regional levels in Mauryan India. The presence of innumerable princely states of various shapes and sizes till the end of British India is an excellent comparable instance of this kind. However, to argue that the writ of the central power did not run more or less uniformly in all parts of the Mauryan kingdom is to forget the detailed implications of the locations of Asokan edicts. We have earlier discussed the geographical implications of each of these locations. We think that not all these edicts have survived or been located, but even the existing locations impress one by their roots in the local context. When viewed in a pan-Indian context, one is invariably stuck by the level of familiarity the Mauryan administration had with all parts of India. The point of their roots in the local context may be explained by one or two examples. The MRE of Rupnath has by its side a rocky cliff of medium height with a thin water flow coming down it. This has created a deep pool at the spot, and as it happens in various parts of India, the pool has acquired a sanctity. This sanctity is recognized by the fact that even now there is an annual fair at the spot. The Asokan edict is quietly announcing its message of Dhamma to the people who have been congregating by this pool in the heart of the Vindhyas for centuries. The fact that it is only within 3 km of the prominent early historic site of Kakrehta means that the pool was regularly frequented by people. The selection of the place well served the purpose for which the edict was set up. If one has to take up a somewhat dissimilar case, one may draw attention to the location of MRE at Bairat on the Delhi-Jaipur road via Alwar. Carved on a set of boulders by the side of the main road leading to the large fortified complex of Bairat, this certainly indicates the general importance of this site in early historic India. One aspect of this importance is well known. There are traces of an early stupa, generally considered Mauryan, a little outside the general habitational area. The second importance of the site is not widely known. Bairat had been a major pre-industrial copper-smelting centre for centuries, with the modern settlement of Bairat standing on a hill which is composed entirely of copper-smelting debris. There is no doubt that the place was an important copper-smelting place in Mauryan India, and as people used to arrive at the place, the royal edict of Dhamma stood for them by the roadside. Examples can be multiplied, but on the whole the locations of the Asokan edicts reveal a remarkably close familiarity with the land throughout the length and breadth of India, from Kalsi at the entry to the Himalayas to the boulder-strewn fields of Karnataka and from Girnar in Gujarat to Sikligarh near Purnea in Bihar. The Mauryan grip over the land cannot be doubted for a moment.

The emphasis on Dhamma or a moral code of life in Asokan edicts has generally led to the impression that barring the war of Kalinga, the Mauryan kingdom had no tension or was entirely peaceful. Even from the common sense point of view, this is unlikely to be true. All that one has to do is to remember the wars which had to be fought by all the large historical kingdoms of India. It is true that in the Mauryan period there were no competing political powers elsewhere in the land, but, as we have noticed before, in the Hindukush and the Karnataka edges of the kingdom there were alien powers—Greeks beyond the Hindukush edge in north Afghanistan and the four southern powers Asoka mentions beyond the kingdom's edge in Karnataka. It is true that the relationship between the Mauryans and the Greeks of Bactria is not known to have been marked by wars after Chandragupta Maurya thwarted the ambition of Seleucas Nicator, but considering that this was at the door of the high plain of Central Asia, things could not be wholly peaceful and were likely to have been characterized by skirmishes of various kinds. We have previously suggested that the concentration of Asokan edicts in this frontier zone indicates an unstable frontier. This may not be the whole truth, but it is a distinct possibility. The same may be said about the Karnataka frontier, beyond which lay the orbit of four southern states. The later history of these states shows that the Pallavas, Cholas, Pandyas, and partly even the Cheras were fighting among themselves for territories, but more than these struggles within their own orbit, they were trying to expand in three directions—in the north-western direction to take possession of places like Mangalore and Banavasi in the south Kanara area; in the northern direction to control the Gulbarga-Bijapur section in south Deccan, and in the north-eastern direction to control the Krishna valley and the coastal tract of Andhra in general. This has been the traditional remit of the southern kingdoms, just as it has been the traditional preoccupation of the powers based around Bijapur-Gulbarga to cross the Gangawadi tract in the south, occupy

Coimbatore-Salem, and proceed as far south as the Kaveri. There is no special ground to think that this traditional political scenario of the south had entirely stopped because of the presence of the Mauryas in south Deccan. The Bellary-Anantapur-Kurnool area marks the general zone where the major conflicts between the southern powers and the powers based in south Deccan. The fact that there is a dense concentration of Asokan edicts precisely in the Bellary-Anantapur-Kurnool area suggests that this section of the Mauryan frontier had suffered from unrest.

The way the south Indian kingdoms formed an orbit of interaction of their own is interesting. Apart from the Mysore tract of Gangawadi or Mahishamandala, the area neatly forms four segments—the Pallava territory around Kanchipuram with links to the Dharmapuri-north Arcot tracts, of which Tagadur was the Satiyaputra capital; the Chola territory between the north and south Vellar rivers in the lower Kaveri; the Pandya territory based on the Vaigai; and the Chera territory of the southern Kerala coast and Kongudesa or Coimbatore-Salem. The main port of the Chera territory was Musiris near modern Craganore, and its capital was Karur located in Konguland. The main Pallava port was Mamallapuram. The main port of the Cholas was Kaveripattinam and their capital Urayur. The Pandya capital was Madura and their main port Alagankulam. The historical antiquity of these areas and states is well understood but the occurrence of the northern black polished pottery (NBP) at Korkai and Alagankulam in the Pandya territory needs highlighting. The lone calibrated date of the NBP-level at Korkai falls in the ninth century BC, and there are grounds to date the Alagankulam NBP around *c.* 500 BC. The point is that this south-easternmost section of the Tamil Nadu coast was exposed to trade with northern India as early as the first half of the first millennium BC, clearly showing that the pearl fisheries of the Gulf of Mannar or the resources of Coimbatore-Salem, which included semi-precious stones like carnelian, agate, and beryl, spices which grew in the southern hills, and possibly *Wootz* steel had got into the trading network between the southern states and the areas to the north quite early in the historical period. South of the south Deccan it was no doubt a separate orbit but in no way was it an orbit separated from the pan-Indian orbit which touched it in the north.

It is doubtful if the collapse of the pan-Indian orbit built by the Mauryas brought about any significant change in the southern orbit. Elsewhere this was the harbinger of a number of significant changes.

From the foot of the Hindukush to the Indus valley, the Oxus-Indus orbit got separate and acted as the most significant orbit in the history of the Ganga plain for a long period—from the end of the second century BC to *c.* AD 300. During the first three centuries AD this orbit as whole, that is, the whole stretch from the Oxus to the Indus, was important.

The second major orbit was the Ganga plain and Malwa. This was the orbit ruled visibly by the Sungas and the Kanvas. In a sense this was going back to the first visible geopolitical orbit.

The third major orbit was the Deccanese orbit presided over by the Satavahanas. It included north and south Deccan, the Konkan coast, Vidarbha, the whole of Andhra including the coast, and possibly a part of south Kosala as well.

And, as we have noted, the southern orbit was there, more or less unchanged.

The interacting and frequently fragmented character of these orbits is clear from the course of post-Mauryan political history. The Sungas may have ruled the Ganga plain-Malwa zone but it was repeatedly subject to attacks by the Indo-Greeks from their base in the Indus valley. These Indo-Greek attacks amply demonstrate the geographical vulnerability of the Ganga plain and predate in a way the pattern of the invasions by Sultan Mahmud of Ghazni in the eleventh century.

In a sense, the starting point of the Muslim expansion in India is the establishment of an independent kingdom by Alptigin in 963 in south Afghanistan with its capital at Ghazni. Sabuktigin, his general, defeated a force of the Hindu Shahis who considered the establishment of an independent kingdom to the south of Kabul unwelcome. This battle took place on the bank of the Lohgar river on the way from Kabul to Ghazni. Sabuktigin ascended the Ghazni throne in AD 977. He fought another successful battle with the Hindu Shahis between Lamghan and Ghazni and annexed the territory between Lamghan and Peshawar. He died in 997, leaving the throne to Mahmud who, before turning his attention to India, consolidated his position north of the Hindukush.

In AD 1000, Mahmud attacked Peshawar and in AD 1001 he defeats Jaipal and conquers the area around Peshawar. He also attacks Udabhandapura, the Hindu Shahi capital of the period, exacting tributes from them. Anandapal succeeds Jaipal on the Hindu Shahi throne.

In AD 1004, Mahmud came through the Sibi plain, crossed the Indus at Multan, attacked Bhatiya, won, and went back to Ghazni in 1005.

In AD 1005–6, Mahmud attacks Multan, defeats Anandapal near Peshawar, and marches back to Multan through the Shahi kingdom. In 1007, he comes back again, mainly to chastise the Hindu Shahis. In 1008, he attacks the Hindu Shahi capital, pursuing the Hindu Shahi army up to Kangra which yielded a rich booty. In 1009, he makes a thrust towards Alwar and in 1010 he attacks again Multan, turning the Hindu Shahi Anandapal into a vassal. In 1011, he carries his attack up to Thaneswar.

In 1013, Mahmud attacks Trilochanapala, Anandapala's son. The Shahis take refuge in Kashmir. Their capital was looted and the western and central parts of the Shahi kingdom annexed. An attack was launched against Kashmir. It was looted and the Shahis fled to eastern Panjab. In 1015, he comes back to Kashmir. In 1018, he crosses Panjab, crosses the Yamuna, and reaches Bulandshahr/ Baran, Mahaban (Mathura), Mathura, and Kanauj. He goes as far east as Fatehpur and returns to Ghazni in AD 1019. In 1020–1, he defeats the Chandella king of Bundelkhand. In 1021–2, he defeats the Kachchhapaghatas of Gwalior and attacks Kalanjar. In 1024, he attacks the Somnath temple of Gujarat and in 1027, Sindh.

The Muslim annexation of northern India waited for some more time.

The Ghurids first set themselves up between Herat and Ghazni and occupy the throne of Ghazni. The process was begun by Muhammad Ghuri who came by the Gomal Pass>Multan and Uch>Mt. Abu route and defeats Mularaja II, the Chalukyan king of Gujarat. Peshawar was taken in 1178 and Sialkot in 1185. The Ghurid general Q. Aibak established a number of garrisons along the route to Delhi—Hansi, Kuhram, Sarsuti, and Sirhind. Delhi was taken in AD 1193. In the same year Jayachandra of the Gahadavalas was defeated at Chandawar on the Yamuna between Etawah and Kanauj, with the Muslim army proceeding up to Banaras and Chandravati. In 1196, Bayana, Ajmer, Gwalior, and Gujarat were attacked, but Gujarat was not annexed this time. The focus of attack and annexation now focussed on northern Doab, Rajputana, and Bundelkhand.

It is not merely the attacks of the Greeks and Indo-Greeks like Demetrius and Menander which are reminiscent of the pattern of Muslim attacks from their base in south Afghanistan. We do not have the details of the Kushana annexation of northern India but if the details were indeed available, one would possibly have got a somewhat similar picture.

Does it mean that the Gangetic orbit got completely lost under the pressure of the forces coming from the Oxus-Indus orbit? The proliferation of numerous coin-issuing authorities in Panjab, Ganga plain, and Malwa in the late centuries BC and early centuries AD testifies to the fact that the process of local territorial formations in the region was not dead due to the impact of the Kushana rule or the attacks by Greeks and Indo-Greeks like Demetrius and Menander. One would call this development a kind of resistance to the forces from the north-west.

Malwa and north Maharashtra including the northern Konkan coast soon assume the character of an orbit on their own because of the rivalry between the Saka Satraps and the Satavahanas. The conflict was natural but for a long time after this, Malwa remained the object of attention of a host of powers right up to the phase of the Marathas in post-Mughal India.

If the vulnerability of the Gangetic-Malwa orbit to the onslaughts emanating from the Oxus-Indus orbit was a conspicuous feature of the post-Mauryan political scenario, perhaps the most important geopolitical orbit of the time was the emergence of the Deccanese orbit and the links it had with the vast region from Malwa, south Kosala, and Orissa to south Deccan. The emergence of the Orissan orbit under Kharavela highlighted the possibilities of the present Bhuvaneswar area as the focus of a state which could go up to Magadha or south Bihar in the Ganga plain, Vidarbha, possibly south Kosala, and a considerable length of the Kalinga and Andhra coasts. The Deccanese orbit is also closely linked with the orbit which covered Sindh, Gujarat, Malwa, some parts of Rajasthan, and northern Maharashtra including its coast and emerged under the Saka satraps of the region. This lasted for the AD first three centuries. The classic Deccanese orbit at the height of the Satavahana power covered the whole of modern Maharashtra, Karnataka (except possibly the portion south of Bellary), and Andhra. Quite naturally, it had various sub-orbits. In Maharashtra, the major sub-orbits are the following—two sections of Vidarbha (Berar and Khandesh, one the area around Nagpur with access to Andhra through Chanda, and the other around Achalpur/Basim/Akola with access to Andhra through Adilabad/Nizamabad); northern Maharashtra around Nasik/Pune/Aurangabad which may be divided into two historical sectors, one based on Nasik-Pune and northern Konkan coast and its extension up to Navsari-Broach area of Gujarat, and the other around Aurangabad; southern Maharashtra with possibly two historical sectors, one around Osmanabad and the other around Kolhapur. In Karnataka, the section which is relevant in the present context is the area roughly north of Chitaldurg extending up to Gulbarga, Bijapur, Badami. In Andhra, it is both the coast and Rayalseema-Telangana. The sub-orbits which frequently occur in the course of Andhra's early political history are the Krishna valley and the Vengi area in the coastal tract. Later, different other pockets (cf. the Kakatiyas of Warangal) appear. The entire region came under the unified leadership of the Satavahanas and after them the sub-orbits decided the flow of historical events under their successors.

The main southern orbit continued to remain confined to the area south of Chitaldurg, but by the end of the AD third century the Pallavas moved up to Bellary.

From the Gupta period onward the main development is the continuous increase in the number of orbits, each shaped by the political forces of the day and their geographical configurations. Under the Guptas, the Gangetic orbit up to the Indus and Malwa-Gujarat came back into its own, but the Guptas themselves demonstrated by their march to Kanchi that the orbits could be stretched by political will. Under the Vakatakas, a new orbit stretched from Bundelkhand to the Krishna valley of Andhra. Various factors such as trade routes, political situations, and so on, created such new orbits and brought about a kind of integration of the different physical territories which were not closely linked before. This process is clearly visible up to *c*. AD seventh century, but soon afterwards the geopolitics of the major dynasties in any case takes a different turn.

The struggle for power over the Ganga plain between the far-flung areas of south Deccan, Kurukshetra-Thaneswar at the head of the Yamuna plain, and Varendri in north Bengal seems to be a new development when the political stage was thrown wide open with no fixed limits. Till the thirteenth century this process continued in various forms. A whirl of political struggle filled up the history of Malwa, Bundelkhand, Rajasthan, and Gujarat throughout this period. The Kalachuris of Tripuri tried their hands in all quarters, even advancing through Central Indian jungles to south Kosala and Vidarbha. The repeated thrusts towards east India from the Kalachuri base of Tripuri were striking. When they attacked Bengal, the Cholas far exceeded the geographic limits of their movements which even otherwise were impressive—from Cape Comorin to Gulbarga on the one hand and the Vengi-Kalinga territory on the other, and this in addition to their Sri Lankan, Maldivian, and South-East Asian conquests. Whether these movements or army marches were successful or not is irrelevant. What is relevant is that for the purpose of conquests geographical limits were steadily ignored, bringing in all kinds of political powers within its vortex. There are, of course, areas where the local powers remained busy within their own contexts. In the later periods, the south Indian powers busied themselves fighting in the area from Cape to Gulbarga and up to Vengi and south Kanara. Many of the new Orissan states did not move out of their own orbit in search of territories. The Assamese state basically remained confined to the Brahmaputra valley, although this does not mean that it was ignorant of the other areas of the subcontinent.

This is not to argue that the geopolitical compulsions disappeared during this period. This is far from being the case. If one has to move from one area to another, the geographical lines of movement will offer the geographical possibilities of the direction of the intended movement. What we are suggesting is that the boundaries of interacting geopolitical orbits become very fluid now. As we wrote earlier:

So politically the diversity of dynastic scaffoldings told, on the one hand, the story of the shaping and consolidation of the political process leading to state formations on both regional and local levels, and showed, on the other, an intense political interaction between them resulting in a much sharper understanding of all parts of India as the components of a political landscape.[1]

Concluding Observations

What we realize is that the geographical lines have both conditioned the lines of movements (political or otherwise) on the subcontinental scale and created a few major orbits within which interactions between different dynasties or territorial formations took place. However, when there is a proliferation of regional and local states, different sub-orbits of interaction take place regularly but not invariably within the earlier major orbits. Throughout this volume we have highlighted these sub-orbits as well as the major early ones. Without trying to put a straight jacket of geographical constraints on the political history of ancient India we have only tried to delineate the range of its geographical possibilities.

Our geographical review of the political events of ancient Indian history may have also succeeded in demonstrating that there were no firm geographical lines of control within the inner frame of Indian history. We have noted how right from the beginning the Ganga plain and Malwa had links with the Deccan, thus making the so-called Narmada-Satpura line a virtual non-issue in Indian history. The political powers of the Chalukyas and Rashtrakutas with their base in southern Deccan were always pushing up to the Konkan coast, Gujarat, Malwa, and the central part of the Ganga plain, besides moving up the Andhra coast up to Vengi and trying to take over the southern domain up to the Kaveri. The Kalachuris of Tripuri controlled the whole of the central Indian forested territory up to south Kosala and Vidarbha, and the way they could penetrate down the Ganga plain up to Bihar and Bengal was impressive. The same is true of the Gurjara-Pratiharas at the height of their power. Not only was their influence in the Gangetic plain noteworthy but also their expedition northward as far as Kangra in the Panjab hills. The Rashtrakutas were knocking at the gates of the Ganga plain not merely through Jhansi and Kalpi in Bundelkhand but also through the Jubbalpore-Maihar-Satna-Kalinjar-Ajaigarh-Banda alignment. If one looks at the distribution of the Maratha princely states in Baroda, Indore, and Gwalior, one realizes that this later Maratha thrust was repeated over a long phase of ancient Indian history—from the Satavahanas to the Chalukyas and the Rashtrakutas. This later Maratha thrust towards the east went through Vidarbha, south Kosala, and the Chhotanagpur plateau and/or Orissa, also repeating some of the movements of the earlier periods.

It would also not be correct to imagine that the southern dynasties lay confined only to the southern domain. The Pallavas always targeted southern Deccan and the Andhra coast, and the Cholas and the Pandyas, whenever they had the chance, came up along these lines. In the case of the Cholas, there was no hesitation to venture beyond Kalinga. We have seen how between c. AD 1000 and c. 1300, the political boundaries within the subcontinent became particularly fluid or unstable and denote only the thrusts and counterthrusts of power.

Without trying to locate a set of relatively permanent lines of political boundaries, perhaps a much more historically fruitful exercise is to mark out the various paths of dynastic movements throughout ancient India. This raises the issue of routes in determining the linkages between the political territories. If the Ganga plain and Malwa were politically or otherwise connected with the Deccan right from the beginning of documented history, this connection was maintained only through certain possible geographical alignments. They could not be arbitrary. Similarly, the repeated thrusts northward from the Gulbarga-Bijapur segment of south Deccan can be marked out reasonably clearly. In a sense, there was a geographically conditioned pattern of route network linking the various political components of ancient India. It is this network which makes possible a proper geographical understanding of the ancient and later Indian dynastic framework. Which parts of this network were significant and became so in which period? Questions like this are likely to infuse an element of ground reality in the study of the political history of ancient India. Some parts of this are no doubt understood, but at the local levels much remains to be done.

Note
   1. Chakrabarti (2006: 432).

References

Aiyangar, S.K. and R.C. Majumdar. 1957. 'The Hoyasalas', in, R.C. Majumdar (ed.), *The Struggle for Empire*. Bombay: Bharatiya Vidya Bhavan, pp. 226–33.

Altekar, A.S. 1955. 'The Rashtrakuta Empire', in R.C. Majumdar (ed.), *The Age of Imperial Kanauj*. Bombay: Bharatiya Vidya Bhavan, pp. 1–18.

Banerjea, J.N. 1957a. 'The Bactrian Greeks in India', in K.A.N. Sastri (ed.), *A Comprehensive History of India, Volume Two: The Mauryas and Satavahanas*. Calcutta: Orient Longman, pp. 158–85.

————. 1957b. 'The Scythians and Parthians in India', in K.A.N. Sastri (ed.), *A Comprehensive History of India, Volume Two: The Mauryas and Satavahanas*. Calcutta: Orient Longman, pp. 263–92.

————. 1957c. 'The Satraps of Northern and Western India', in K.A.N. Sastri (ed.), *A Comprehensive History of India, Volume Two: The Mauryas and Satavahanas*. Calcutta: Orient Longman, pp. 263–92.

Banerjea, J.N. and Professor Jagannath. 1957. 'The Rise and Fall of the Kushana Power', in K.A.N. Sastri (ed.), *A Comprehensive History of India, Volume Two: The Mauryas and Satavahanas*. Calcutta: Orient Longman, pp. 222–62.

Chakrabarti, Dilip K. 2006. *The Oxford Companion to Indian Archaeology*. New Delhi: Oxford University Press.

————. 2005. *The Archaeology of the Deccan Routes: The Ancient Routes which Linked the Ganga Plain with the Deccan*. Delhi: Munshiram Manoharlal.

————. 2001 (Dhaka edition). *Ancient Bangladesh*. Dhaka: University Press Limited.

————. 1988. *Theoretical Issues in Indian Archaeology*. Delhi: Munshiram Manoharlal.

————. 1977. 'India and West Asia—An Alternative Approach', *Man and Environment*, Volume 1, pp. 25–38.

Chattopadhyay, S. 1974. *The Achaemenids in India*. Delhi: Munshiram Manoharlal.

Dandamaev, M.A. 1989. *A Political History of the Achaemenid Empire*. Leiden: Brill.

Day, W.M. 1949. 'Relative Permanence of Former Boundaries in India', *Scottish Geographical Magazine*, Volume 45, pp. 113–22.

Falk, H. 2006. *Asokan Sites and Artefacts: A Sourcebook with Bibliography*. Mainz am Rhein: Philipp von Zabern.

———. 2004. 'The Kanishka era in Gupta records', *Silk Road Art and Archaeology*, Volume 10, pp. 167–76.

———. 2001. The Yuga of Sphujiddhvaja and the Era of the Kushanas', *Silk Road Art and Archaeology*, Volume 7, pp. 121–56.

Ganguly, D.C. 1957a. 'Northern India during the Eleventh and Twelfth Centuries', in R.C. Majumdar (ed.), *The Struggle for Empire*. Bombay: Bharatiya Vidya Bhavan, pp. 24–103.

———. 1957b. 'The Age of Prithviraja', in R.C. Majumdar (ed.), *The Struggle for Empire*. Bombay: Bharatiya Vidya Bhavan, pp. 104–15.

———. 1957c. 'Later Chalukyas and Kalachuris of Kalyana', in R.C. Majumdar *The Struggle for Empire*. Bombay: Bharatiya Vidya Bhavan, pp. 161–83.

———. 1957d. 'Dynasties of Eastern Deccan', in R.C. Majumdar *The Struggle for Empire*. Bombay: Bharatiya Vidya Bhavan, pp.198–209.

———. 1955. 'Central and Western India', in R.C. Majumdar (ed.), *The Age of Imperial Kanauj*. Bombay: Bharatiya Vidya Bhavan, pp. 82–131.

Gopalachari, K. 1957. 'The Satavahana Empire', in K.A.N. Sastri (ed.), *A Comprehensive History of India, Volume Two: The Mauryas and Satavahanas*. Calcutta: Orient Longman, pp. 293–327.

Holdich, T.H. 1910. *The Gates of India*. London: Macmillan and Co.

Hultzsch, H. 1925. *Corpus Inscriptionum Indicarum I. Inscriptions of Asoka*. Oxford: Clarendon Press.

Jagannath, Professor. 1957. 'Post-Mauryan Dynasties (184 BC to AD 200)', in K.A.N. Sastri (ed.), *A Comprehensive History of India, Volume Two: The Mauryas and Satavahanas*. Calcutta: Orient Longman, pp. 94–115.

Magee, Peter, Cameron Petrie, Robert Knox, Farid Khan, and Ken Thomas. 2005. 'The Achaemenid Empire in South Asia and Recent Excavations at Akra in Northwest Pakistan, *American Journal of Archaeology*, 109(4): 711–41.

Mahadevan, I. 2003. *Early Tamil Epigraphy*. Chennai: Cre-A.

Majumdar, R.C. (ed.). 1957. *The Struggle for Empire*. Bombay: Bharatiya Vidya Bhavan.

Majumdar, R.C. (ed.). 1955a. *The Age of Imperial Kanauj*. Bombay: Bharatiya Vidya Bhavan.

———. 1955b. 'Rise and Fall of the Pratihara Empire', in R.C. Majumdar (ed.), *The Age of Imperial Kanauj*. Bombay: Bharatiya Vidya Bhavan, pp. 19–43.

———. 1955c. 'The Palas', in R.C. Majumdar (ed.), *The Age of Imperial Kanauj*. Bombay: Bharatiya Vidya Bhavan, pp. 44–57.

———. 1955d. 'Eastern India during the Pala Period', in R.C. Majumdar (ed.), *The Age of Imperial Kanauj*. Bombay: Bharatiya Vidya Bhavan, pp. 58–81.

———. 1954a. *The Classical Age*. Bombay: Bharatiya Vidya Bhavan.

———. 1954b. 'The Rise of the Guptas', in R.C. Majumdar (ed.), *The Classical Age*. Bombay: Bhartaiya Vidya Bhavan, pp. 1–6.

———. 1954c. 'The Foundation of the Gupta Empire', in R.C. Majumdar (ed.), *The Classical Age*. Bombay: Bhartaiya Vidya Bhavan, pp. 7–16.

———. 1954d. 'The Fall of the Gupta Empire', in R.C. Majumdar (ed.), *The Classical Age*. Bombay: Bhartaiya Vidya Bhavan, pp. 42–5.

———. 1954e. 'Harsha-Vardhana and His Time', in R.C. Majumdar (ed.), *The Classical Age*. Bombay: Bhartaiya Vidya Bhavan, pp. 96–123.

———. 1954f. 'Northern India during AD 650–750', in R.C. Majumdar (ed.), *The Classical Age*. Bombay: Bhartaiya Vidya Bhavan, pp. 124–76.

——— (ed.). 1953. *The Age of Imperial Unity*. Bombay: Bharatiya Vidya Bhavan.

——— (ed.). 1951. *The Vedic Age*. London: Allen and Unwin.

McCrindle, J.W. 2004 (reprint). *The Invasion of India by Alexander the Great as Described by Arrian, Q. Curtius, Diodorus, Plutarch and Justin*. Portland, Oregon: Kessinger Publishing.

Mukherjee, B.N. 1995. 'The Great Kushana Testament', *Indian Museum Bulletin*, pp. 1–105.

———. 1988. *The Rise and Fall of the Kushana Empire*. Calcutta: Firma K.L.Mukhopadhyay.

Pargiter, F.E. 1922. *Ancient Indian Historical Tradition*. London: Humphrey Milford Oxford University Press.

———. 1913. *The Purana Text of the Dynasties of the Kali Age with Introduction and Notes*. London: Humphrey Milford Oxford University Press.

Pusalker, A.D. 1951a. 'Traditional History from the Earliest Time to The Accession of Parikshit', in R.C. Majumdar (ed.), *The Vedic Age*. London: Allen and Unwin, pp. 267–318.

———. 1951b. 'Traditional History from the Accession of Parikshit to the End of the Barhadratha Dynasty', in R.C. Majumdar (ed.), *The Vedic Age*. London: Allen and Unwin, pp. 319–29.

Raychaudhuri, H.C. 1953 (6th ed). *Political History of Ancient India, from the Accession of Parikshit to the Extinction of the Gupta Dynasty*. Calcutta: University of Calcutta.

Richards, F.J. 1933. 'Geographical Factors in Indian Archaeology', *Indian Antiquary*, Volume 62, pp. 235–43.

Sastri, A.M. 1999. *The Age of the Satavahanas*. 2 vols Delhi: Aryan Books.

———. 1997–8. 'A (lost?) Asokan edict from Vidarbha', *Puratattva*, Volume 28, pp. 55–8.

Sastri, K.A.N. 1958 (2nd ed). *A History of South India from Prehistoric Times to the Fall of Vijayanagar*. Madras: Oxford University Press.

———. (ed.) 1957a. *A Comprehensive History of India, Volume Two: The Mauryas and Satavahanas*. Calcutta: Orient Longman.

———. 1957b. 'Minor States of the North, Monarchical and Non-monarchical', in K.A.N. Sastri (ed.), *A Comprehensive History of India, Volume Two: The Mauryas and Satavahanas*. Calcutta: Orient Longman, pp. 116–37.

———. 1957c. 'South India—Part I', in K.A.N. Sastri (ed.), *A Comprehensive History of India, Volume Two: The Mauryas and Satavahanas*. Calcutta: Orient Longman, pp. 498–532.

———. 1957d. 'South India—Part II', in K.A.N. Sastri (ed.), *A Comprehensive History of India, Volume Two: The Mauryas and Satavahanas*. Calcutta: Orient Longman, pp. 533–67.

———. 1935–7. *The Colas*. Madras: University of Madras.

Sathianathaiyer, R. 1957a. 'The Cholas', in R.C. Majumdar (ed.), *The Struggle for Empire*. Bombay: Bharatiya Vidya Bhavan, pp. 234–55.

———. 1957b. 'The Later Pandyas', in R.C. Majumdar (ed.), *The Struggle for Empire*. Bombay: Bharatiya Vidya Bhavan, pp. 256–60.

———. 1955. 'South India', in R.C. Majumdar (ed.), *The Age of Imperial Kanauj*. Bombay: Bharatiya Vidya Bhavan, pp. 159–64.

———. 1954. 'Dynasties of South India', in R.C. Majumdar (ed.), *The Classical Age*. Bombay: Bharatiya Vidya Bhavan, pp. 255–74.

Schwartzberg, J.E. (ed.). 1992 (2nd edn). *A Historical Atlas of South Asia*. Oxford: Oxford University Press.

Sims-Williams, N. and J. Cribb. 1995–6. 'A New Bactrian Inscription of Kanishka the Great', *Silk Road Art and Archaeology*, Volume 4, pp. 75–142.

Sircar, D.C. 2000. *Asokan Studies*. Calcutta: Indian Museum.

———. 1957. 'The Deccan after the Satavahanas (c. AD 200–300)', in K.A.N. Sastri (ed.), *A Comprehensive History of India, Volume Two: The Mauryas and Satavahanas*. Calcutta: Orient Longman, pp. 328–38.

———. 1955. 'The Deccan', in R.C. Majumdar (ed.), *The Age of Imperial Kanauj*. Bombay: Bharatiya Vidya Bhavan, pp. 132–49.

Sircar, D.C. 1954a. 'Deccan in the Gupta Age', in R.C. Majumdar (ed.), *The Classical Age*. Bombay: Bharatiya Vidya Bhavan, pp. 177–222.

———. 1954b. 'The Chalukyas', in R.C. Majumdar (ed.), *The Classical Age*. Bombay: Bharatiya Vidya Bhavan, pp. 227–54.

———. 1953a. 'The Yavanas', in R.C. Majumdar (ed.), *The Age of Imperial Unity*. Bombay: Bharatiya Vidya Bhavan, pp. 101–119.

———. 1953b. 'The Sakas and the Pahlavas', in R.C. Majumdar (ed.), *The Age of Imperial Unity*. Bombay: Bharatiya Vidya Bhavan, pp. 120–35.

———. 1953c. 'The Kushanas', in R.C. Majumdar (ed.), *The Age of Imperial Unity*. Bombay: Bharatiya Vidya Bhavan, pp. 136–53.

———. 1953d. 'Northern India after the Kushanas', in R.C. Majumdar (ed.), *The Age of Imperial Unity*. Bombay: Bharatiya Vidya Bhavan, pp. 159–77.

———. 1953e. 'The Saka Satraps of Western India', in R.C. Majumdar (ed.), *The Age of Imperial Unity*. Bombay: Bharatiya Vidya Bhavan, pp. 178–90.

———. 1953f. 'The Satavahanas and the Chedis', in R.C. Majumdar (ed.), *The Age of Imperial Unity*. Bombay: Bharatiya Vidya Bhavan, pp. 191–216.

———. 1953g. 'The Deccan after the Satavahanas', in R.C. Majumdar (ed.), *The Age of Imperial Unity*. Bombay: Bharatiya Vidya Bhavan, pp. 217–27.

Smith, V.A. 1924. *The Early History of India*. Oxford: Clarendon Press.

Spate, O.H.K. 1957 (2nd edn). *India and Pakistan: A General and Regional Geography*. London: Methuen and Co.

Thapar, R. 2002. *Asoka and the Decline of the Mauryas* (paperback edn). New Delhi: Oxford University Press.

Vogelsang, W.J. 1992. *The Rise and Organization of the Achaemenid Empire: the Eastern Iranian Evidence*. Leiden: Brill.

Index